Fluency Doesn't Just Happen with Addition and Subtraction

Fluency in math doesn't just happen! It is a well-planned journey. In this book, you'll find practical strategies and activities for teaching your elementary students basic addition and subtraction facts. The authors lay out the basic framework for building math fluency using a cycle of engagement (concrete, pictorial, abstract) and provide a multitude of examples illustrating the strategies in action.

You'll learn how to:

- help students to model their thinking with a variety of tools;
- keep students engaged through games, poems, songs, and technology;
- assess student development to facilitate active and continuous learning;
- implement distributed practices throughout the year;
- boost parental involvement so that students remain encouraged even as material becomes more complex.

A final chapter devoted to action plans will help you put these strategies into practice in your classroom right away. Most importantly, you'll open the door to deep and lasting math fluency.

Dr. Nicki Newton has been an educator for 30 years, working both nationally and internationally with students of all ages. She has worked on developing Math Workshops and Guided Math Institutes around the country; visit her website at www.drnickinewton.com. She is also an avid blogger (www.guidedmath.wordpress.com), tweeter (@drnickimath), and Pinterest pinner (www.pinterest.com/drnicki7).

Ann Elise Record has been an educator for over 18 years as a classroom teacher, math coach and specialist, adjunct faculty member of Plymouth State University, and, currently, as a national speaker and independent math consultant. She can be found on Facebook (www.facebook.com/groups/2022849141262766/) facilitating the Math Running Records group as well as on Twitter (@AnnEliseRecord).

Dr. Alison J. Mello has been in education for over 25 years as a classroom teacher, math specialist, director of curriculum, and, currently, as the Assistant Superintendent of Foxborough Public Schools, MA. In addition to her work in the district, Alison is a national speaker, math consultant, and graduate instructor of in-service teachers. She can be found on Twitter (@alisonmellomath).

Fluency Doesn't Just Happen with Addition and Subtraction

Strategies and Models for Teaching the Basic Facts

Dr. Nicki Newton
with Ann Elise Record and
Dr. Alison J. Mello

Routledge
Taylor & Francis Group

NEW YORK AND LONDON

First published 2020
by Routledge
52 Vanderbilt Avenue, New York, NY 10017

and by Routledge
2 Park Square, Milton Park, Abingdon, Oxon, OX14 4RN

Routledge is an imprint of the Taylor & Francis Group, an informa business

Library of Congress Cataloging-in-Publication Data
Names: Newton, Nicki, author. | Record, Ann Elise, author. | Mello, Alison J., author.
Title: Fluency doesn't just happen with addition and subtraction:
strategies and models for teaching the basic facts / Dr. Nicki Newton with Ann Elise Record and Dr. Alison J. Mello
Description: New York, NY : Routledge, 2020. | Includes bibliographical references.
Identifiers: LCCN 2019034612 (print) | LCCN 2019034613 (ebook) | ISBN 9780367151836 (hardback) | ISBN 9780367151850 (paperback) | ISBN 9780429055553 (ebook)
Subjects: LCSH: Addition--Study and teaching (Elementary) | Subtraction--Study and teaching (Elementary)
Classification: LCC QA115 .N49 2020 (print) | LCC QA115 (ebook) | DDC 372.7--dc23
LC record available at https://lccn.loc.gov/2019034612
LC ebook record available at https://lccn.loc.gov/2019034613

ISBN: 978-0-367-15183-6 (hbk)
ISBN: 978-0-367-15185-0 (pbk)
ISBN: 978-0-429-05555-3 (ebk)

Typeset in Berling and Futura
by Swales & Willis, Exeter, Devon, UK

I dedicate this book to my Auntie Lizzie.

– Nicki Newton

Dedicated to Mom, Dad, Dan, Matthew, and Kathryn for their endless love and support.
– Ann Elise Record

I dedicate this book to my amazing colleagues who got behind me to transform the way we approach fluency. I also dedicate this to my wonderful family who patiently waited while I spent many days, nights, and weekends behind the screen of my computer and writing. Nothing I do is possible without your support and I am so blessed to have you all cheering me on.

– Alison J. Mello

Contents

Meet the Authors

Dr. Nicki Newton has been an educator for 30 years, working both nationally and internationally, with students of all ages. Having spent the first part of her career as a literacy and social studies specialist, she built on those frameworks to inform her math work. She believes that math is intricately intertwined with reading, writing, listening, and speaking. She has worked on developing Math Workshop and Guided Math Institutes around the country. Most recently, she has been helping districts and schools nationwide to integrate their State Standards for Mathematics and think deeply about how to teach these within a Math Workshop Model. Dr. Nicki works with teachers, coaches, and administrators to make math come alive by considering the powerful impact of building a community of mathematicians who make meaning of real math together. When students do real math, they learn it. They own it, they understand it, and they can do it. Every one of them. Dr. Nicki is also an avid blogger (www.guidedmath.wordpress.com) and Pinterest pinner (www.pinterest.com/drnicki7/).

Ann Elise Record has been an educator for over 18 years as a classroom teacher, math coach and specialist, adjunct faculty member of White Mountains Community College and Plymouth State University, and currently as a national speaker and consultant. She holds a Master's degree in Education and is a certified NH Elementary Math Specialist. Ann Elise is passionate about sharing growth mind-set messages with anyone she meets (yes, even grocery store cashiers who tell her that they were never good at math) that everyone can learn math, making mistakes is part of the learning process, and you don't need to be fast to be good at math. She wholeheartedly believes that there is nothing elementary about teaching elementary math! She continues to learn every day and understands that when we know more, we do better! She loves every opportunity to share current research-based best practices for teaching math and has witnessed the power of teaching through the use of strategies in transforming entire school climates and the achievement of their students. She is an avid believer that when we explore strategies with math facts, we are providing our students with a foundation of strategic thought that will follow them throughout their math journeys, since those very same strategies can then be used for larger numbers and even, down the road, decimals and fractions. When she isn't working on math at home or consulting in schools, you will probably find her at Walt Disney World making magical memories with her family.

Dr. Alison J. Mello has been in education for over 25 years as a classroom teacher, math specialist, director of curriculum and, currently, as the Assistant Superintendent of Foxborough Public Schools, MA. She holds an EdD in educational leadership and her research focuses on classroom learning environments and relationship to mathematical disposition. In addition to her work in the district, Alison is a national speaker, math consultant, and graduate instructor of in-service teachers.

Alison enjoys working to develop practical strategies to address issues that teachers face in their classrooms every day. She uses her understanding of curriculum and best practices to assist teachers in using the resources at their disposal to deliver the standards in ways that are meaningful, engaging, and truly impact student learning. Her passion for equity and access for all students drives her to continue to spend time during the summer offering graduate courses on Guided Math and Math Workshops. Her hope is that more teachers will use these powerful mechanisms to differentiate instruction and, as a result, will more effectively meet the wide variety of needs that students present. Aside from engaging with students, which will always be the best part of working in education, Alison absolutely loves working with teachers and seeing them get excited about transforming their practice.

Preface

I am so excited to be writing this great book with extraordinary friends. We all share a deep love for the teaching of math. We are especially interested in how the research and the actual practice of teaching mathematics intersects in classrooms. We have written a book grounded in the research-based continuum for teaching math facts that is situated in the 21st century and offers practical strategies for success. We respectfully applaud those who have trailed a path before us and now we would like to further the discussion by looking at exactly what we know about teaching and learning math facts today and what 21st century technologies can be incorporated into that journey. A 21st century framework is essential because teaching and learning today offer completely new and exciting opportunities than ever before.

We have divided this book up into ten chapters:

Part I: Introduction

Chapter 1: Introduction

In Chapter 1 we discuss the research and frameworks for teaching addition and subtraction facts. I call them the "Dolch words of math" (Newton, personal communication, 2008). Dolch words are all the basic words that students need to know to become fluent readers. In the same way, the "Dolch words of math" are the strategies that students need to know so that they can do higher level mathematics without being bogged down in the basic fact stuff. In this chapter we discuss the basic framework for building fact power.

Chapter 2: Modeling Math Facts

In this chapter we are going to delve deep into what it means and how to teach strategies using various models. We will discuss:

- classroom as a tool kit;
- individual student tool kits;
- teacher's tool kit;
- digital tool kit.

We explain the importance of how tools help students to model their thinking and how they have the potential to help students understand the math they are doing.

Part II: Introduction to Exploring and Learning Addition Strategies

Chapter 3: Exploring and Learning Addition Facts within 10

In this chapter we are going to delve deep into what this means and how you teach strategies within 10. We will discuss:

- add 1;
- add 0;
- add 2 and 3;
- adding within 5 and making 5;
- add within 10;
- making 10.

We explain a cycle of engagement which looks at teaching and learning using concrete, pictorial, and abstract representations. We will talk about which activities to use and how to develop a deep level of understanding. We will also discuss picture books, songs, poems, videos, and spotlight activities for teaching these strategies.

Chapter 4: Exploring and Learning Facts above 10

In this chapter we are going to delve deep into what this means and how you teach addition strategies from 10 to 20. We will discuss:

- doubles;
- doubles plus 1;
- doubles plus 2;
- add 10;
- bridging 10 with 7, 8, or 9.

We discuss a cycle of engagement which looks at teaching and learning using concrete, pictorial, and abstract representations. We will talk about which activities to use and how and when to develop a deep level of understanding. We will also discuss picture books, songs, poems, videos, and spotlight activities for teaching these strategies.

Part III: Introduction to Exploring and Learning Subtraction Strategies

Chapter 5: Exploring and Learning Subtraction within 10

In this chapter we are going to delve deep into what this means and how you teach strategies within 10. We will discuss:

- subtract 0;
- subtract 1;

- subtract a number from itself;
- subtract within 5;
- subtract from 5;
- subtract within 10;
- subtract from 10.

We discuss a cycle of engagement which looks at teaching and learning using concrete, pictorial, and abstract representations. We will talk about which activities to use and how to develop a deep level of understanding. We will also discuss picture books, songs, poems, videos, and spotlight activities for teaching these strategies.

Chapter 6: Exploring and Learning Subtraction within 20

In this chapter we are going to delve deep into what this means and how you teach strategies from 10 to 20. We will discuss;

- subtract 10 from a teen and 1 from a teen number;
- subtract half facts;
- subtract by bridging 10 with higher facts;
- fact families;
- subtract from 20.

We discuss a cycle of engagement which looks at teaching and learning using concrete, pictorial, and abstract representations. We will talk about which activities to use and how to develop a deep level of understanding. We will also discuss picture books, songs, poems, videos, and spotlight activities for teaching these strategies.

Part IV: Other Crucial Elements

Chapter 7: Assessing Basic Fact Fluency

In this chapter we look at the many different aspects of assessment that take place along the way as students learn strategies. We will explore:

- assessing conceptual understanding;
- assessing procedural fluency;
- assessing adaptive reasoning;
- strategic competence;
- productive disposition.

We want to emphasize that the assessment of learning facts should be a "scrapbook rather than a snapshot" of what students know how to do and what they need to learn next (Wiggins & McTighe, 2005 – see Chapter 1).

Chapter 8: Doing Daily Fluency Routines

In this chapter we will discuss engaging activities that can be used to distribute practice across the year rather than just massed practice in a unit of study:

- subitizing;
- what doesn't belong?;
- I was walking down the street;
- number talks;
- true or false;
- I love math;
- virtual dice;
- splat!;
- the power of color;
- circle map facts.

Chapter 9: Parental Involvement

In this chapter we discuss the crucial element of home support. We talk about how to set parents up to be able to help their students learn addition and subtraction strategies:

- making the most of the home–school connection;
- getting parents on board;
- sharing the strategies;
- addressing parental concerns;
- parents as partners.

We strongly believe that if parents or guardians know how to help their students then they will. Empowering parents with the right language, tools, and understanding will reinforce all of our efforts in school.

Chapter 10: Action Plan

In this chapter we discuss making and carrying out an action plan. If you plan and write it down then you are much more likely to get started and continue doing it. So we help you navigate some of the key elements of making a plan that you can use:

- mission statement;
- fluency vision statements;
- fluency plans and template.

It is with great joy that we have written this book to continue an ongoing discussion about teaching students their basic math facts. We wish you many "Aha" moments along the way.

Acknowledgments

My journey with fact fluency has been long and filled with so many learning opportunities and aha moments. I am fortunate to work with incredible teachers and specialists who agreed long ago that fluency and speed are not synonymous, and that strategies are the key to building true numeracy through flexibility. I applaud them for their willingness to try different approaches and to think outside of the box about how to achieve fluency for every student. Our classrooms today look radically different from ten years ago, and I am so proud that the changes we have implemented honor the research, respect different learning styles, and foster positive and productive math dispositions. I hope that anyone who reads this book and makes changes gets to experience the wonderful outcomes that we have seen not only in the fluency of their students, but in their overall satisfaction of teaching in a way that promotes curiosity, instills pride, and allows students to experience the joy of mathematics.

I thank everyone who has researched this topic, led professional development to make powerful changes for students, and Dr. Nicki Newton, especially, for giving these ideas a platform. I am so grateful for her friendship, inspiration, and unwavering efforts to push me to scale my impact. Her influence on me and my work is immeasurable, and I am eternally grateful.

– Alison J. Mello

I am so grateful to all the people who have helped me on my math journey. First, I want to thank the Berlin Public School system for providing me many professional development opportunities as well as the privilege of becoming a Math Coach. Many thanks to the dedicated teaching staff, both past and present, of Brown and Hillside Elementary Schools who welcomed me into their classrooms with open minds. Thanks also to the amazing online community of math educators whom I continue to learn from every day. Finally, thanks to my treasured family and friends who have been with me every step of the way. One of the most dramatic steps on my journey was attending a conference with Dr. Nicki Newton who blew my mind with ways of teaching math that I have never heard of before. Choosing her session was a decision that literally changed my life. To say that I have collaborated with her on a book is beyond anything I ever dreamed of! I am awed by the extent of her knowledge of research-based best practices, her incredible generosity, and her continual sense of wonder at the way children learn and grow. She is my math mentor and, I'm so grateful to say, my close friend. Whenever I am pondering an educational concern, I always hear her voice saying, "What does the research say? You've got to know the research." Thank you so very much, Dr. Nicki Newton!

– Ann Elise Record

I am so grateful to have had the opportunity to work with two outstanding educators, Ann Elise and Dr. Mello on this book. It has been a real joy to work and learn together. I am thankful for all the teachers and students that I have had the opportunity to work with over the past three decades, they have taught me so much about teaching and learning. I thank my family and friends for continuous support and encouragement. I have been blessed with the best editor in the entire world, Lauren Davis. I thank Janet Nuzzie for being the math editor on this book. I thank the entire editorial team that makes it all come to fruition.

– Nicki Newton

PART I

Introduction

CHAPTER 1

Introduction

Do not be content with the right answer. Always demand explanation.

(Van de Walle, 2001, p. 425)

INTRODUCTION

Fluency doesn't just happen! It is a well-planned journey. This book is meant to help you navigate that journey. Fluency is a multidimensional concept. We like to think of it as a four-legged stool: accuracy, flexibility, efficiency, and automaticity. Ann Elise once said that "Automaticity has hijacked fluency." We love this because it is so true. Students need to be able to instantly recall their facts at some point so that they don't get bogged down in the little stuff when they are working on multi-digit operations and fractions, decimals, and integers. BUT, students must learn their facts through a variety of engaging, ongoing, interactive, rigorous, student-friendly activities that build a fundamental understanding of how numbers are in relationship with each other. The research resoundingly states that computational fluency is multidimensional (speed and accuracy, flexibility and efficiency) (Brownell, 1956/1987; Brownell & Chazal, 1935; Kilpatrick et al., 2001; National Council of Teachers of Mathematics, 2000).

Fluency is a four-legged stool

If one of the legs is missing – then students only have partial fluency. Students can know all their facts instantly and not have any number sense.

The four legs of fluency are:

Accuracy, Flexibility, Efficiency, and Automaticity.

DOLCH WORDS OF MATH

Students should *learn* their facts rather than *memorize* them. If you just memorize them, then you can easily forget them. If you learn them, then you can always access them through a variety of strategies based in place value, properties, and the relationships between the operations. There is a continuum for learning basic facts. Baroody (2006) calls it the "Phases of Mastery." Battista (2012) calls it the *"Levels of Sophistication."* This continuum has been discussed by many researchers and guides our work in this book. Basic facts for addition and subtraction are sums and differences within 20. (See Figure 1.1.)

Addition	Subtraction
Plus 1	Minus 1
Plus 0	Minus 0
Count On 1,2,3	Take a number away from itself
Add within 5	Count Back 1,2,3
Make 5	Subtract within 5
Add within 10	Subtract from 5
Make 10	Subtract within 10
Add 10	Subtract from 10
Doubles	Subtract 10 from a teen number
Doubles Plus 1	Subtract 1s from a teen number
Doubles Plus 2	Subtracting differences of 1 or 2
Adding 7,8,9	Subtract by bridging 10
Adding within 20	Fact Families
Make 20	Subtract from 20

FIGURE 1.1 Addition and Subtraction Strategies

STRATEGY TALK

As students are learning their facts, there are different approaches to working with numbers. These strategies have names. (See Figure 1.2.)

Strategies				
Counted All	**Counted on**	**Known Facts**	**Derived Facts**	**Automatic Facts**
Students count out the first addend, then they count out the second addend, then they count the total. Sounds like: 1,2,3,4,5 then 1,2,3 then 1,2,3,4,5,6,7,8	There are different types of counting on… one is when students start at whatever addend comes first, the next level is when students consistently start with the higher addend. Sounds like: 7 – 8,9,10,11,12	These are facts that students just know… often times they are intermittent they could be random facts. But they could be things like doubles… many students know that 5 + 5 is 10 without thinking about it.	These are facts where students use what they know to figure out new facts. So to figure out 6 + 6, a student might say, well 5 + 5 is 10 and 2 more is 12.	This is when students know their facts without having to think about them. Logan calls this the "instant popping into of mind." (1991)

FIGURE 1.2 Basic Fact Strategies

CYCLE OF ENGAGEMENT: CONCRETE, REPRESENTATIONAL, ABSTRACT

We strongly believe that students should go through the cycle of engagement so that they have several opportunities to learn about the ways in which numbers are related and work together (see Figure 1.3). Many researchers maintain that this cycle gives students access to deeper understanding of mathematical concepts (Anstrom, n.d.; Bender, 2009; Devlin, 2000; Maccini & Gagnon, 2000; Van de Walle, 2001). This cycle, known as C-R-A or C-P-A, is a three-step instructional process that allows students to gain conceptual understanding of a strategy by first working with manipulatives or concrete objects. The second part of the cycle is for students to do pictorial representations of the math. The third part of the cycle is for students to work at an abstract level with the concepts.

Each stage builds on the previous stage. It is important to give all students an opportunity to work through the stages because otherwise some students can get the answer but don't understand the concept. For example, if we were teaching students how to double a number, we would give them plenty of opportunities to actually pull objects and make the doubles fact. Next, we would have students draw out doubles facts and work with them on scaffolded strategy flashcards that have visual supports. Finally, we would have students play a variety of dice, domino, card, and board games where they just have to recall the facts.

Concrete Activities	Pictorial Activities	Abstract Activities
2 Colored Counters	Pictures	Board Games
Cubes	Tally marks	Dice Games
Bears	Stickers	Domino Games
Beans	Number Bonds	Flashcards
Playdoh	Part-Part Whole Mats	Card Games
Popsicle Sticks	Number Frames	Sorting Games

FIGURE 1.3 C-R-A Cycle

As students are working through this cycle of engagement – concrete, pictorial, and abstract – they are building their number sense. They are developing familiarity with numbers and the way they work. As Van de Walle (2007) noted:

> A rich and thorough development of number relationships is a critical foundation for mastering of basic facts. Without number relationships, facts must be rotely memorized. With number understanding, facts for addition and subtraction are relatively simple extensions.
>
> (p. 120)

Mastery of basic facts occurs as students have ongoing experiences working with number combinations. When students have achieved mastery they are efficient, flexible, accurate, and automatic. They understand when and how to use appropriate strategies. Basic facts are the linchpin of learning mathematics because students will build on this foundational knowledge to do everything else in math. Van de Walle and Lovin point out that mastery is when "a child can give a quick response without resorting to nonefficient means, such as counting" (2006, p. 24). Furthermore, they note that "all children are able to master the basic facts – including children with learning disabilities" (2006, p. 24).

MAKING THE CONNECTION BETWEEN ADDITION AND SUBTRACTION

Throughout this book we will spend some time talking and thinking about subtraction as it relates to addition. Subtraction is much more difficult for many students throughout the grades. A firm foundation in subtraction will do wonders for students later on. The research discusses the need for students to understand the relationship between addition and subtraction.

> "A good understanding of the operations can firmly connect addition and subtraction so that subtraction facts are a natural consequence of having learned addition. For example, 12 - 5 is 7 since 5 + 7 is 12"
>
> (Van de Walle, 2007, p. 143)

It is important to work with students so that they understand we can use *count up strategies* to subtract as well as *take away strategies*. Students should do various activities where they explore addition as a whole in terms of putting parts together to find the sum and subtraction as a missing part by taking away, removing, or comparing to find the difference (Van de Walle, 2007). "Recognizing the inverse relationship between addition and subtraction can allow students to be flexible in using strategies to solve problems" (NCTM, 2000, p. 83).

21ST CENTURY COMPONENTS

The students that we teach are called "digital natives" (Prensky, 2001). We are called "digital immigrants." Our students were born into a world where the internet is ever present. They have learned much of the stuff they know from the internet. We must incorporate the teaching and learning of the basic facts into our daily routines. Students should be not only consumers but also producers of technology. This means that, yes, they should practice their basic facts on games (but most of these games are working mainly on accuracy and instant recall). Also, students should be using technology to show what they know. They can make podcasts, screencasts, videos, and narrated slides to show what they know. Even the kindergarteners can do it!

PURPOSEFUL PRACTICE

Practice should be meaningful. Students should practice number combinations in ways that build understanding and familiarity. Over time, students become automatic with various number combinations. Van de Walle and Lovin (2006) warn us that we shouldn't start by drilling students, but instead focus on the acquisition of efficient strategies. We think this is more about having students work towards automaticity. After students understand the concept and are comfortable with the number combinations, they then can play games that work on instant recall. Students don't have to do drills to work on instant recall; I think board games, card games, dice games, and domino games help students work on instant recall as well. Ask yourself: what would you rather do, rote drills or games?

Leveling workstations addresses the idea that meaningful practice should be individualized (Van de Walle & Lovin, 2006). When students are working in their zone of proximal development (Vygotsky, 1978), then they are not bored or frustrated. They can actually build a solid foundation of understanding. This specifically looks like some students working on making ten facts and other students working on making doubles. Everyone is working towards the grade level standard *but at their own pace*. In literacy we would never say that everyone has to read the same books at the same time, but in math we do exactly that! It doesn't work for literacy and it doesn't work for math either. Students will progress towards grade level standards at different times and that should be expected and respected.

Part of purposeful practice entails students engaging in self-monitoring. There are different ways to do this. Students might have a Fact Fluency Folder or Fact Practice Rings (see Figure 1.4).

Fact Fluency Folder	Fact Fluency Ring	Fact Practice Wallet

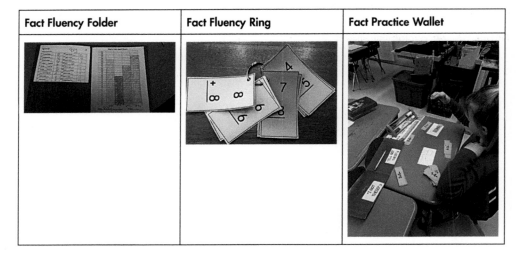

FIGURE 1.4 Fact Fluency Options

ACCOUNTABILITY

Students have to be accountable to the work they are doing in workstations (see Figure 1.5). We should never do worksheets but we should have students recording the work they are doing. Sometimes they use templates and other times they just record their work on a piece of paper.

Roll the dice and fill in the spaces!	Largest Number Instructions: Roll the dice. Record your roll. Compare your numbers with symbols.
1. ____ + ____ = 10	
2. 10 = ____ + ____	Partner 1 Partner 2
3. 7 = ___ + ____	
4. 8 + ___ = 10	
5. ____ + 5 = 10	
6. 6 + 2 = ____	
7. 4 + ____ = 10	
8. 1 + ___ = 10	
9. ___ + 3 = 10	
10. 9 + ___ = 10	

FIGURE 1.5 Accountability Sheets

ENGAGING APPROACHES

Our students are diverse learners. Building on the theories of learning styles and multiple intelligences, we suggest a variety of ways to engage students in learning their basic facts. Through poems, songs, picture books, and videos students can learn their facts. Not all of these things are great. Some of them rely on mnemonic devices that teach students isolated facts but don't build number sense. We don't recommend that you do those! However, there is some really good, catchy, fun stuff out there that builds number sense. We highly recommend that you do those!

Throughout the chapters, we will look at how literature can serve as a springboard into unpacking various strategies. We will look at different ways that students can work on their facts, from individual games to partner games and small-group games. We will also discuss how various energizers and routines can help students to engage in distributed practice over time.

MATH LITERATURE

Children's picture books and poems can be a great springboard into teaching and learning the basic math facts (see Research Connection). They provide an understandable context so students can follow the story. They often intentionally teach a skill or concept. These books are engaging and have many extension possibilities. There is a great deal of research supporting the idea that using literature to teach math can be very powerful (Burns, 1992, 1995; Whitin & Whitin, 2004; Whitin & Wilde, 1992, 1995; Zambo, 2005). Scholars note that stories help students to understand the math and construct meaning through the story (Burns, 1995; Whitin & Whitin, 2004). Draper (2002) noted that "literacy and literacy instruction are necessary parts of mathematics instruction" (p. 523). Math literature "allows students to think deeply, discuss, debate" (Ducolon, 2000); and "gain experience with solving word problems in familiar stories" (Ward, 2005; Wilburne & Napoli, 2008).

> Integrating literature within mathematics lessons not only develops literacy skills, but also promotes mathematical language and problem solving. Moreover, the visual representation in the literature books not only stimulates readers, but also provides informative story lines that foster children's curiosity. The power of children's literature and mathematics provide readers with opportunities to try different strategies and to scaffold previous experiences to broaden one's learning.
>
> (Wilburne & Napoli, 2008, p. 2)

RESEARCH CONNECTION

"Many children's books present interesting problems and illustrate how other children solve them. Through these books, students see mathematics in a different context while they use reading as a form of communication" (p. 28).

(NCTM, 1989)

GAMIFICATION

Games are a great vehicle to get students to practice their facts. Research shows that students will spend 100 hours getting good at a video game (Gee, 2005). There are certain elements of game theory that students connect with. After writing extensively about game theory and education, Gee said:

> So the suggestion I leave you with is not "use games in school" – though that's a good idea – but: How can we make learning in and out of school, with or without using games, more game-like in the sense of using the sorts of learning principles young people see in good games every day when and if they are playing these games reflectively and strategically?
>
> (p. 11)

Dr. Nicki calls it the *purple popsicle stick theory*. She notes that,

> If you give students something that they need to do but don't want to do on a worksheet, there is resistance. But, if you put it on a purple popsicle stick and you tell students that whoever gets 5 first wins, they are all in!

The point is that students love games. They want to play games. Teachers just have to offer students academically rigorous, standards-based games that are engaging. Students love bonus rounds! When students love what they are doing they will stay engaged in what is called "infinite play" which means that they will play a game over and over until they master it because they are intrigued by it (Knewton, n.d.).

Why do games work? Students know where they are, what they are trying to do, what the endgame is, and what they need to do to get there. They engage and reflect. They monitor their progress. They do all the stuff we want them to do in school! Gee (2005) notes that students take on a particular identity in a game:

- commitment;
- interaction;
- production;
- risk-taking;
- customization;
- agency;
- well-ordered problems;
- challenge and consolidation;
- "just-in-time" or "on demand";
- pleasantly frustrating – idea of doable but challenging;
- performance before competence.

Hello! Are we listening? How do we, as educators, "Up our game!" Imagine if students worked on their facts with the same determination and engagement of a video game!

Imagine a classroom where when you tried to stop math class, the students begged to play just a few more minutes! Imagine a space where everyone knew exactly where they were on the learning continuum and what they needed to do to get better and they had a plan! This can happen, and it is happening! Hopefully, with some of the suggestions in this book, we will help you to get closer to creating those spaces or to enhancing what you already have.

KEY POINTS

- Dolch words of math
- cycle of engagement
- 21st century technologies
- engaging approaches
- math literature
- gamification.

SUMMARY

Basic facts are the foundation for most of the math that students will learn in school. There is a specific developmental approach to teaching and learning facts. We all need to learn the sequence and assess according to it so that we can address the specific needs of our students. The cycle of engagement builds a strong understanding of the facts by having students first work concretely, then pictorially, and finally abstractly. It is important to integrate 21st century technologies into the teaching and learning of facts so that students can practice in engaging and rigorous ways. We must be ever cognizant of applying multiple approaches so that we tap into the different ways that students learn. We need to consider the implications of game theory on our own pedagogy to see how we might better capture and keep the attention of our students.

REFLECTION QUESTIONS

1. How is fluency currently defined in your school?
2. What are your particular challenges around fluency?
3. What new ideas are you taking away from this chapter?

REFERENCES

Anstrom, T. (n.d.). *Supporting students in mathematics through the use of manipulatives.* Washington, DC: Center for Implementing Technology in Education. Retrieved November 15, 2017.

Baroody, A. J. (2006). Why children have difficulties mastering the basic number combinations and how to help them. *Teaching Children Mathematics, 13,* 22–31.

Battista, M. (2012). *Cognition-based assessment and teaching of addition and subtraction: Building on students' reasoning.* Portsmouth, NH: Heinemann.

Bender, W. (2009). *Differentiating math instruction: Strategies that work for K-* classroom.* Thousand Oaks, CA: Corwin Press.

Brownell, W. A. (1956/1987). Meaning and skill: Maintaining the balance. *Arithmetic Teacher,* 34(8), 18–25.

Brownell, W. A., & Chazal, C. B. (1935). The effects of premature drill in third-grade arithmetic. *The Journal of Educational Research,* 29(1), 17–28.

Burns, M. (1992). *Math and literature: (K-3). Book one.* Sausalito, CA: Math Solutions.

Burns, M. (1995). *Writing in math class.* Sausalito, CA: Math Solutions.

Devlin, K. (2000). Finding your inner mathematician. *The Chronicle of Higher Education,* 46, B5.

Draper, R. (2002). School mathematics reform, constructivism and literacy: A case for literacy instruction in the reform-oriented math classroom. *Journal of Adolescent & Adult Literacy,* 45(6), 520–529.

Ducolon, C. (2000). Quality literature as a springboard to problem solving. *Teaching Children Mathematics,* 6(7), 442–447.

Gamification. Retrieved November 20, 2017 from www.knewton.com/infographics/gamification-education/.

Gee, J. P. (2005). *Why video games are good for your soul: Pleasure and learning.* Melbourne: Common Ground.

Kilpatrick, J., Swafford, J., & Findell, B. (2001). *Adding it up: Helping children learn mathematics.* Washington, DC: National Academy Press.

Knewton (n.d.). Retrieved March 23, 2019 from www.knewton.com.

Logan, G. D. (1991). Automaticity and memory. In W. E. Hockley & S. Lewandowsky (Eds.), *Relating theory and data: Essays on human memory in honor of Bennett B. Murdock* (pp. 347–366). Hillsdale, NJ: Lawrence Erlbaum.

Maccini, P., & Gagnon, J. C. (2000). Best practices for teaching mathematics to secondary students with special needs. *Focus on Exceptional Children,* 32(5), 1–21.

National Council of Teachers of Mathematics. (1989). *Curriculum and evaluation standards for school mathematics.* Reston, VA: Author.

National Council of Teachers of Mathematics. (2000). *Principles and standards for school mathematics.* Reston, VA: National Council of Teachers of Mathematics.

Prensky, M. (2001). Digital natives, digital immigrants part 1. *On the Horizon,* 9(5), 1–6. doi:10.1108/10748120110424816.

Van de Walle, J. A. (2001). *Elementary and middle school mathematics: Teaching developmentally* (4th ed.). Boston, MA: Addison Wesley Longman, Inc.

Van de Walle, J. A. (2007). *Elementary and middle school mathematics: Teaching developmentally.* Boston, MA: Pearson/Allyn and Bacon.

Van de Walle, J. A., & Lovin, L. H. (2006). *Teaching student-centered mathematics: Grades K-3.* New York: Pearson.

Vygotsky, L. S. (1978). *Mind in society: The development of higher psychological processes.* Cambridge, MA: Harvard University Press.

Ward, R. (2005). Using children's literature to inspire K-8 preservice teachers' future mathematics pedagogy. *The Reading Teacher,* 59(2), 132–143.

Whitin, D. J., & Whitin, P. (2004). *New visions for linking literature and mathematics.* Urbana, IL: National Council of Teachers of English.

Whitin, D. J., & Wilde, S. (1992). *Read any good math lately? Children's books for mathematical learning, K-6*. Portsmouth, NH: Heinemann.

Whitin, D. J., & Wilde, S. (1995). *It's the story that counts: More children's books for mathematical learning, K-6*. Portsmouth, NH: Heinemann.

Wilburne, J., & Napoli, M. (2008). Connecting mathematics and literature: An analysis of pre-service elementary student teachers' changing beliefs and knowledge. *IUMST: The Journal, 2*.

Zambo, R. (2005). The power of two: Linking mathematics and literature. *Mathematics Teaching in the Middle School, 10*(8), 394–399.

CHAPTER 2

Modeling Math Facts

The evidence indicates, in short, that manipulatives can provide valuable support for student learning when teachers interact over time with the students to help them build links between the object, the symbol, and the mathematical idea both represent.

(Kilpatrick et al., 2001, p. 354)

Modeling addition and subtraction math strategies helps build conceptual understanding. Manipulatives are essential in the teaching and learning of mathematics (see the two Research Connections that follow). Concrete manipulatives are objects that students can touch, hold, feel, move around, and think with. Digital manipulatives are virtual tools that students can view and move around on the screen to show their thinking. Van de Walle et al. (2013) define a math tool as:

Any object, picture, or drawing that represents a concept or onto which the relationship for that concept can be imposed. Manipulatives are physical objects that students and teachers can use to illustrate and discover mathematical concepts, whether made specifically for mathematics (e.g., connecting cubes) or for other purposes (e.g. buttons).

(p. 24)

RESEARCH CONNECTION: CONSISTENTLY USE TOOLS

"[I]n order to develop every student's mathematical proficiency, leaders and teachers must systematically integrate the use of concrete and virtual manipulatives into classroom instruction at all grade levels" (NCSM, 2013).

Manipulatives allow students to see the math they are doing, model the math that they are learning, making the abstract more concrete, and they also provide a way for students to talk about their thinking (Hartshorn & Boren, 1990; Ruzic & O'Connell, 2001). Manipulatives can be engaging and inviting. We say inviting because they "invite" students to toodle around with the math they are learning. Students who work with manipulatives have been found to be more interested in math and students who are more interested have been found to tend to stick with it longer and achieve more (Sutton & Krueger, 2002).

RESEARCH CONNECTION: A HANDS-ON APPROACH

Wenglinsky (2000) found that "when students are exposed to hands-on learning on a weekly rather than a monthly basis, they prove to be 72% of a grade level ahead in mathematics" (p. 27).

The 2009 *Doing What Works Clearinghouse* report notes that visual models and manipulatives are one of the research-based recommendations to develop understanding. More specifically, the Concrete Representational Abstract (CRA) approach is supported. In this approach, students use concrete manipulatives to build understanding and see patterns, structure, and number relationships. After students work with manipulatives, they then begin to record their work with manipulatives through mathematical drawings and sketching. They represent the thinking they are doing with the manipulatives. As students are working with concrete, pictorial and abstract representations, they begin to deeply understand the math they are doing.

STRATEGIES AND MODELS

There is a difference between strategies and models. Strategies are what we do with numbers, such as composing and decomposing them. Models are how we show our thinking. Oftentimes, charts will use the term "strategies" but they are actually showing models. Be sure that your students know the difference and label them correctly. Here is a sample of some anchor charts to illustrate the difference. (See Figures 2.1 and 2.2.)

Models for Addition and Subtraction

1. Use your fingers

2. Make tallies

3. Use a 10 frame

4. Use a numberline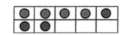

5. Use a <u>rekenrek</u>

FIGURE 2.1 Model Poster

Addition Strategies

Add 0	Adding 0 to a number results in the same number. $3 + 0 = 3$
Count on 1, 2, or 3	Count up when adding on small numbers like 1, 2, or 3.
Make Ten Pairs	Practice knowing all the number pairs for 10. $10 + 0$ $9 + 1$ $8 + 2$ $7 + 3$ $6 + 4$ $5 + 5$
Doubles	Add the number to itself for doubles.
Doubles Plus 1	Double the number and add 1 more.
Doubles Plus 2	Double the number and add 2 more OR double the number in the middle.
Bridge 10	Break apart one of the numbers to make a 10 with the other number.

FIGURE 2.2 Strategy Poster

CLASSROOM AS A TOOL KIT

First, the classroom should be a tool kit (see Figures 2.3 and 2.4). It should have several of the tools that are used in big, student-size form. For example, there should be number lines and number tracks that students can walk on. There should be a large hundreds grid and large five and ten frames that students can act out problems inside of. There should be a large part-part whole mat as well as a large number bond for students to act out problems. Acting out a problem is different than modeling it with the manipulatives. Students should have an opportunity to do both.

5 Frame	10 Frame	Double Ten Frame	Part-Part Whole Mat
	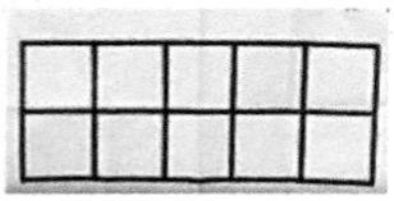	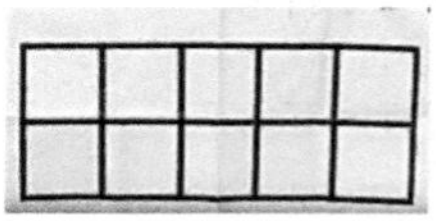 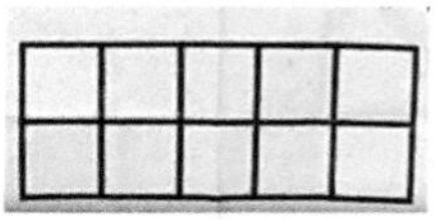	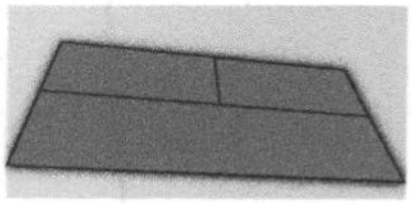

FIGURE 2.3 Classroom as a Tool Kit

Number Bond	Number Line/ Number Ladder	Large Unifix Cubes Get here:	Large Hundreds Grid Get here:	Large Hundreds Grid Get here:
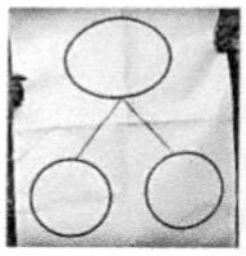		http://www. didax.com/ jumbo-unifix-cubes-set-of-100-vp.html	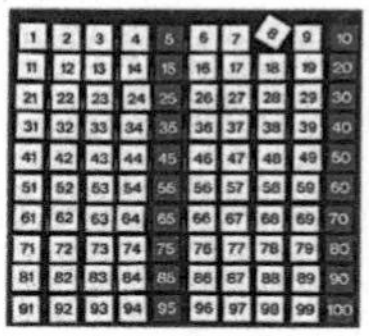 http://www.didax. com/catalogsearch/ result/?q=hundred+chart	http://www.technolog yrocksseriously.com/ 2009/12/big-printable-playing-cards.html#. WqqTw5P4_Us

FIGURE 2.4 More Big Classroom Materials, Templates, and Mats

INDIVIDUAL STUDENT TOOL KITS

We believe that students need tool kits that they can turn to and use at any moment. We also think that individual tool kits are an important part of math class. (See Figures 2.5–2.7.) They don't have to be specific to each student, although they could be. However, there should be a place where the templates and the tools are centrally located so that when the teacher pulls up the ten frame on the smartboard, students can open up to their laminated ten frames and either act out the same problem with manipulatives or draw it out. Students need tool kits so when the teacher pulls out the number line, students can pull out their number lines and hop and draw on them. Students need tool kits because *Math is NOT a Spectator Sport* and they need to play the game not watch it!

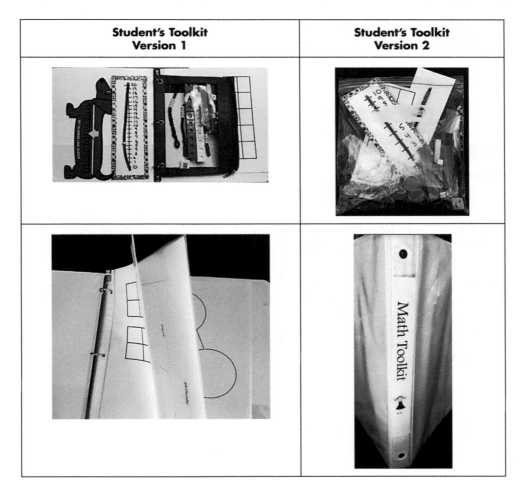

Student's Toolkit Version 1	Student's Toolkit Version 2

FIGURE 2.5 Tool Kits

Top 10 Tools to Teach Basic Addition and Subtraction				
Red/white or red/yellow counters	**Unifix cubes/ snap cube**	**Bears**	**Base ten blocks**	**Rekenrek**
One inch tiles	**Cuisenaire© rods**	**Cards**	**Dice**	**Dominos**

FIGURE 2.6 Tools

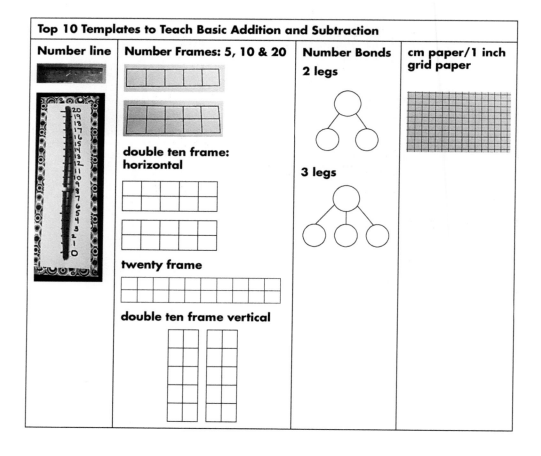

Top 10 Templates to Teach Basic Addition and Subtraction			
Number line	**Number Frames: 5, 10 & 20**	**Number Bonds** **2 legs** **3 legs**	**cm paper/1 inch grid paper**
	double ten frame: horizontal		
	twenty frame		
	double ten frame vertical		

Part-Part Whole Mat	Number Ladder	Addition Mat	Subtraction Mat	Rekenrek paper
	10 9 8 7 6 5 4 3 2 1		Subtraction Mat 5 – 2 minuend subtrahend □ – ○ ↓ difference	

Hundred Grids: 20, 50, 100, 120

1	2	3	4	5	6	7	8	9	10
11	12	13	14	15	16	17	18	19	20
21	22	23	24	25	26	27	28	29	30
31	32	33	34	35	36	37	39	39	40
41	42	43	44	45	46	47	48	49	50
51	52	53	54	55	56	57	58	59	60
61	62	63	64	65	66	67	67	69	70
71	72	73	74	75	76	77	78	79	80
81	82	83	84	85	86	87	88	89	90
91	92	93	94	95	96	97	98	99	100
101	102	103	104	105	106	107	108	109	110
111	112	113	114	115	116	117	118	119	120

1	2	3	4	5	6	7	8	9	10
11	12	13	14	15	16	17	18	19	20
21	22	23	24	25	26	27	28	29	30
31	32	33	34	35	36	37	39	39	40
41	42	43	44	45	46	47	48	49	50

1	2	3	4	5	6	7	8	9	10
11	12	13	14	15	16	17	18	19	20

FIGURE 2.7 Templates

TEACHER'S TOOL KIT

The teacher should have a tool kit ready to go. In this way the teacher isn't running around every time trying to get the basic tools to model something. The teacher's tool kit should mirror the students' tool kits. One of the things that the teacher should have in their tool kit is magnetized manipulatives. These can be bought or made. To make them, you simply have to buy magnet tape and glue it onto the manipulatives.

DIGITAL TOOL KIT

There are so many wonderful digital tools out there now. We are amazed at how many there are and the different types of things that you can do with them (see Figures 2.8 and 2.9). In the figures that follow are some of our favorites.

Virtual Number Frames	Virtual Number Lines Open and Marked Lines	Virtual Rekenrek	Virtual Number Bead
https://apps.mathlearningcenter.org/number-frames/ 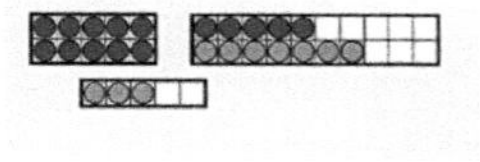	https://apps.mathlearningcenter.org/number-line/ 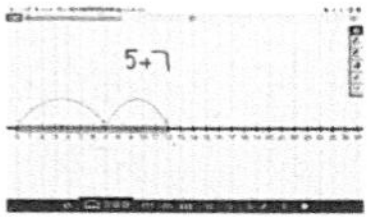	https://apps.mathlearningcenter.org/number-rack/ 	https://mathsframe.co.uk/en/resources/resource/69/itp-beadstring
Virtual Cuisenaire rods	Virtual Hundreds Grid	Virtual Bears in a Boat and other manipulatives	Virtual Money
https://www.mathplayground.com/mathbars.html	http://www.abcya.com/interactive_100_number_chart.htm	http://www.glencoe.com/sites/common_assets/mathematics/ebook_assets/vmf/VMF-Interface.html	https://www.mathlearningcenter.org/resources/apps/money-piece 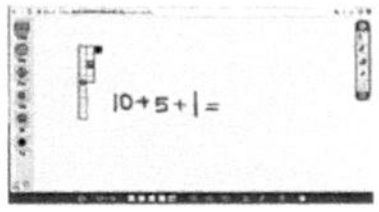

FIGURE 2.8 Digital Tools

Top Ten Math Fluency Apps
Fast Facts Early Addition
Fast Facts Math
Math Slide (+/-)
Splash Math Bingo
Math Dots
Sushi Monster
Mathmateer
Mental Math: Addition & Subtraction
Number Bubbles
Addimals

FIGURE 2.9 Apps

ANCHOR CHARTS

It is important that the teacher makes anchor charts with the students so that they can discuss, explain, and understand the different strategies. Teachers should put a QR code on these charts, take a picture, and send them home to parents so that parents can watch videos of the strategies in action. These videos can be made by the teacher, the students, or pulled from YouTube, TeacherTube or SchoolTube. (See Figure 2.10.) There should be a place in the classroom where these can stay up for most, if not all, of the year. Moreover, students should have an opportunity to make their own charts. Students should keep their charts in their math journal under the Math Strategy Section.

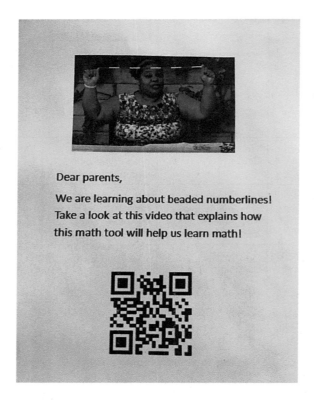

FIGURE 2.10 Example Digital Parent Explanation

KEY POINTS

- strategies and models
- cycle of engagement – concrete, pictorial, and abstract
- concrete tools
- classroom as a tool kit
- individual student tool kits
- teacher tool kits
- digital tools.

SUMMARY

Modeling math facts is an essential part of developing a conceptual understanding of how numbers work together. We model our thinking with tools. We want students to go through the cycle of engagement – concrete, pictorial, and abstract. We need tools and tool kits to help to do this. There should not only be the concrete tools but also digital tools. Students should have their own tool kits, with templates that they can write on and tools that they have at their fingertips. Teachers should have their own tool kits as well, so that they can have easy access to the templates and tools that they need during mini-lessons and guided math lessons. This is not to say that everything is in a tool kit. Rather, this is to say that there is a specific set of everyday tools that students have instant access to when they need them.

REFLECTION QUESTIONS

1. In what ways are you modeling facts currently?
2. Are you using your classroom as a tool kit with big models of the tools?
3. What are some takeaways you have from this chapter?

REFERENCES

Hartshorn, R., & Boren, S. (1990). *Experiential learning of mathematics: Using manipulatives*. Martin, TN & Charleston, WV: ERIC Clearinghouse on Rural Education and Small Schools.

Institute of Educational Science (2009). *Doing What Works Clearinghouse*. Retrieved March 23, 2019 from https://ies.ed.gov/ncee/wwc/Docs/InterventionReports/wwc_earobics_011309.pdf.

Kilpatrick, J., Swafford, J., & Findell, B. (2001). *Adding it up: Helping children learn mathematics*. Washington, DC: National Academy Press.

National Council of Supervisors of Mathematics (2013). *Improving student achievement in mathematics by using manipulatives with classroom instruction.* Aurora, CO: NCSM Position Paper.

Ruzic, R., & O'Connell, K. (2001). *Manipulatives.* National Center on Accessing the General Curriculum. Retrieved from www.cast.org/ncac/index.cfm?i=1666.

Sutton, J., & Krueger, A. (2002). *What we know about mathematics teaching and learning.* Aurora, CO: Mid-continent Research for Education and Learning.

Van de Walle, J. A., Karp, K. S., & Bay Williams, J. M. (2013). *Elementary and middle school mathematics: Teaching developmentally* (8th ed.). Boston, MA: Pearson.

Wenglinsky, H. (2000). *How teaching matters: Bringing the classroom back into discussions of teacher quality.* Princeton, NJ: Educational Testing Service.

PART II

Introduction to Exploring and Learning Addition Strategies

CHAPTER 3

Exploring and Learning Addition Facts within 10

"To many, the word basic implies something that is 'simple,' 'straightforward,' or 'easy.' In mathematics classrooms, however, teaching and learning the 'basic' facts is anything but simple."

(Crespo et al., 2005)

INTRODUCTION

In this chapter we will discuss different strategies to work on adding within 10 (Henry & Brown, 2008; Van de Walle, 2007). When introducing these early math concepts, real-life objects like actual pencils or toy cars support thinking and help students to model the situation and accurately calculate. From there, students may use cubes or other items that can represent these objects.

As we progress through the chapter we will look at the sophistication of the strategies (Baroody, 2006). It is developmentally appropriate for students in the early stage of direct modeling to build the problem by putting out objects to represent the first addend, and then putting out the amount of the second addend, and then counting them all. While we work with our students, we want to help students transition to counting on by helping them to notice that we can count on from the larger amount to make it easier for our brain.

COMMUTATIVE PROPERTY OF ADDITION

As we are working on addition strategies, it is incredibly helpful to spend some time exploring the Commutative Property of Addition since it will cut the number of math facts in half. Once children understand that they can change the order of the addends without changing the sum, they are on their way to being efficient math thinkers. Cuisenaire© rods are a very helpful tool to explore this, since you can visually see how the two equations are equal to each other. This part-part whole visual model really illustrates the power of concrete models in building understanding. Here's an example:

We can begin by saying yellow plus purple is the same as purple plus yellow. Then, we can progress the concept to 5 plus 4 equals 4 plus 5. Finally, we can record this situation using a number sentence: 5 + 4 = 4 + 5. (See Figure 3.1.)

FIGURE 3.1 Commutative Property Example

EXPLORING AND LEARNING TO ADD 1

There is an ongoing discussion in the literature about what is tougher to teach, adding 1 or adding 0. Many researchers note that adding 0 is much more difficult because it is the concept of "no quantity" (Merritt & Brannon, 2012). So, oftentimes, teachers will introduce adding 1 first. The Add 1 strategy provides an exciting opportunity for students to discover that the resulting sum is always the next counting number.

Similar to learning the ABCs, students are able to recite the counting numbers long before they understand that the words for the numbers represent a quantity. It is important to note that this is not an indication of understanding. Because of this, we need to assist them as they attach the word for a number to the quantity represented, and then connect that to the written numeral. Knowing the correct number order sequence helps with adding 1 to a number.

A great way to introduce Add 1 is through poems, songs, and picture books. Students must have a variety of experiences to develop understanding by modeling the Add 1 facts using a variety of concrete and digital tools within the context of real-life situations (see Figures 3.3–3.12). We want students to develop automaticity with their Add 1 facts and also generalize what will happen when we add 1 to any number. After students are comfortable with the idea of just knowing that it is the number that follows when adding 1, then we can move onto counting on with 2 and 3.

WHOLE CLASS MINI-LESSON: USING A MATH ANCHOR TEXT

Launch: *Teacher has seated students in a circle on the class rug.*

Teacher: *We're going to read a book now called Fish Eyes by Lois Ehlert. In this book, we are going to be meeting a little gray fish. He adds himself to different numbers of fish. I'd like your help to figure out how many fish there are on many of these pages. We can act out the story. (Teacher reads Fish Eyes. She has fish cut out. Three students go to the front of the class. One more student comes up.)*

Teacher: *Tell me how many fish are there now?*

Justina: *3.*

Teacher: *What did we learn in this word problem?*

Justina: *There were 3 fish swimming.*

Teacher: *What else did we learn?*

Justina: *1 more joins them.*

Teacher: *How can you figure out how many there are now?*

Justina: *I can count them all. 1–2–3–4. There are 4. Oh, there aren't 3, there are 4. (Students then act out several pages of the book. 6 students go to the front of the class. 1 more joins them.)*

Teacher: *OK could someone tell me how many fish there are now?*

Jaritza: *7.*

Teacher: *How did you figure that out, Jaritza?*

Jaritza: *I counted them all up.*

Teacher: *Could you come to the front and show us?*

(Jaritza points to each student and counts 1–2–3–4–5–6–7.)

Teacher: Thank you Jaritza, does anyone have another way to figure out how many fish there are?

Zoeigh: I know that there are 6 fish to start so I know that I can put that number in my head and then count 1 more to get to 7.

Teacher: Who agrees with Zoeigh that we can start with six and then add one more to figure out the answer? (Show of hands – teacher calls on a student who is raising his hand.) How do you know that adding 1 more to 6 is 7?

Michael: It's the next number. I say 6 and then 7.

Teacher: So in both cases we have figured out that there are 7 fish. It's just that one way is a little quicker, isn't it? Let me show you how we can write this as an equation. (Teacher writes 3 + 1 = 4.)

Next day The teacher reads Fish Eyes and uses the ten frames to act out the pages where the gray fish adds himself to the number of fish on the two-page spreads. The teacher can also record the equations on the side of the board to keep track of all the equations in the book. There are a variety of resources to support the teaching of this concept (see Figures 3.8 and 3.9).

 SPOTLIGHT ACTIVITY

Ten Apples Up on Top by Theo LeSieg

Reading the book *Ten Apples Up on Top* will help students explore what happens when we add 1 more to a number. For each page, count the number of apples on top. Record on the board how many there are on each page. After a few pages, ask the students if they have noticed a pattern to the new number of apples on the heads of the characters. On each new page another apple is added. Once this pattern is discussed, have students predict what number of apples will come next and have students defend their predictions (see Figure 3.2).

Red Counters	Plus 1 apple picture	Cuisenaire© rod build	Resources and Lesson Plans
Students are given a paper with the characters from the story and they act out the story with red counters as the apples.	Students are given a paper with animal faces. They draw a certain number of red apples on top. Then, they draw a green apple on the very top. Students record the equation that represents that situation of adding one more.	While reading the book, students will build the Cuisenaire© rod representation of the number of apples on the heads. They will add the one cube to the current Cuisenaire© rod and discuss the addition equation.	**https://www. education.com/ lesson-plan/ten-apples-up-on-top/**
			http://www. kindergarten-lessons.com/ ten-apples-up-on-top/

FIGURE 3.2 *Ten Apples Up on Top* Examples

MATH WORKSTATIONS

Workstations to Explore Add 1		
Concrete	**Pictorial**	**Abstract**
Roll or Pull and Build an Add 1 fact on a Ten Frame	Draw on Ten Frame Model	Add 1 Clip Flashcards
Roll and Build an Add 1 fact on a Rekenrek	Draw on Rekenrek Model	Spin and Add 1 to 5 or 10
Roll and Build an Add 1 fact with the Cubes	Draw on Cube Template	Add 1 Board Game
Roll and Build an Add 1 fact in a Part-Part Whole Mat	Draw in a Part-Part Whole Mat	Add 1 War
Roll and Show an Add 1 fact in a Number Bond	Draw and Show in a Number Bond	Add 1 Tic-Tac-Toe
Add 1 with Play-Doh©	Add 1 Domino Sort & Record	Pull and Add 1
Spin and Build an Add 1 to 5	Add 1 Booklet	Add 1 Four in a Row
Spin and Build an Add 1 to 10	Savvy Subitizing Pull and 1	Show or Record on Number Path
Flashcard build		Show or Record on Number Line
Show with Cuisenaire© rods		Power Towers
		Add 1 Bingo

FIGURE 3.3 Math Workstations

CONCRETE ACTIVITIES

Add 1 Concrete Activities		
Roll and Build with Cubes	**Roll and Build Part-Part Whole Mat**	**Roll and Show in a Number Bond**
Students roll a dice and add 1 more to model it.	Students roll the dice and add 1 more to model it on the Part-Part Whole Mat.	Students roll the dice and add 1 more to model it in a number bond.
	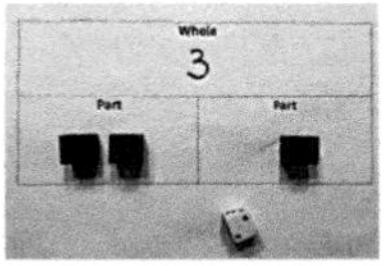	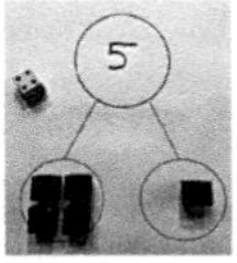

FIGURE 3.4 Concrete Activities

PICTORIAL ACTIVITIES

Add 1 Pictorial Activities		
Roll and Draw on a Number Bond	Savvy Subitizing Cards Pull (deck of cards available from https://buildmathminds.com/shop/)	Class Book Project Based on Fish Eyes by Lois Ehlert
Students roll a dice, add 1 more and model it on a number bond.	Students pull one card from the deck and then add 1 more.	Having students make a big class book of fish eyes is a great way to use math literature. This book can then be in the math workstation library and students can reread it throughout the year.
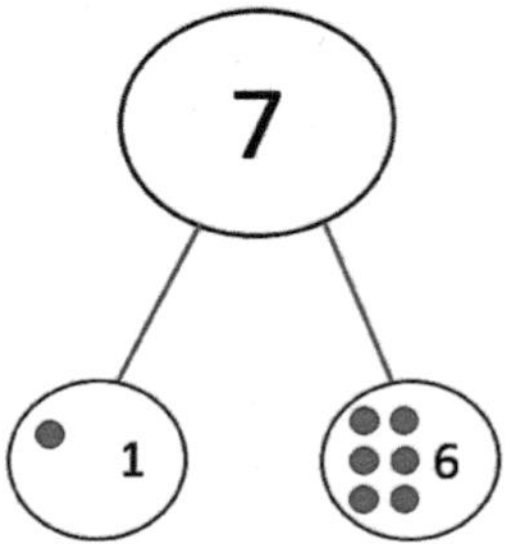	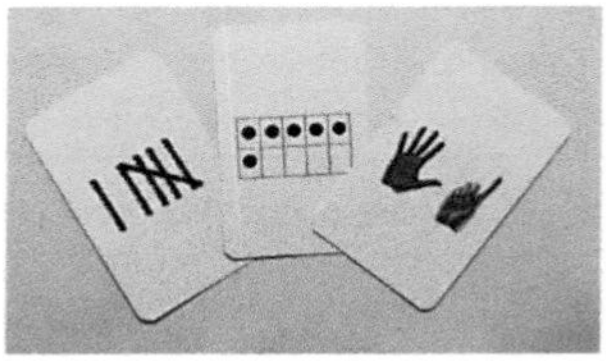	Draw a picture to match the situation on your page of the book. Next, write the equation that matches the situation on your page. _____ + 1 = _____

FIGURE 3.5 Pictorial Activities

ABSTRACT ACTIVITIES

<table>
<tr><th colspan="3">Add 1 Abstract Activities</th></tr>
<tr><th>Clip Flashcards</th><th>Tic-Tac-Toe</th><th>Pull a Card</th></tr>
<tr><td>Students use a clothespin to clip the correct sum. On the back is a dot indicating the correct answer.</td><td>Students play Tic-Tac-Toe as usual but they have to answer the question in the space before they can put an x or an o. Whoever gets 3 in a row first wins.</td><td>Students pull a card and add 1 to that number. They record the answer on a recording sheet or in their math journal.</td></tr>
<tr><td>
<table>
<tr><th colspan="3">Clip the correct sum.
3 + 1</th></tr>
<tr><td>4</td><td>2</td><td>5</td></tr>
</table>
</td><td>
<table>
<tr><th colspan="3">Plus 1 Tic-Tac-Toe</th></tr>
<tr><td>2 + 1</td><td>3 + 1</td><td>4 + 1</td></tr>
<tr><td>7 + 1</td><td>5 + 1</td><td>6 + 1</td></tr>
<tr><td>8 + 1</td><td>9 + 1</td><td>10 + 1</td></tr>
</table>
</td><td>

____ + 1 = _____
</td></tr>
</table>

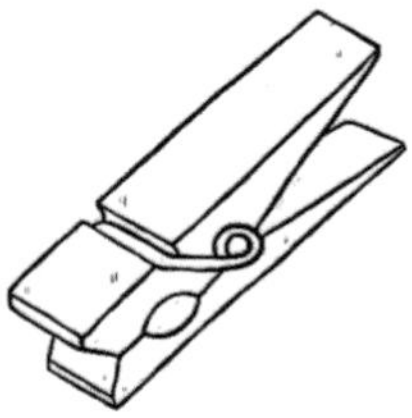

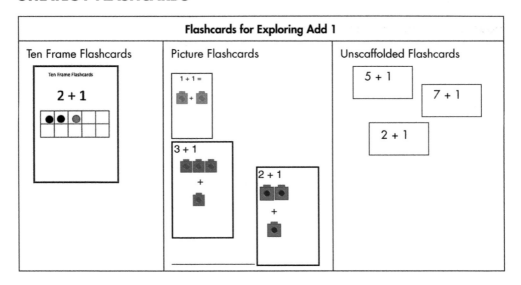

FIGURE 3.6 Abstract Activities

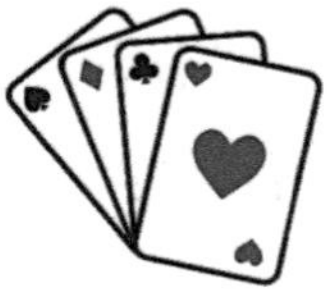

STRATEGY FLASHCARDS

<table>
<tr><th colspan="3">Flashcards for Exploring Add 1</th></tr>
<tr><td>Ten Frame Flashcards
</td><td>Picture Flashcards
</td><td>Unscaffolded Flashcards
5 + 1
7 + 1
2 + 1</td></tr>
</table>

FIGURE 3.7 Strategy Flashcards for Exploring Add 1

WORD PROBLEMS

In every fluency module there should be a focus on word problems. Here are a few examples of the types of word problems for Add 1.			
My Add 1 Story Problems Booklet	**Marquis had 3 fish. He caught 1 more. How many fish does he have now?**	**There were 6 chickens and 1 pig on a farm. How many animals were there altogether?**	**There were 4 giraffes eating leaves. 1 more giraffe joined them. How many giraffes were there?**
	Write the set-up equation:	**Write the set-up equation:**	**Write the set-up equation:**
	Show your thinking with a model.	**Show your thinking with a model.**	**Show your thinking with a model.**
	Write the solution equation.	**Write the solution equation.**	**Write the solution equation.**

FIGURE 3.8 Word Problems

RESOURCES

Picture Books

Books about Add 1				
Fish Eyes by Lois Ehlert Video reading: https://youtu.be/3YWKHo1Bghl	One Hungry Monster: Counting Book in Rhyme by Susan Heyboer O'Keefe	Mouse Count by Ellen Stoll Walsh	Ten Black Dots by Donald Crews	Feast for 10 by Cathryn Falwell
Counting Crocodiles by Judy Sierra	One Guinea Pig is Not Enough - Katie Duke			

FIGURE 3.9 Picture Books

Videos

 Video - Add 1

Ann Elise video on math tools to use to teach the Add 1 strategy:
https://youtu.be/XMB-oon6Rrg
PISD Mathematics, Fact Fluency Video Count On & Count Back: https://youtu.be/N36t_sSZPww
Harry Kindergarten videos on adding 1: https://youtu.be/INHYb1RNaMM

FIGURE 3.10 Videos

Anchor Charts

Anchor charts support the teaching and learning of Add 1. Here are a few examples of what they might look like. It is important that the teacher make the charts with the students, but also that students have an opportunity to make their own charts. Students should keep their charts in their math journal under the Math Strategy Section.

Strategy: Add 1

When we add one, the sum is the 'neighbor number'

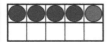

When we add 1, it is the next number on the number line.

FIGURE 3.11 Anchor Chart

Quiz

Add 1 Quiz

Name: Date:

3 + 1 = Model with a drawing.	8 + 1 = Model on the ten frame. (ten frame grid)	Solve. Hannah had 6 marbles. She was given 1 more. How many marbles does she have now? Write the equation: Answer: _____
Solve. Jillian had 2 princess dolls. She was given 1 more. How many does she have now? Write the equation: Answer: _____	Solve. 5 + ____ = 6 ____ + 1 = 4 8 = 7 + _____ ____ = 8 + 1	Interview Question: What is the Add 1 strategy? Explain with numbers, words and pictures.

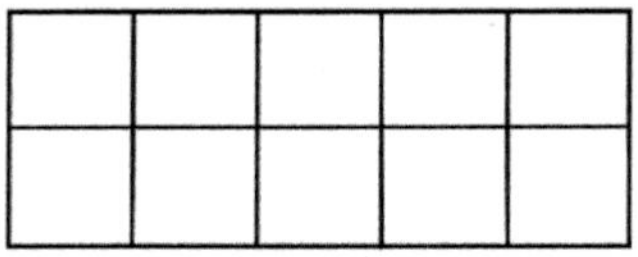

6 + 1 =

Model on the number line.

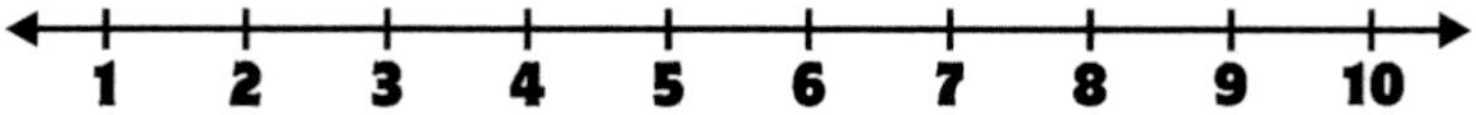

```
◄──┬───┬───┬───┬───┬───┬───┬───┬───┬───►
   1   2   3   4   5   6   7   8   9   10
```

Circle how good you think you are at doing Add 1 facts!

Great   Good    OK, still thinking

FIGURE 3.12 Quiz

EXPLORING AND LEARNING HOW TO ADD 0

Adding 0 to a number is a tricky idea. We have to make sure that students have plenty of opportunities to act it out, work on it with concrete materials, and draw it before we just work on abstract problems. We have outlined specific activities to engage students in how to Add 0 that supports understanding (see Figures 3.16–3.25).

WHOLE CLASS MINI-LESSON

Launch: *Teacher passes out 4 connecting cubes to one student.*

Teacher: *Good morning, class. Today we are going to be learning about how to add 0 to a number. Can anyone tell me how many cubes Joey has? (Calling on a student who raised her hand.)*

Melissa: *4.*

Teacher: *How do you know he has 4 cubes?*

Melissa: *I counted them. 1–2–3–4.*

Teacher: *Thumbs up if you agree with Melissa that Joey has 4 cubes. (Checks to see that students agree.) How would I write that amount as a number?*

Teacher: *What if I didn't give him anymore? How many would he have now? (Teacher does this with a few students.)*

Teacher pulls up a virtual ten frame (see Figure 3.13).

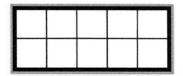

(From the Math Learning Center Virtual Number Frame App
https://www.mathlearningcenter.org/resources/apps/number-frames)

FIGURE 3.13 Virtual Ten Frame

Teacher: *Let's try this situation with our ten frame counters. There were 4 penguins on the rock. Then no more penguins came. How many penguins are there? (See Figure 3.14.)*

Melissa: *4.*

Teacher: *How do you know?*

Melissa: *I counted them.*

Teacher: *That's right. So how could we write that using numbers? (Teacher calls on volunteers to determine that 4 + 0 = 4 can represent this situation.) We have discussed the number 0 and why it is so important. It is a way we can talk about not having anything. I'm going to read you a story called Zero that talks about this special number.*

Follow-up next day: *Teacher reads Zero is the Leaves on the Trees by Betsy Franco and Shino Arihara (see Figure 3.22).*

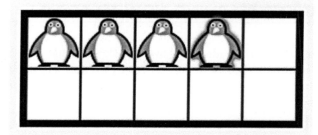

(From the Math Learning Center Virtual Number Frame App
https://www.mathlearningcenter.org/resources/apps/number-frames)

FIGURE 3.14 Ten Frame

 SPOTLIGHT ACTIVITY

Poems and songs are great ways to capture students' attention. This poem is just a fun chanting poem, where students can act out some examples. Students should do several activities where they experience 0. For example, as they say this poem they can act it out on their fingers and then discuss it and give other examples (see Figure 3.15).

ZERO ZERO
THAT'S ITS NAME!
WHEN YOU ADD A NUMBER TO IT... THE NUMBER STAYS THE SAME.....
0 + 1 = 1
0 + 2 = 2
0 + 3 = 3
THAT'S JUST THE WAY IT'S ALWAYS GOING TO BE!
ZERO ZERO
THAT'S ITS NAME!
WHEN YOU ADD A NUMBER TO IT... THE NUMBER STAYS THE SAME.....

FIGURE 3.15 Zero Poem

MATH WORKSTATIONS

Workstations to Explore Add 0		
Concrete	**Pictorial**	**Abstract**
Roll or Pull and Build an Add 0 fact on a Ten Frame	Draw on Ten Frame Model	Add 0 Clip Flashcards
Roll and Build an Add 0 fact on a Rekenrek	Draw on Rekenrek Model	Spin and Add 0 to 5 or 10
Roll and Build an Add 0 fact with the Cubes	Draw on Cube Template	Add 0 War
Roll and Build an Add 0 fact in a Part-Part Whole Mat	Draw in a Part-Part Whole Mat	Add 0 Tic-Tac-Toe
Roll and Show an Add 0 fact in a Number Bond	Draw and Show in a Number Bond	Pull and Add 0
Add 0 with Play-Doh©	Add 0 Domino Sort & Record	Add 0 Four in a Row
Spin, Build and Add 0 to 5	Add 0 Booklet	Show or Record on a number path
Spin, Build and Add 0 to 10	Savvy Subitizing Pull and Add 0	Show or Record on a number line
Add 0 Flashcard Build		Power Towers
Show with Cuisenaire© rods		Add 0 Bingo
		Flashcards

FIGURE 3.16 Math Workstations

CONCRETE ACTIVITIES

Add 0 Concrete Activities		
Roll or Pull and Build on a Ten Frame	**Spin and Build with Cubes**	**Roll and Build on a Rekenrek**
Students roll a dice or pull a card and build on a ten frame. Students will develop the understanding through many experiences the generalization that any number we add to 0 results in the same number.	Students spin the spinner and build with cubes to add 0.	Students roll a dice and build on a rekenrek to model adding 0.
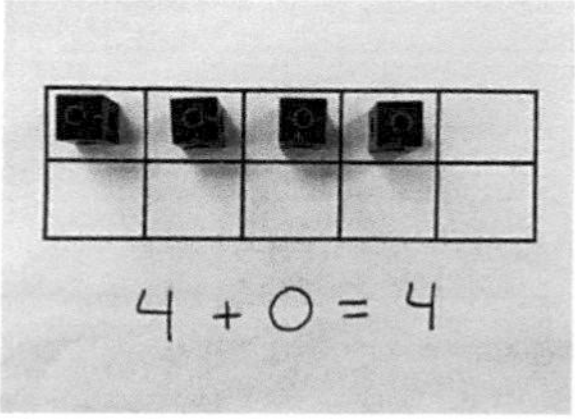 $4 + 0 = 4$	 $3 + 0 = 3$	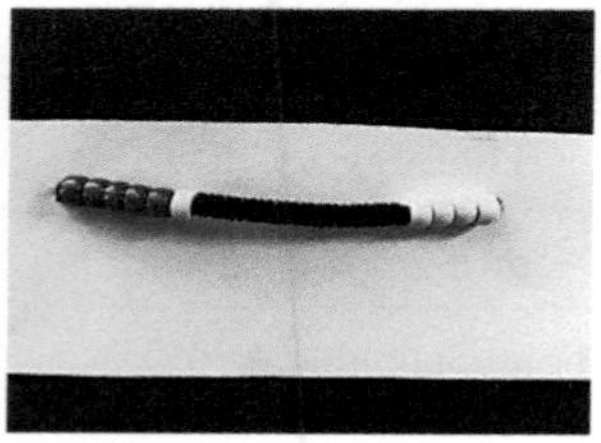 $6 + 0 = 6$

FIGURE 3.17 Concrete Activities Add 0

PICTORIAL ACTIVITIES

Add 0 Pictorial Activities		
Roll or Pull a Card and Draw on a Ten Frame	**Roll or Pull a Card and Draw on a Part-Part Whole Mat**	**Savvy Subitizing Cards Pull (deck of cards available from https://buildmathminds.com/shop/)**
Students roll a dice or pull a card and draw on a ten frame to model adding 0.	Students roll a dice or pull a card and draw on a part-part whole mat to model adding 0.	Students pull a card and add 0 to it.
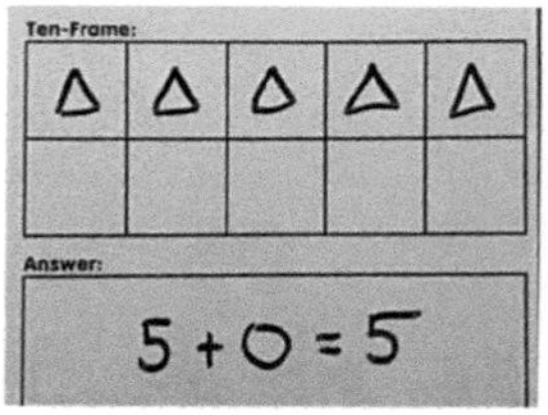 $5 + 0 = 5$	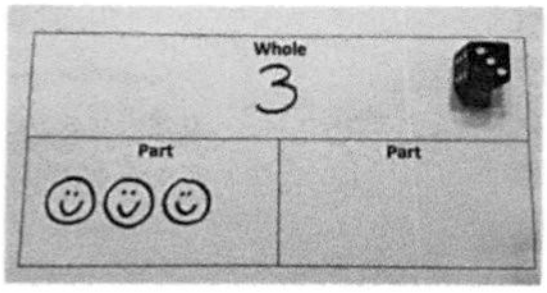	

FIGURE 3.18 Pictorial Activities Add 0

ABSTRACT ACTIVITIES

Add 0 Abstract Activities		
War	**Roll or Pull and Record on a Number Path**	**Four in a Row**
Students each pull a flashcard and whoever has the largest sum wins that hand and gets the two cards. Whoever has the most cards at the end of the game is the winner. Or you could roll a die with only "more" or "less" on it to determine the winner.	Students roll a dice or pull a card and record adding 0 on a number path.	Students pull a card, add 0, and cover the sum on the gameboard. 4 in a row wins.

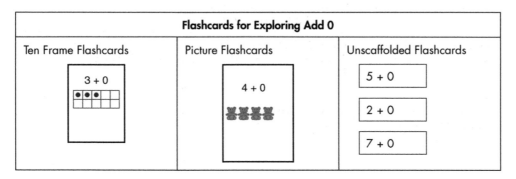

FIGURE 3.19 Abstract Activities Add 0

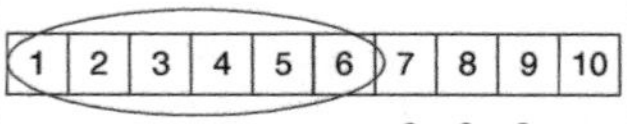

STRATEGY FLASHCARDS

Flashcards for Exploring Add 0		
Ten Frame Flashcards	Picture Flashcards	Unscaffolded Flashcards

Ten Frame Flashcards:

$3 + 0$

Picture Flashcards:

$4 + 0$

Unscaffolded Flashcards:

$5 + 0$

$2 + 0$

$7 + 0$

FIGURE 3.20 Strategy Flashcards Add 0

WORD PROBLEMS

In every fluency module there should be a focus on word problems. Here are a few examples of the types of word problems for Add 0.			
My Add 0 Story Problems Booklet	**Dan had 4 pairs of sneakers. He didn't buy any more of them. How many pairs of sneakers does he have now?** **Write the set-up equation:** **Show your thinking with a model.** **Write the solution equation.**	**There were 4 pigs rolling in the mud and no more pigs joined them. How many pigs were rolling in the mud?** **Write the set-up equation:** **Show your thinking with a model.** **Write the solution equation.**	**Rod had 5 plants. He did not buy any more. How many plants does he have now?** **Write the set-up equation:** **Show your thinking with a model.** **Write the solution equation.**

FIGURE 3.21 Word Problems

RESOURCES

Picture Books

Books about Zero	
Zero by Kathryn Otoshi	Zero is the Leaves on the Trees by Betsy Franco

FIGURE 3.22 Picture Books

Videos

 Videos about Add 0

Sesame Street video exploring the concept of the number 0: https://youtu.be/xjHSPyFjZpc
Adding 0 song: https://youtu.be/wy389QGYe4I
Homeschool Pop video on adding 0: https://youtu.be/UGXp5GjqifQ
PISD Mathematics, +/- 0 Facts Part–Part Whole Mat: https://youtu.be/rNyKFP8WEag

FIGURE 3.23 Videos

Anchor Chart

Anchor charts support the teaching and learning of Add 0. Here is an example of what one might look like. It is important that the teacher makes the charts *with* the students, but also that the students have an opportunity to make their *own* charts. Students should keep their charts in their math journal under the Math Strategy Section.

Strategy: Add 0
When we add 0 to a number the number stays the same! **1 + 0 = 1** **2 + 0 = 2** **3 + 0 = 3**

FIGURE 3.24 Anchor Chart

Quiz

Add 0 Quiz

Name:

Date:

$2 + 0 =$ Model with a drawing.	$7 + 0 =$ Model on the ten frame.	Solve. Matthew had 4 shirts with Goofy on them. He got 0 more. How many does he have now? Write the equation: Answer: _____
Solve. Kathryn had 3 paintings. She got 0 more. How many does she have now? Write the equation: Answer: _____	Solve. $6 + \_\_\_\_ = 6$ $\_\_\_\_ + 0 = 9$ $5 = 5 + _____$ $\_\_\_\_\_ = 4 + 0$	Interview Question: What is the Add 0 strategy? Explain with numbers, words and pictures.

$5 + 0 =$

Model on the number line.

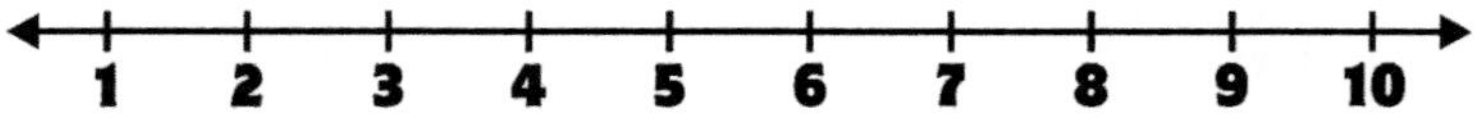

```
◄——┼——┼——┼——┼——┼——┼——┼——┼——┼——┼——►
    1   2   3   4   5   6   7   8   9   10
```

Circle how good you think you are at doing Add 0 facts!

Great   Good    OK, still thinking

FIGURE 3.25 Add 0 Quiz

EXPLORING AND LEARNING TO ADD 2 AND 3

After students learn to add on 1, then this understanding is extended to counting on 2 and 3 from the largest addend. For example, when given the expression 2 + 6, we want students to recognize that since the 6 is larger they should begin there and count on 2. They can determine the sum of 8 quickly using this strategy. A great way to introduce it is through poems, songs, and picture books.

Model this strategy with any counting objects you may have. It is best to use two colors of objects so that students can see the two addends and how they make the total amount all together. Once they have modeled the situation with the objects, encourage them to determine the sum by starting with the larger amount as a group and then count on the 2 or 3. As children develop their early number sense, they will initially count all the objects, so as often as you can, point out that counting them all takes longer than counting on, yet it results in the same total amount.

A powerful instructional routine is to have students subitize a number and then count up 1 or 2 or 3 from that number. As with all strategy work, we are trying to help students become flexible and efficient so that they can free up working memory. We want them to conserve mental energy for more difficult problems. They learn this by working through a variety of activities (see Figures 3.27–3.37).

WHOLE CLASS MINI-LESSON: COUNTING ON

Launch: *Teacher has seated students in a circle on the class rug. Teacher has given a rekenrek to each student and has one demonstration-sized rekenrek. Teacher writes this word problem on the board: Maya had 4 marbles, then her mom gave her 2 more. Teacher reads the problem to the students two times.*

Teacher: *Tell me one piece of information we are given in this problem.*

Zachary: *Maya had 4 marbles.*

Teacher: *What else do we know?*

Hannah: *She got 2 more.*

Teacher: *Boys and girls, what number should I start working with first and why?*

Mary: *4.*

Teacher: *Why?*

Tim: *Because it is the greater number?*

Teacher: *Why do I want to start with the greater number?*

Conner: *Because you can add it fast that way.*

Teacher: *Can you all model that on your rekenrek? Who wants to come to the board and model it on the virtual one?*

Tami: *Here I moved over 4 and then added 2 more. I got 6.*

Teacher: *Did you all get the same sum as she did?*

(Students say yes and the teacher continues to practice different count on problems with them.) (see Figure 3.26).

SPOTLIGHT ACTIVITY

Counting on cards are great scaffolds for students. Here is an example of how these cards can help scaffold student learning of this very important idea. Students have a visual reminder to start with the greater number. The greater number is actually in green and has a frog by it. These cards can also be done by giving the students an actual paper frog to do the jumping.

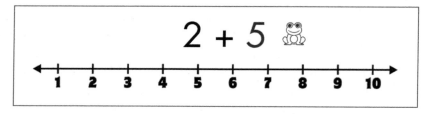

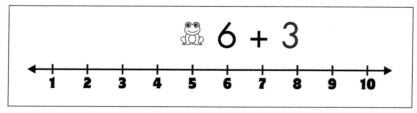

Newton, 2018 personal collection

FIGURE 3.26 Counting Cards

MATH WORKSTATIONS

Workstations to Explore Add 2 or 3		
Concrete	**Pictorial**	**Abstract**
Roll or Pull and Build an Add 2 or 3 fact on a Ten Frame	Draw on Ten Frame Model	Add 2 or 3 Clip Flashcards
Roll and Build an Add 2 or 3 fact on a Rekenrek	Draw on Rekenrek Model	Spin and Add 2 or 3 within 5 or 10
Roll and Build a Add 2 or 3 fact with the Cubes	Draw on Cube Template	Add 2 or 3 Board Game
Roll and Build an Add 2 or 3 fact in a Part-Part Whole Mat	Draw in a Part-Part Whole Mat	Add 2 or 3 War
Roll and Show an Add 2 or 3 fact in a Number Bond	Draw and Show in a Number Bond	Add 2 or 3 Tic-Tac-Toe
Add 2 or 3 with Play-Doh©	Add 2 or 3 Domino Sort	Pull and Plus 2 or 3
Spin and Build Add 2 or 3 within 5 or 10	Add 2 or 3 Booklet	Add 2 or 3 Four in a Row
Add 2 or 3 Flashcard Build	Savvy Subitizing Pull and Add 2 or 3	Show or Record on Number Path
Show with Cuisenaire© rods		Show or Record on Number Line
Build and Record on Number Line		Power Towers
		Add 2 or 3 Bingo

FIGURE 3.27 Math Workstations

CONCRETE ACTIVITIES

Add 2 or 3 Concrete Activities		
Roll or Pull and Build on a Ten Frame	**Build with Cuisenaire© rods**	**Build and Record on Number Line**
Students roll a dice or pull a card and build on a ten frame to model the equation.	Students roll a dice or pull a card and use Cuisenaire© rods to model the equation.	Students build the count on fact on a mat and then add it on the number line.
$4 + 3 = 7$ It is helpful to use two different colors for the two addends. Students can then use the benchmark number of 5 to help them determine the sum.	$5 + 3 = 8$ By using Cuisenaire© rods, students can see the first amount existing as a group rather than a collection of ones.	

FIGURE 3.28 Concrete Activities

PICTORIAL ACTIVITIES

Add 2 or 3 Pictorial Activities		
Pull, Build & Draw on a Rekenrek	**Pull, Build & Draw on a Part-Part Whole Mat**	**Pull, Build & Draw on the Cube Template**
Students pull a scaffolded flashcard, build the count on fact using a rekenrek and then draw on a rekenrek template.	Students pull a scaffolded flashcard, build the count on fact using a part-part whole mat and then draw on the part-part whole mat.	Students pull a scaffolded flashcard, build the count on fact using cubes and then draw it on a cube template.

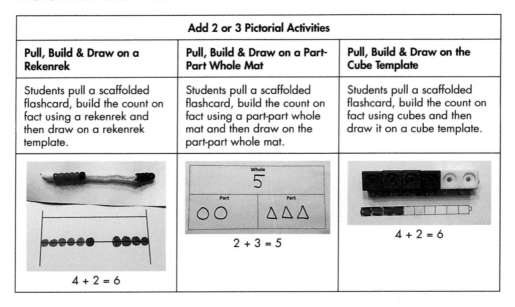

FIGURE 3.29 Pictorial Activities

ABSTRACT ACTIVITIES

Add 2 or 3 Abstract Activities		
Finger Card Count On	**War**	**Interactive Number Lines**
Teacher passes out number cards and finger cards. Students choose a card from pile a (number card) and then a card from pile b (count on cards). Students color in the two amounts on their ten frame using a different color for each addend.	Pull 2 flashcards and whoever has the largest sum wins that hand and gets the two cards. Whoever has the most cards at the end of the game is the winner. 4 + 2 7 + 3	Using interactive number lines is another way to reinforce starting at the highest number and counting on.
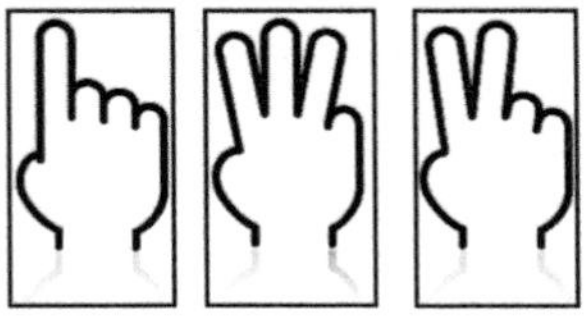		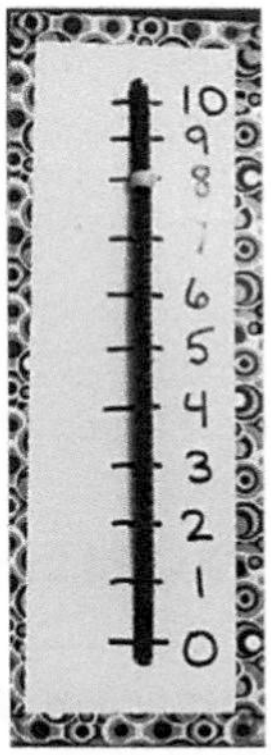

FIGURE 3.30 Abstract Activities

STRATEGY FLASHCARDS

Flashcards for Exploring Add 2 or 3		
Ten Frame Flashcards We want students to always remember to count on from the greater number. 6 + 2 	Picture Flashcards We focus on getting students to count on from the greater number.	Unscaffolded Flashcards 4 + 2 6 + 3 5 + 3

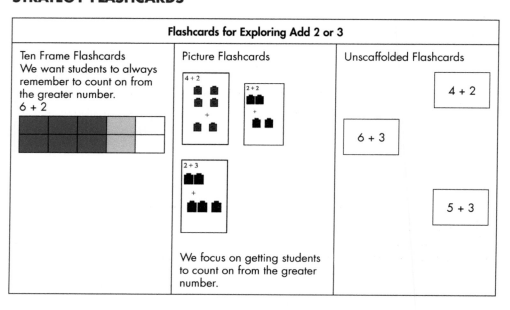

FIGURE 3.31 Strategy Flashcards

WORD PROBLEMS

In every fluency module there should be a focus on word problems. Here are a few examples of the types of word problems for Add 2 or 3.

My Add 2 or 3 Story Problems Booklet	**Deb had 6 lollipops. She was given 2 more. How many lollipops does she have now?** **Write the set-up equation:** **Show your thinking with a model.** **Write the solution equation.**	**Benjamin did 3 science experiments on Saturday and 4 on Sunday. How many did he do in all?** **Write the set-up equation:** **Show your thinking with a model.** **Write the solution equation.**	**Jeff made 7 baskets and then 3 more baskets. How many baskets did he make altogether?** **Write the set-up equation:** **Show your thinking with a model.** **Write the solution equation.**

FIGURE 3.32 Word Problems

RESOURCES

Picture Books

Books about Add 2 or 3		
Rooster's Off to See the World by Eric Carle	My Sister Ate One Hare by Bill Grossman	Quack and Count by Keith Baker

FIGURE 3.33 Picture Books

Videos

Video Add 2 or 3
Ann Elise describing the various math tools to help teach about Add 2 or 3: https://youtu.be/-OfzK22K7Yk PISD Mathematics, Fact Fluency Video Count On & Count Back: https://youtu.be/N36t_sSZPww PISD Mathematics, + 0 1 2 3 on a Number line: https://youtu.be/x87vvAXjEyw

FIGURE 3.34 Videos

Online Games

Online Games about Add 2 or 3
https://www.mathgames.com/skill/P.36-add-two-numbers-up-to-5

FIGURE 3.35 Online Games

Anchor Chart

Anchor charts support the teaching and learning of Add 2 or 3. Here are a couple of examples of what they might look like. It is important to make the charts with students, but also ensure that students have an opportunity to make their own charts. Students should keep their charts in their math journal under the Math Strategy Section.

Anchor Chart
Counting on is easy peasy .... start at the greater number and hop on!
Class Made Models

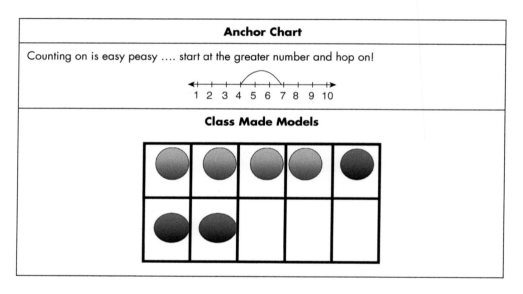

FIGURE 3.36 Anchor Chart

Quiz

Add 2 or 3 Quiz		
Name:		Date:
4 + 2 = Model with a drawing.	6 + 3 = Model on the ten frame. 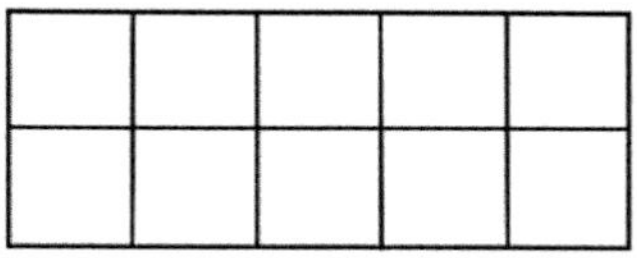 [ten frame grid]	Solve. There were 4 ducks in a pond. 2 more flew in to join them. How many ducks are in the pond now? Write the equation: Answer: _____
Solve. Janice bought 4 ice cream cones and 3 ice cream sandwiches for her friends. How many treats did she buy in all? Write the equation: Answer: _____	Solve. 3 + ____ = 5 ____ + 3 = 8 6 = 4 + _____ ____ = 6 + 3	Interview: What is the Add 2 or 3 strategy? Explain with numbers, words and pictures.

5 + 3 =

Model on the number line.

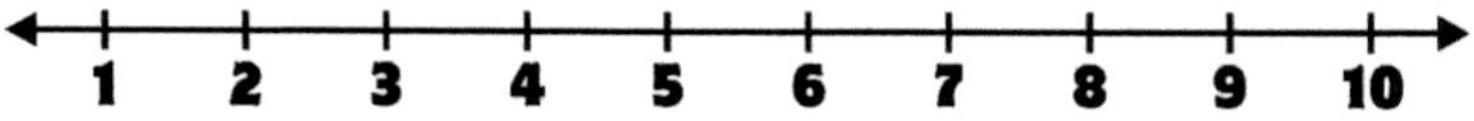

```
<---+----+----+----+----+----+----+----+----+----+--->
    1    2    3    4    5    6    7    8    9    10
```

Circle how good you think you are at doing Add 2 or 3 facts!

Great   Good    OK, still thinking

FIGURE 3.37 Quiz

EXPLORING AND LEARNING ADDING WITHIN 5 AND MAKING 5

5 is a benchmark number. Students must be able to know and understand 5 fluently. At this point in the progression of strategies, we want to ensure that the math facts within 5 are fluent. This means that students exhibit relative speed, accuracy, efficiency, and flexibility with the aforementioned facts and strategies within 5 (Add 0, Add 1, Count on 2 or 3). In addition to these, students should explore all pairs of numbers that combine to make 5 (see Figures 3.38–3.48). 5 is the first benchmark number that students can use to explore thinking strategically. Ten frames are organized with 2 rows of 5 so that students can see the structure of the numbers within 10 and how they can use that "fast 5" to determine sums over 5. Fluency with these math facts is expected within most state standards by the end of kindergarten.

WHOLE CLASS LESSON

Teacher: Today we are going to look at all of our make 5 facts. We are going to make individual books of ways to make 5. Let's talk about it and then everyone gets to do a book.

Teacher: Who wants to model making 5 on the cubes?

Jamal models 2 + 3 using cubes. (Teacher shows a strip of five frames.) OK. We did this lots of times.

(Teacher continues discussing various ways to make 5. Students are excited for their turn to work in the center making their 5 books.)

 ## SPOTLIGHT ACTIVITY

Use the Math Learning Center App to Spotlight ways of making 5. Tell a story of butterflies on a log. Discuss how there are 2 different colors. We are looking for all the combinations that they could be in.

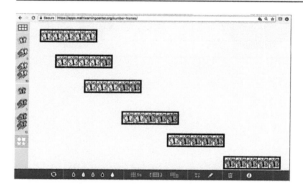

FIGURE 3.38 Spotlight Activity

MATH WORKSTATIONS

Workstations to Review Add within 5 facts and Add Make 5 facts		
Concrete	**Pictorial**	**Abstract**
Roll or Pull and Build an Add within 5 fact on a Five Frame	Draw on Five Frame Model	Add within 5 Clip Flashcards
Roll and Build an Add within 5 fact on a Rekenrek	Draw on Rekenrek Model	Spin and Make 5
Roll and Build an Add within 5 fact with the Cubes	Draw on Cube Template	Bump Game
Roll and Build an Add within 5 fact in a Part-Part Whole Mat	Draw in a Part-Part Whole Mat	Add within 5 Bingo
Roll and Show an Add within 5 fact in a Number Bond	Draw and Show in a Number Bond	Add within 5 Board Game
Add w/in 5 fact with Play-Doh©	Domino Strategy Sort	Add within 5 War
Shake and Spill	Add within 5 Booklet	Add within 5 Tic-Tac-Toe
Show with Cuisenaire© rods	Savvy Subitizing Make 5 game	Pull and Make 5
Math Fact Flashcards Build		Add w/in 5 Four in a Row
Number bracelet game		Flashcards
Cup hiding game		Roll & Make 5
Split machine		Show or Record on Number Path
		Show or Record on Number Line
		Power Towers

FIGURE 3.39 Math Workstations

CONCRETE ACTIVITIES

Add within 5 and Make 5 Concrete Activities		
Cuisenaire© rods Build	**Shake and Spill**	**Addition Story Mat**
Students make a 5 house with Cuisenaire© rods to explore the pairs of numbers that make 5. By systematically making the pairs, we can be assured we have them all.	Students put five 2-sided counters in a cup. Shake and spill and record how many are red and how many are yellow. Repeat and see how many combinations there are. Students can record equations as well.	Students model a story situation using a story mat and then write the equation that matches the situation.
	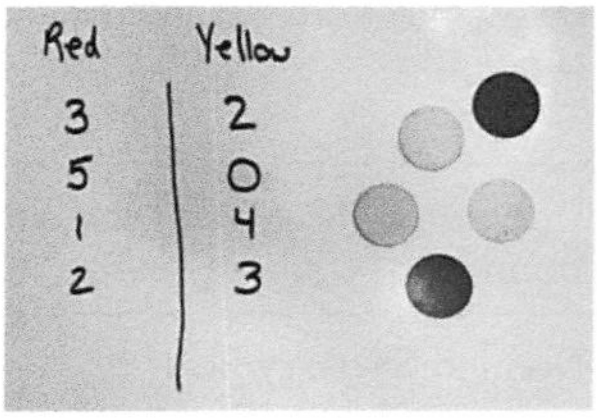	

FIGURE 3.40 Concrete Activities

PICTORIAL ACTIVITIES

Add within 5 and Make 5 Pictorial Activities		
Draw on a 5 frame	**Roll and Show a Make 5 & Draw it in a Number Bond**	**Domino Strategy Sort**
Students pull a scaffolded flashcard and draw on a 5 frame to model the expression.	Students pull a number card up to 5 and model it on the number bond in different ways.	Students pull a domino and determine which strategy can used to solve the expression. Students can then draw the fact in that strategy box.
	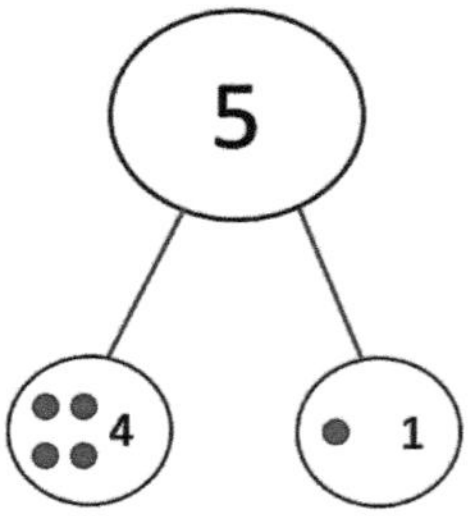	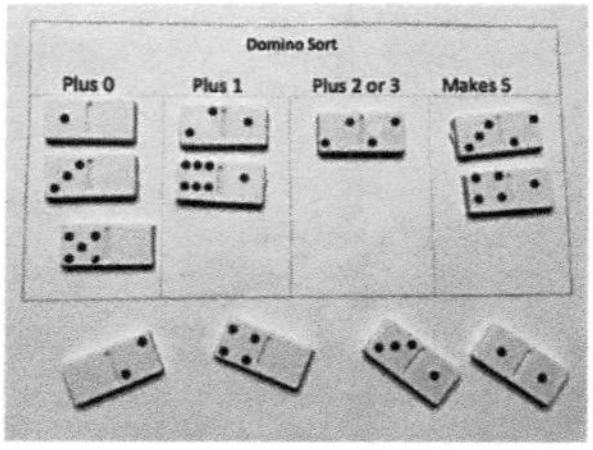

FIGURE 3.41 Pictorial Activities

ABSTRACT ACTIVITIES

Add within 5 and Make 5 Abstract Activities		
Record on Number Path	**Bump Board Game**	**Power Towers**
Students pull a flashcard and model the expression on a number path. 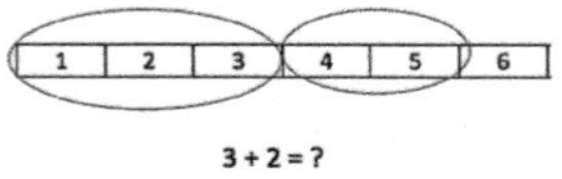	Students pull a flashcard or domino and place a marker on the sum. If there is one marker already on a sum, the opposing player can bump off the marker. If a player has two markers on the same spot, they cannot be bumped. 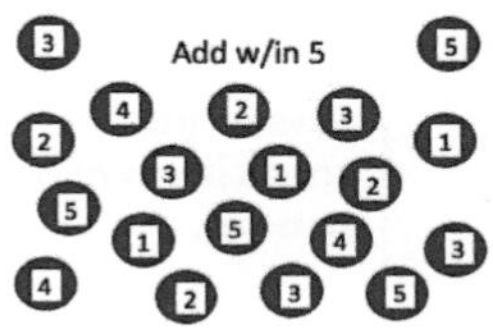	Mix together all the cups that have Add 0, Add 1 or Add 2 or 3 facts on them with sums within 5. Students take turns answering the math fact and, if correct, get to add it to the tower. If it is incorrect it just goes back in the pile. No one is ever out. 

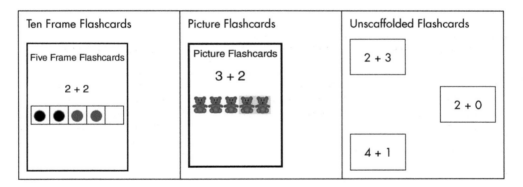

FIGURE 3.42 Abstract Activities

STRATEGY FLASHCARDS

Ten Frame Flashcards	Picture Flashcards	Unscaffolded Flashcards
Five Frame Flashcards 2 + 2 ● ● ● ●	Picture Flashcards 3 + 2	2 + 3 2 + 0 4 + 1

FIGURE 3.43 Strategy Flashcards

WORD PROBLEMS

In every fluency module there should be a focus on word problems. Here are a few examples of the types of word problems for Add within 5 and Make 5.

| My Add within 5 and Make 5 Story Problems Booklet | Ann had 2 butterflies on her arm. 3 more butterflies landed on her. How many does she have on her now?

Write the set-up equation:

Show your thinking with a model.

Write the solution equation. | There were 3 red grapes and 2 green grapes. How many grapes were there altogether?

Write the set-up equation:

Show your thinking with a model.

Write the solution equation. | Kate had 2 headbands. Her mom gave her 2 more. How many headbands does she have now?

Write the set-up equation:

Show your thinking with a model.

Write the solution equation. |

FIGURE 3.44 Word Problems

RESOURCES

Picture Books

Books about Adding within 5 and Make 5			
Five Green and Speckled Frogs by Priscilla Burris	Five Little Monkeys Jumping on the Bed by Eileen Christelow	Five Little Ducks by Rafi and Jose Aruego	Five Little Pumpkins by Dan Yaccarino

FIGURE 3.45 Picture Books

Online Games

Online Games about Adding within 5
https://www.mathgames.com/skill/P.36-add-two-numbers-up-to-5 https://www.mathgames.com/skill/K.66-add-two-numbers-up-to-5 https://www.mathgames.com/skill/K.65-addition-with-pictures-up-to-5 https://www.mathgames.com/skill/K.67-choose-addition-pictures-up-to-5

FIGURE 3.46 Online Games

Anchor Chart

Anchor charts support the teaching and learning of Adding within 5. Here is an example of what one might look like. It is important that the teacher makes the charts with the students, but also that the students have an opportunity to make their own charts. Students should keep their charts in their math journal under the Math Strategy Section.

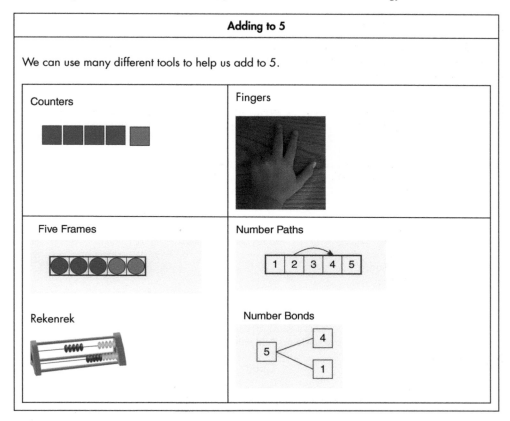

FIGURE 3.47 Anchor Chart

Quiz

Add within 5 and Make 5 Quiz		
Name:		Date:
3 + 2 = Model with a drawing.	4 + 1 = Model on the ten frame. 	Solve. Kay had 2 bows. She was given 3 more. How many bows does she have now? Write the equation: Answer: _____
Solve. There was one bird in a tree. 4 more birds flew in. How many birds are in the tree now? Write the equation: Answer: _____	Solve. 2 + ____ = 5 ____ + 2 = 4 3 = 1 + _____ _____ = 1 + 4	Interview: What is the Add within 5 strategy? Explain with numbers, words and pictures.

2 + 3 =

Model on the number line.

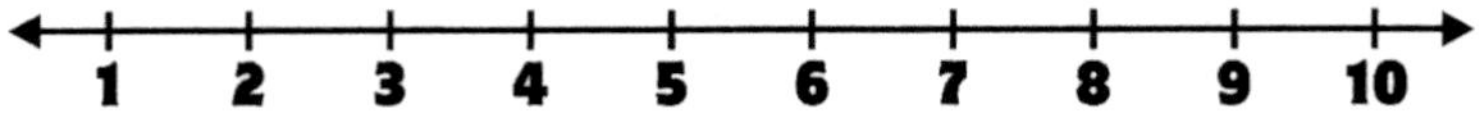

Circle how good you think you are at doing Add within 5 facts!

Great	Good	OK, still thinking

FIGURE 3.48 Quiz

EXPLORING AND LEARNING TO ADD WITHIN 10

Once students have developed fluency within 5, they can progress to mastering their math facts within 10 (see Figures 3.49–3.60). This may begin with a review of all of the previously introduced strategies within the greater context of sums to 10. Once again, we will use the concrete, pictorial, and abstract progression to explore these facts to develop fluency. A big emphasis for adding within 10 should be on composing and decomposing numbers within 10. If students can flexibly build numbers and take them apart, then they can more easily approach unfamiliar quantities and more successfully add and subtract. As the numbers get larger, students should remember to start with the greater number and count on. We should continue to work with the commutative property as well.

 SPOTLIGHT ACTIVITY

Teacher reads *Quack and Count* by Keith Baker to the class. Students should have yellow beaded number bracelets of 7 on a blue pipe cleaner. For each page, students will move the beads around to represent how the ducks have rearranged themselves. Teacher and students can record the equation representations for each decomposition of 7 and discuss various strategies for determining the sums, paying particular attention to adding up from the larger number.

Read it!	Watch it!	Act it Out!	More Activities
<u>Quack and Count</u> by Keith Baker	Look up various video readings of the book.	Give the students a mat of blue paper with 7 small rubber ducks so they can reenact the story.	http://www. cpalms.org/Public/ PreviewResourceLesson/ Preview/65687 https://www.uen.org/ lessonplan/view/16221 http://mathathome. org/lessons/ quack-and-count/

FIGURE 3.49 Spotlight Activity

MATH WORKSTATIONS

Workstations to Explore Adding within 10		
Concrete	**Pictorial**	**Abstract**
Roll or Pull and Build an Add within 10 fact on a Ten Frame	Draw on Ten Frame Model	Add within 10 Clip Flashcards
Roll and Build an Add within 10 fact on a Rekenrek	Draw on Rekenrek Model	Spin and Add within 10
Roll and Build an Add within 10 fact with the Cubes	Draw on Cube Template	Add within 10 Board Game
Show with Cuisenaire© rods	Draw in a Part-Part Whole Mat	Add within 10 War
Roll and Build an Add within 10 fact in a Part-Part Whole Mat	Draw and Show in a Number Bond	Add within 10 Tic-Tac-Toe
Roll and Show an Add within 10 fact in a Number Bond	Domino Strategy Sort	Pull and Add within 10
Add within 10 with Play-Doh©	Add within 10 Booklet	Add within 10 Four in a Row
Number bracelet Game	Savvy Subitizing Add 0, 1, 2, or 3	Add within 10 Flashcards
Spin and Add within 10		Roll & Add within 10
Add within 10 Flashcard Build		Bump Game
Cup Hiding Game		Show or Record on Number Path
Shake and Spill		Show or Record on Number Line
Split machine		Power Towers
		Add within 10 Bingo
		Missing Number Card Game
		Matching Game Commutative Property

FIGURE 3.50 Math Workstations

CONCRETE ACTIVITIES

Add within 10 Concrete Activities		
Roll and Build on a Rekenrek	**Pull and Build on a Ten Frame**	**Splitsville Machine**
Students roll two dice and build on a rekenrek.	Students pull a flashcard and then build the fact on a ten frame.	With this Splitsville machine, the students start with all the beads at the top and count to three and then split them into 2 parts. For example, in the one below there were 7 beads. When they split the beads, they get 4 and 3. Students then say, "4 and 3 make 7."
5 + 3 = 8 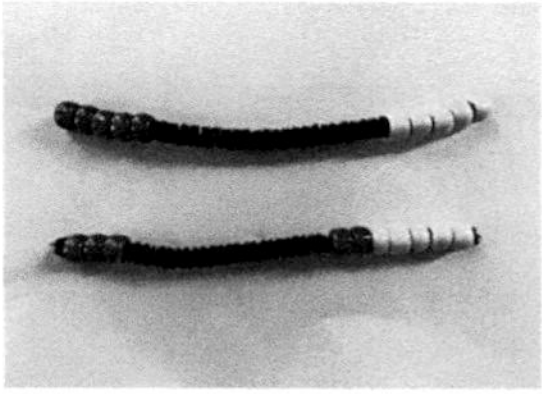 OR 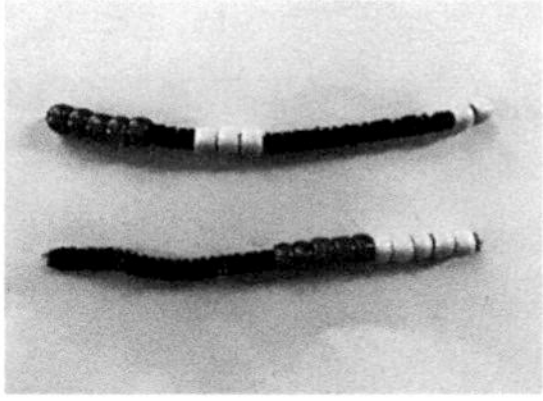	 4 + 4	

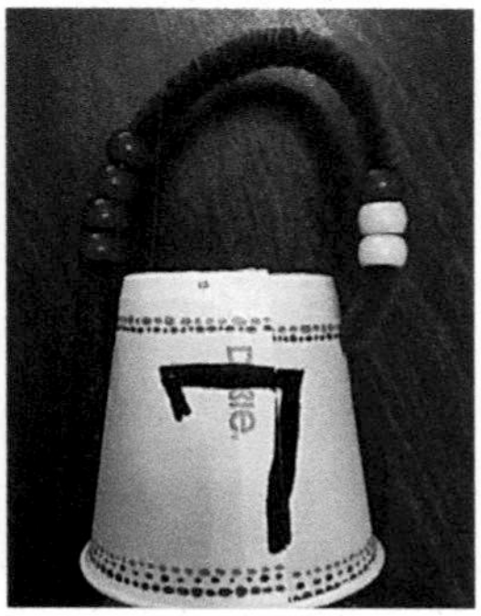

FIGURE 3.51 Concrete Activities

PICTORIAL ACTIVITIES

Add within 10 Pictorial Activities		
Roll it, Draw it, Add it, Draw it on a Number Bond	**Roll it, Build it, Add it & Draw it on a Rekenrek**	**Savvy Subitizing Cards Pull two cards and Determine the Sum (deck of cards available from https:// buildmathminds.com/ shop/)**
Students roll two dice and draw the fact on a number bond.	Students roll two dice, build the fact on a rekenrek, and then draw the fact on a rekenrek template.	Students pull two cards and determine the sum.
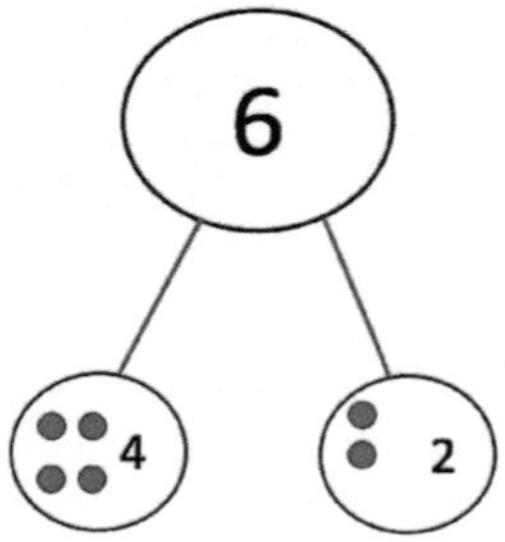	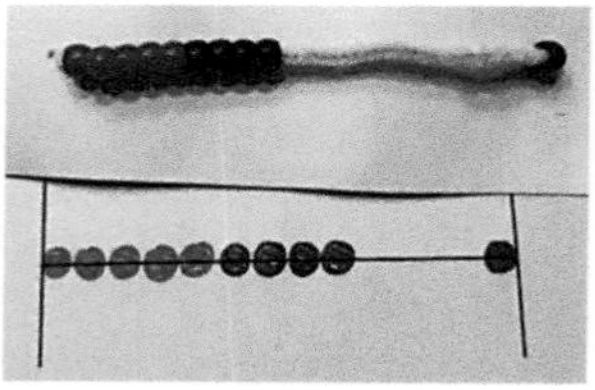 5 + 4 = 9	 4 + 2 = ?

FIGURE 3.52 Pictorial Activities

ABSTRACT ACTIVITIES

Add within 10 Abstract Activities		
Number Bond Roll and Fill in Games	Matching Game Exploring Commutative Property	Missing Number Game
Students are given a number and they need to determine all the pairs of numbers that have a sum of that number.	Students play a matching game to pair the two expressions that demonstrate the commutative property.	You need at least three students, one is the person in charge. Without looking at the card, the other two students flip a card off the pile to their forehead with card facing outward. The person in charge says, "The sum of the two addends is ___." Each student is able to see the number on the other student's forehead and using that information and the sum, figures out the number (missing addend) on their own forehead. First student to correctly give their answer becomes the person in charge.
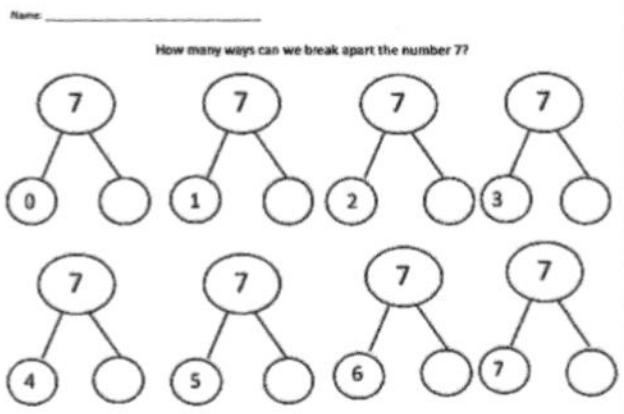	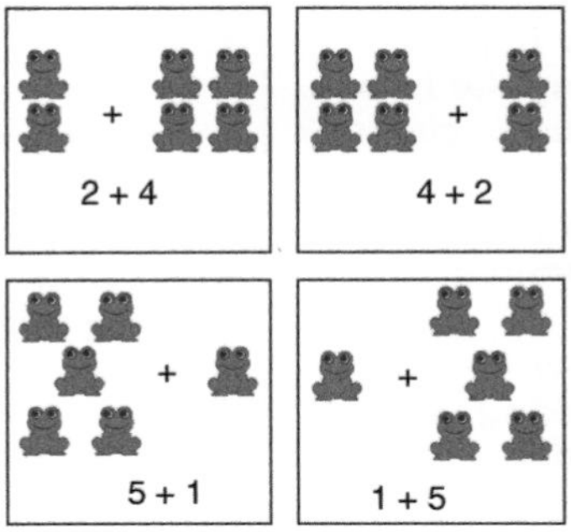	

FIGURE 3.53 Abstract Activities

STRATEGY FLASHCARDS

Flashcards for Exploring Add within 10		
Ten Frame Flashcards	Picture Flashcards	Unscaffolded Flashcards
		5 + 1 7 + 2 3 + 4

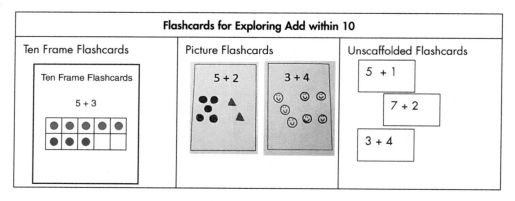

FIGURE 3.54 Strategy Flashcards

WORD PROBLEMS

In every fluency module there should be a focus on word problems. Here are a few examples of the types of word problems for Add within 10.

My Add within 10 Story Problems Booklet	**Justin saw some seagulls at the beach. He then saw 3 more. Altogether he saw 8. How many did he see in the beginning?** **Write the set-up equation:** **Show your thinking with a model.** **Write the solution equation.**	**Vivi had 4 necklaces and 4 bracelets. How many pieces of jewelry did she have?** **Write the set-up equation:** **Show your thinking with a model.** **Write the solution equation.**	**Mary ran 4 miles. Chris ran 2 more miles than Mary. How many miles did Chris run? How many miles did they run all together?** **Write the set-up equation:** **Show your thinking with a model.** **Write the solution equation.**

FIGURE 3.55 Word Problems

RESOURCES

Picture Books

Books about Adding within 10				
Two Ways to Count to Ten: A Liberian Folktale retold by Ruby Dee and Susan Meddaugh	How Many Birds by Don L. Curry	What Comes in 2's, 3's and 4's? by Suzanne Aker and Bernie Karlin	The Very Hungry Caterpillar by Eric Carle	Anno's Counting Book by Mitsumasa Anno
If You Were a Plus Sign by Trisha Speed Shaskan	Jack the Builder by Stuart Murphy and Michael Rex	Domino Addition by Lynette Long	12 Ways to get to 11 by Eve Merriam	Mission: Addition by Loreen Leedy
The Grapes of Math by Greg Tang online version: http://gregtangmath.com/thegrapesofmath	Mathterpieces by Greg Tang online version: http://gregtangmath.com/mathterpieces			

FIGURE 3.56   Picture Books

Videos

Video Songs about Adding within 10
Mr R's Songs for Teaching, Tens Frame Song: https://youtu.be/RLiwP_hxdQc Jack Hartmann's Addition Song for Kids: https://youtu.be/UqQ1VkBvuRs Harry Kindergarten Music, When You Add with a Pirate: https://youtu.be/WT_wvvEvkw4 Umigo: https://www.youtube.com/watch?v=R__VKQRYcDg

FIGURE 3.57   Videos

Online Games

Online Games about Add within 10
Greg Tang's fluency games are some of the best games available online! http://www.gregtangmath.com/tenframemania http://www.gregtangmath.com/mathlimbo http://www.gregtangmath.com/numtanga https://www.mathgames.com/skill/K.57-add-two-numbers-up-to-10 https://www.mathgames.com/skill/K.58-choose-addition-pictures-up-to-10 https://www.mathgames.com/skill/K.62-addition-with-sums-up-to-10 https://www.mathgames.com/skill/K.64-how-to-make-a-number-with-sums-up-to-10

FIGURE 3.58 Online Games

Anchor Chart

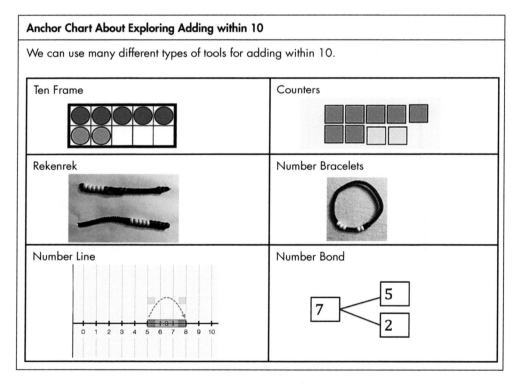

Anchor Chart About Exploring Adding within 10
We can use many different types of tools for adding within 10.

FIGURE 3.59 Anchor Chart

Quiz

Add within 10 Quiz

Name:

Date:

2 + 7 = Model with a drawing.	5 + 3 = Model on the ten frame.	Solve. Sandy baked 2 apple pies and 5 pumpkin pies. How many pies did she bake? Write the equation: Answer: _____
Solve. Delia had 4 pineapple slices and 4 orange slices. How many slices of fruit did Delia have? Write the equation: Answer: _____	Solve. 6 + ____ = 9 ____ + 2 = 8 7 = 3 + _____ ____ = 5 + 4	Interview: What is the Add within 10 strategy? Explain with numbers, words and pictures.

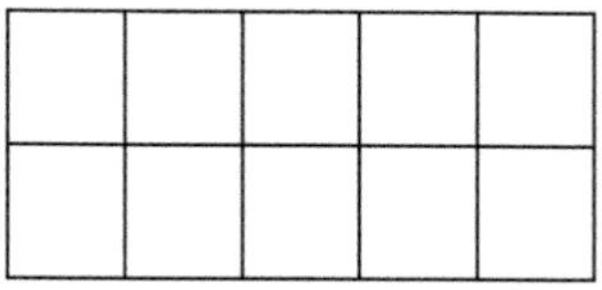

4 + 2 =

Model on the number line.

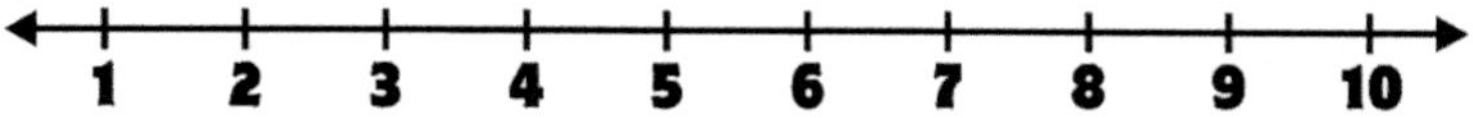

1 2 3 4 5 6 7 8 9 10

Circle how good you think you are at doing Add within 10 facts!

Great

Good

OK, still thinking

FIGURE 3.60 Quiz

EXPLORING AND LEARNING MAKING 10

After students have mastered all the abovementioned strategies, they should work on building fluency with Partners of 10. The Make 10 strategy is called by a variety of names, including Ten Friends and Pairs of Ten. 10 is an important benchmark number. Knowing how to make 10, get to 10, get from 10, break apart 10 and put it together is the way many students around the world work on fluency (Henry & Brown, 2008). Students will build on this initial understanding of 10, when working with larger numbers. They will "bridge 10" either when adding such numbers as 7, 8, or 9. For example, while adding 9 + 5, we want students to use 9 + 1 more makes 10 and then add 4 more. When subtracting, we want students to hop back to 10 and then down. For example, 14 - 6 would be 14 - 4 to get to a 10 and then subtract 2 more.

Without having the pairs of numbers that make 10 automatized, students will have a much harder time working with larger numbers. Students need to know all the pairs of numbers that combine to make 10 with automaticity. You simply can't do enough practice of these combinations of numbers. Students need to have a lot of practice using concrete objects and visually seeing these combinations of numbers, before they are rushed to do them abstractly (see Figures 3.61–3.72).

WHOLE CLASS MINI-LESSON: MAKE 10

Launch   *Teacher sits students in the gathering spot in the classroom. Teacher reads the story Ten Flashing Fireflies by Philemon Sturges. The teacher will then record on the board any of the noticings of the students. Then, the teacher will pass out papers that have a big jar drawn on them as well as 10 connecting cubes. The teacher will read the book again and as he/she does, students move 1 of their cubes inside the jar and discuss how many there are outside of the jar. The teacher may also record a numerical expression or a number bond to show all the combinations that make 10.*

 SPOTLIGHT ACTIVITY

Read It!	Watch it!	Act it Out!	Other Resources
Ten Flashing Fireflies by Philemon Sturges	There are different versions on YouTube.	http://www.fun365. orientaltrading.com/ article/ways-to-make-ten-activity	https://www. illustrativemathematics. org/content-standards/ tasks/1151 http://www. catchthepossibilities. com/2012/06/flannel-friday-ten-flashing-fireflies.html [PDF]Kindergarten Ten Flashing Fireflies by Philemon Sturges - BCAMT

FIGURE 3.61 Spotlight Activity

MATH WORKSTATIONS

Workstations to Explore Make 10		
Concrete	**Pictorial**	**Abstract**
Roll or Pull and Build a Make 10 fact on a Ten Frame	Draw on Ten Frame Model	Make 10 Clip Flashcards
Roll and Build a Make 10 fact on a Rekenrek	Draw on Rekenrek Model	Spin and Make 10
Roll and Build a Make 10 fact with the Cubes	Draw on Cube Template	Make 10 Board Game
Show with Cuisenaire© rods	Draw in a Part-Part Whole Mat	Go Ten Card Game
Roll and Build a Make 10 fact in a Part-Part Whole Mat	Draw and Show in a Number Bond	Pull and Make 10
Roll and Show a Make 10 fact in a Number Bond	Domino Strategy Sort	Bump game
Make 10 with Play-Doh©	Make 10 Booklet	Show or Record on Number Path
Cup hiding game	Savvy Subitizing Make 10 game	Show or Record on Number Line
Spin and Make 10		Power Towers
Make 10 Flashcard Build		Flashcards
Hiding game with 10 beaded bracelet		Roll & Make 10
Make 10 Shake and Spill		Birds and Worms Make 10
Split Machine		
Clothes Pins on Hanger Activity		

FIGURE 3.62 Math Workstations

CONCRETE ACTIVITIES

Make 10 Concrete Activities		
Cuisenaire© rods Build	**Cup Hiding Game**	**Clothes Pins on Hanger Activity**
Students will use Cuisenaire© rods to systematically determine all the combinations of numbers that make 10 including the ones that show the commutative property. In this way, they can see the pattern that is happening.	Partners count out 10 objects. One partner hides some of them under a cup. The other partner then needs to guess how many are under the cup. For example, Partner A shows 10 bears. Then, Partner B looks away and Partner A hides 8. When Partner B looks back, there are only 2 bears visible. Partner B has to calculate that 8 are hidden because 2 and 8 make 10. Students can use ten frames, rekenreks, and number paths to help them with their calculations.	Using a clothes hanger ten maker is great. Students can compose and decompose ten easily on this "tool". See a great video of this in action.... https://youtu.be/OkW1Y11tGxw
		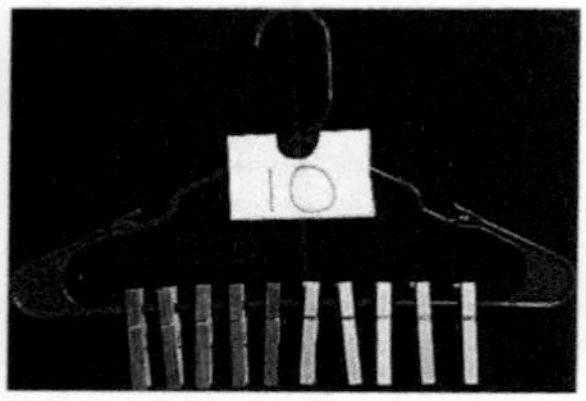

FIGURE 3.63 Concrete Activities

PICTORIAL ACTIVITIES

Make 10 Pictorial Activities		
Roll and Draw on a Ten Frame	**Roll, Build & Draw on a Part-Part Whole Mat**	**Savvy Subitizing Go Ten Game**
Students roll a ten-sided die and draw shapes on a ten frame to show the first addend and then focus on the amount that is needed to complete the ten frame.	Students roll a ten-sided die and draw that number on one side of the Part-Part Whole Mat and then the pair that makes ten with it on the other side.	Using the Savvy Subitizing Cards, students play Go Fish card game but rather than asking for the pair of the same card, they ask for the card that will make 10 with the card they have. Savvy Subitizing Cards are available from https://buildmathminds.com/shop/)
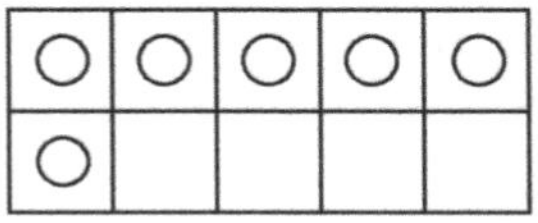	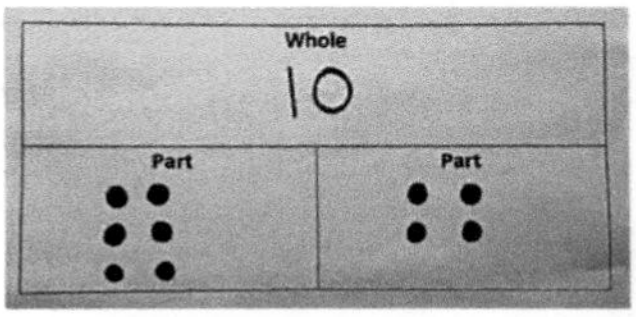	

FIGURE 3.64 Pictorial Activities

ABSTRACT ACTIVITIES

Make 10 Abstract Activities		
Record on a Number Path	**Birds and Worms Make 10**	**Spin and Make 10**
Students roll a ten-sided die and then record that number as well as its pair that makes ten on a number path.	Students play the Birds and Worms game to find combinations of dice or cards that add to make ten and score a point for making an apple. There are worms that will eat apples and birds that will eat the worms for an extra element of fun. https://guidedmath.wordpress.com/2018/05/29/the-birds-and-worms-math-game-k-5/	Students will spin a spinner and determine the number that makes ten with it and then record the equation on the bottom part of the sheet.
		Spin and Make 10

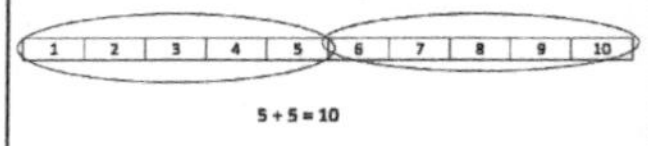

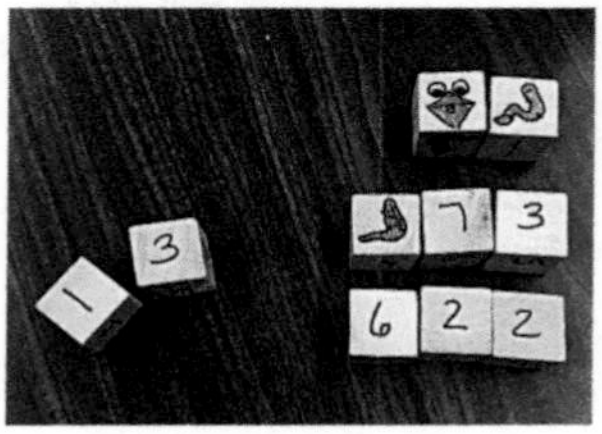

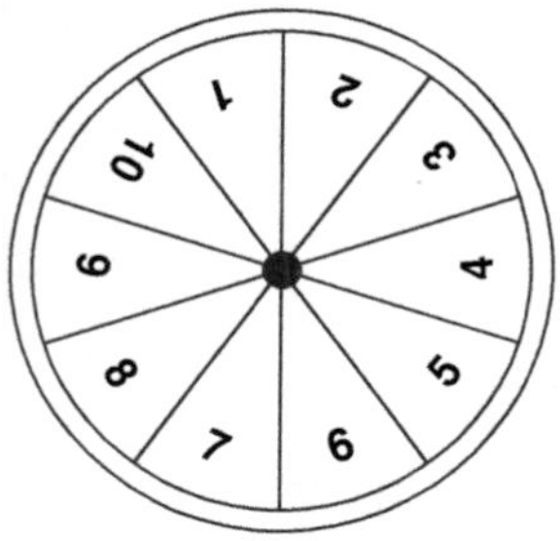

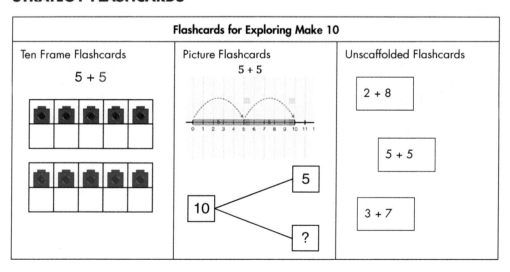

FIGURE 3.65 Abstract Activities

STRATEGY FLASHCARDS

Flashcards for Exploring Make 10		
Ten Frame Flashcards 5 + 5 	Picture Flashcards 5 + 5 	Unscaffolded Flashcards 2 + 8 5 + 5 3 + 7

FIGURE 3.66 Strategy Flashcards

WORD PROBLEMS

In every fluency module there should be a focus on word problems. Here are a few examples of the types of word problems for Add Make 10.

My Add Make 10 Story Problems Booklet	**Meg had 4 cat treats and 6 dog treats. How many pet treats did she have?** **Write the set-up equation:** **Show your thinking with a model.** **Write the solution equation.**	**Linda had some sweaters. Holly gave her 3 more. Now she has 10. How many did she have in the beginning?** **Write the set-up equation:** **Show your thinking with a model.** **Write the solution equation.**	**Don had 2 toys in his sandbox. His grandmother put some more in the sandbox. Now there are 10. How many toys did his grandmother put in the sandbox?** **Write the set-up equation:** **Show your thinking with a model.** **Write the solution equation.**

FIGURE 3.67 Word Problems

RESOURCES

Picture Books

Books to teach Make 10				
Ten Flashing Fireflies by Philemon Sturges	Ten Friends by Bruce Goldstone	Ten in the Bed by Penny Dale	Math-terpieces by Greg Tang	Ten Apples Up on Top by Dr. Seuss

FIGURE 3.68 Picture Books

Videos

 Video Songs about Make 10

Ann Elise's video on math tools we can use to teach Make 10 facts: https://youtu.be/ibQ6rigG2W4
Jack Hartmann song about the numbers that make 10: https://youtu.be/YBkpC29_GaI
Another Jack Hartmann song about numbers that make 10: https://youtu.be/73av5oijolU
Another Jack Hartmann song using number bonds: https://youtu.be/GyK8iEO5-GI
Mr R's Math Songs for Teaching numbers that make 10: https://youtu.be/RiFRb_Uoa3U
UMIGO: Math Mania - That makes 10: https://youtu.be/KaTSpMPpfnY
Fun Songs with UMIGO: https://youtu.be/cdlxSwokZRw
Rocking Dan Teaching Man Friends of 10: https://youtu.be/QS5w8LRnnp0
Rocking Dan Teaching Man Let's All Do the 10 Dance: https://youtu.be/UD_RUVLPvTY

FIGURE 3.69 Videos

Online Games

Online Games about Make 10

https://www.mathplayground.com/number_bonds_10.html

FIGURE 3.70 Online Games

Anchor Chart

Anchor charts support the teaching and learning of Make 10 facts. Here are a few examples of what they might look like. It is important that the teacher makes the charts with the students, but also that the students have an opportunity to make their own charts. Students should keep their charts in their math journal under the Math Strategy Section.

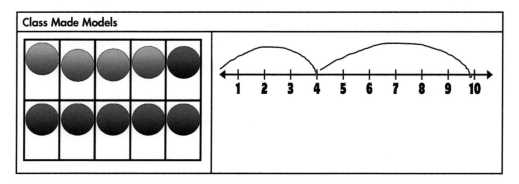

FIGURE 3.71 Anchor Chart

Quiz

Make 10 Quiz

Name
Date:

---

2 + 8 =

Model with a drawing.

---

7 + 3 =
Model on the ten frame.

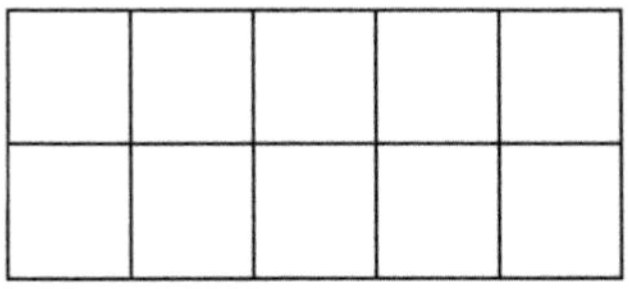

Solve.
There were 4 bananas and some apples in a basket. There are 10 pieces of fruit. How many apples are there?

Write the equation:

Answer: _____

Solve.
3 children were playing in a playground. Some more children joined them and now there are 10. How many students joined them?

Write the equation:

Answer: _____

Solve.
6 + ____ = 10

____ + 2 = 10

10 = 5 + _____

10 = 3 + _____

Interview Questions:
What are some number pairs that make 10? Explain with numbers, words and pictures.

---

9 + 1 =

Model on the number line.

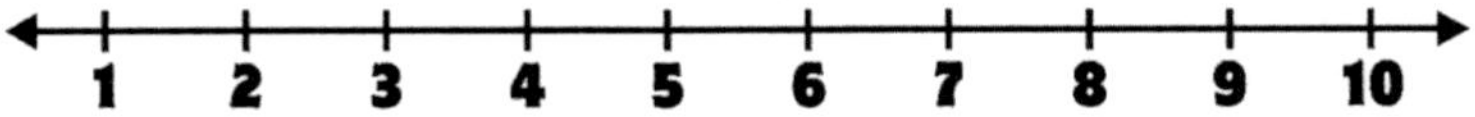

```
←——+——+——+——+——+——+——+——+——+——+——→
   1   2   3   4   5   6   7   8   9   10
```

Circle how good you think you are at doing Add Make 10 facts!

Great   Good    OK, still thinking

FIGURE 3.72 Quiz

KEY POINTS

There is a continuum for learning lower sums:
- plus 1
- plus 0
- facts within 5 and making 5
- facts within 10
- making 10.

SUMMARY

Learning the basic facts is anything but basic as (Crespo et al., 2005) stated. There is a continuum. These "Dolch words of math" (Newton, personal communication, 2008) are the foundation for becoming proficient in math. We shouldn't rush students through this learning process because, if given the time, they can learn these facts well and be set up to do great mathematical work later. If students know the lower sum strategies, it only makes the higher sums much easier. It also greatly shapes their experiences with subtraction. We have to be cognizant of the continuum and take the time to know which students are working on which fact strategies in our classes so that all students are given the opportunity to progress through the levels with deep understanding.

REFLECTION QUESTIONS

1. What did you learn from this chapter?
2. How is it going to affect your pedagogy?
3. Do you currently have detailed information about your students' knowledge of the lower sums? If you do, do you use that information to differentiate your workstations? If not, how are you going to start letting that information inform your teaching and learning moves?

REFERENCES

Baroody, A. J. (2006). Why children have difficulties mastering the basic number combinations and how to help them. *Teaching Children Mathematics*, 13(1), 22–32.

Crespo, S., Kyriakides, A. O., & McGee, S. (2005). Nothing "basic" about basic facts: Exploring addition facts with fourth graders. *Teaching Children Mathematics*, 12(2), 60–67.

Henry, V., & Brown, S. (2008). First-grade basic facts: An investigation into teaching and learning of an accelerated, high demand memorization standard. *Journal for Research in Mathematics Education*, 39(2), 153–183.

Merritt, D., & Brannon, E. (2012). Nothing to it: Precursors to a zero concept in preschoolers. Retrieved December 2, 2018 from www.ncbi.nlm.nih.gov/pmc/articles/PMC3582820/.

Van de Walle, J. A. (2007). *Elementary and middle school mathematics: Teaching developmentally*. Boston, MA: Pearson/Allyn and Bacon.

CHAPTER 4

Exploring and Learning Facts above 10

Before moving on to sums between 10 and 20, let's pause for a second and review the progression that students will go through for both addition and subtraction. In most states, the standards expect fluency for addition and subtraction within 5 in kindergarten, within 10 for 1st grade, and within 20 for 2nd grade. We have found it to be a powerful practice to work with students on their strategy development through Add Make 10 and then to begin students on the Subtraction within 10 progression rather than continuing on with the addition strategies. This allows students to develop and understand the relationship between addition and subtraction, and not view them separately. This also supports flexibility and safeguards against the overemphasis on addition which often leads to significantly lower proficiency in subtraction (LeFevre et al., 2003). Once students have mastered subtracting numbers from 10, the addition progression resumes with sums in the teens.

EXPLORING AND LEARNING DOUBLES

Teaching Doubles is an important strategy because it lays the foundation for additional strategies that allow students to acquire a larger collection of facts (Steinberg, 1985). We want students to understand we refer to doubles when we add two groups of the same amount. As always, this should follow the concrete–pictorial–abstract progression which will support deeper understanding of the relationship between the numbers. When introducing doubles, begin with doubles facts 0 to 5 and then 6 to 9. This helps to break up the teaching of doubles and build a scaffold for learning. As stated earlier, as you move through the progression do not waste the opportunity to reinforce the relationship between addition and subtraction. Do this by highlighting "half facts" along with doubles facts and integrating the idea of half facts into your fact family work.

A great way to introduce doubles is through poems, songs, and picture books. Another fun and messy idea involves using a piece of manila paper folded in half. Students open the paper and use paint or bingo daubers to make a set number of spots on one side. They then fold the paper so that the image will mark the other side and be "doubled" when you open the paper. It is great to have students predict how many total dots will be seen when the paper is opened, and then to reinforce that with the written number sentence. This is just one example. Be sure to model the doubles facts on a variety of concrete and digital tools so that students can discover patterns among this collection of facts. It is important for students to develop automaticity with their doubles facts since these facts are the building blocks for the next couple of strategies. This automaticity will naturally happen after lots of practice and exposure to the patterns within these sums (see Figures 4.2–4.13). Our essential questions for this strategy are: (1) What does it mean to double a number?; (2) How does this strategy help us to add? These questions frame the acquisition of facts in thinking, not rote memory. As Daniel Willingham notes "memory is the residue of thought" (2009).

WHOLE CLASS ACTIVITIES

Routines

Use virtual dice to roll a number and have students double that number. Use jumbo cards and have students double that number. Play Doubles bingo with the whole class. Students can either have their own boards or they can play with partners. Also play Doubles tic-tac-toe as a whole class game. The class divides up into two teams and they take turns picking a square and stating the answer.

Virtual Dice

www.curriculumbits.com/prodimages/details/maths/mat0005.html

WHOLE CLASS MINI-LESSON: TWO OF EVERYTHING

Introduction

Launch: Teacher shows the students a "magic pot." The pot should have several items already put inside of it.

Teacher: Hi, today I am going to show you a magic pot. I want you to tell me what you think is happening. Watch very carefully. (The teacher then does the following without speaking. Puts in 1 potato (represented by a brown cube) – out comes 2 (brown cubes). Puts in 2 carrots (represented by 2 orange cubes) – out comes 4 (orange cubes). Puts in 3 bananas (represented by 3 yellow cubes) – out comes 6 (yellow cubes).) What do you notice?

Stevie: It's doubling.

Teacher: Who noticed what Stevie noticed? Show me with your hands. Thumbs up if you noticed the same thing. Thumbs down if you noticed something different. Thumbs sideways if you are not sure. Well, today I am going to read you a story about a magic pot.

(Teacher reads the story about the doubling pot. Then the teacher asks the students to retell the story. As the teacher rereads the story and students retell it, the teacher acts out what is happening. After they have done this, draw a visual table of what is happening.)

Explicit Instruction/Teacher Facilitating

Teacher: I want us to look at what was happening in this story with a visual table (see Figure 4.1).

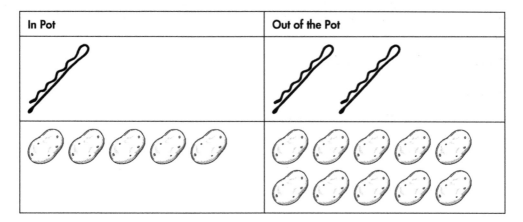

In Pot	Out of the Pot

FIGURE 4.1 Magic Pot Chart

Teacher:	What do we notice? What's the rule?
Marta:	Whatever you put in doubles?
Teacher:	Who agrees? (Many students agree with Marta.)

Guided Practice/Interactive Modeling

Teacher:	Ok, let's see if you all can show me that on your whiteboard ten frames. I am going to say a number of coins and you draw how many would come out in your ten frame. 1 … Show me your boards … Tim, why did you shade 2?
Tim:	Because if you double 1 you get 2.
Teacher:	Ok, what if I put in 3 … shade what is going to come out. Susana why did you shade 6? Are you correct? Can you defend your thinking?
Susana:	Yes, I can show it here … 3 + 3 more is 6 total.
Teacher:	Today we have looked at a doubles story to learn about doubles. Doubles is an addition strategy that we can use especially when adding numbers within 20. We will be looking at some other doubling pot stories this week and doing several doubles activities in our guided math groups and our workstations. Tomorrow, we are going to look at how we can show this pattern with a table. Ok, get ready to go to workstations and guided math.

 SPOTLIGHT ACTIVITY

There are many different versions of the magic pot. You can use this book as a "mentor text" and have the students compare and contrast different versions of the stories.

The Magic Pot	Two of Everything	The Magical Pot	Resources and Lesson Plans
https://www.youtube.com/watch?v=cYRo0o1sZ9o	https://www.youtube.com/watch?v=TY_NP528ph4	https://www.youtube.com/watch?v=AEP6-opdhio	https://illuminations.nctm.org/Lesson.aspx?id=3294 http://www.mathwire.com/games/algebragames.html

FIGURE 4.2 Spotlight Activity

MATH WORKSTATIONS

 Workstations to Explore Doubles

Concrete	Pictorial	Abstract
Roll or Pull and Build & Draw a Double fact on a Double Ten Frame	Roll, Build and Draw it on a double ten frame model	Doubles Clip Flashcards
Roll and Build a Double fact on a Rekenrek	Roll, Build and Draw it on a Rekenrek	Spin and Double to 5
Roll and Build a Double fact with Cubes	Roll, Build and Model it on the Cube Template	Spin and Double to 10
Roll and Build a Double fact in a Part-Part Whole Mat	Roll, Build and Draw in a Part-Part Whole Mat	Doubles Board Game 1
Roll and Show a Double fact in a Number Bond	Roll, Show, and Draw in a Number Bond	Doubles War
Double it with Play-Doh©	Doubles Domino Sort, Draw and Record	Doubles Tic-Tac-Toe
Spin, Build and Double to 5	Doubles Booklet	Pull and Double Flashcards
Spin, Build and Double to 10	Build and Draw on 1cm paper with Cuisenaire© rods	Doubles Four in a Row
Roll and Build it with Cuisenaire© rods	Doubles Poster	Missing Number Flashcards
		Bump
		Interactive Number Line

FIGURE 4.3 Math Workstations

CONCRETE ACTIVITIES

Doubles Concrete Activities		
Roll or Pull and Build Doubles on a Double Ten Frame	Roll and Build a Double in a Part-Part Whole Mat	Roll and Build a Double on a Rekenrek
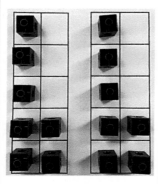		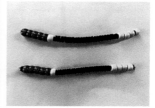

Students can see 7 + 7 is made up of 2 fives and 2 twos for a total of 14.

We can orient the two 10 frames vertically to better see the decomposition within each of the addends of a doubles fact and encourage the use of the benchmark of 5's until some higher sums are learned.

Notice how 6 + 6 can be thought of as 5 + 5 and 1 + 1 when looking at this representation on the rekenrek.

Rekenreks are another powerful concrete math tool to show the doubles facts. Each addend can be shown on its own row on the rekenrek so that students can use the benchmark of 5 to help them visualize the teen double facts.

Once they have learned 6 + 6 and 7 + 7, students can then use those sums to figure out higher sums. If a student knows that 7 + 7 = 14, then they can see that 8 + 8 is two more than the 14.

FIGURE 4.4 Concrete Activities

PICTORIAL ACTIVITIES

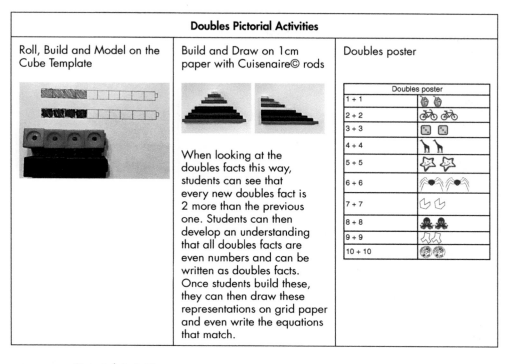

Doubles Pictorial Activities

Roll, Build and Model on the Cube Template	Build and Draw on 1cm paper with Cuisenaire© rods	Doubles poster

When looking at the doubles facts this way, students can see that every new doubles fact is 2 more than the previous one. Students can then develop an understanding that all doubles facts are even numbers and can be written as doubles facts. Once students build these, they can then draw these representations on grid paper and even write the equations that match.

Doubles poster

1 + 1	
2 + 2	
3 + 3	
4 + 4	
5 + 5	
6 + 6	
7 + 7	
8 + 8	
9 + 9	
10 + 10	

FIGURE 4.5 Pictorial Activities

ABSTRACT ACTIVITIES

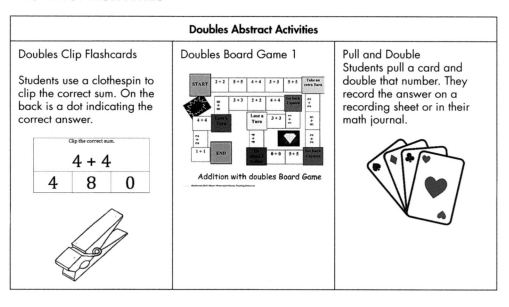

Doubles Abstract Activities

Doubles Clip Flashcards	Doubles Board Game 1	Pull and Double
Students use a clothespin to clip the correct sum. On the back is a dot indicating the correct answer.		Students pull a card and double that number. They record the answer on a recording sheet or in their math journal.

Clip the correct sum.

4 + 4

| 4 | 8 | 0 |

Addition with doubles Board Game

FIGURE 4.6 Abstract Activities

STRATEGY FLASHCARDS

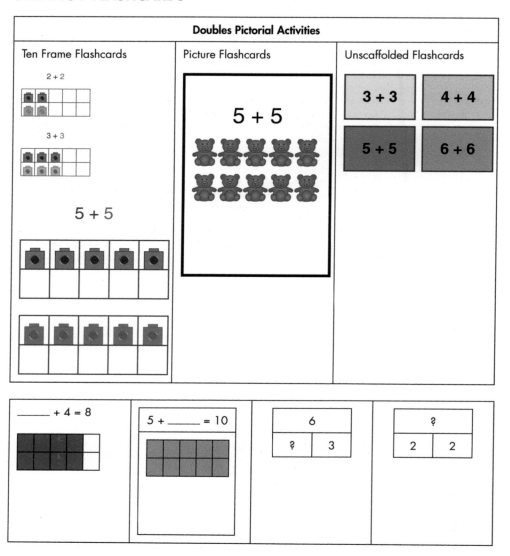

FIGURE 4.7 Strategy Flashcards

WORD PROBLEMS

In every fluency module there should be a focus on word problems. Here are a few examples of the types of word problems for doubles.			
My Doubles Story Problems Booklet	**Burgess read 4 short stories on Monday and 4 short stories on Tuesday. How many short stories did he read altogether?** **Write the set-up equation:** **Show your thinking with a model.** **Write the solution equation.**	**There were 7 red pencils and 7 yellow ones. How many pencils were there altogether?** **Write the set-up equation:** **Show your thinking with a model.** **Write the solution equation.**	**Ashton played 8 songs on his guitar, then took a break, and then played 8 more songs. How many songs did Ashton play altogether?** **Write the set-up equation:** **Show your thinking with a model.** **Write the solution equation.**

FIGURE 4.8   Word Problems

RESOURCES

Picture Books

Books about Doubles			
Double the Ducks by Stuart J. Murphy	Two of Everything by Lily Toy Hong	One Potato Two Potato by Andrea U'Ren	Minnie's Diner by Dayle Ann Dodds

FIGURE 4.9   Picture Books

Videos

 Video Songs about Doubles

Ann Elise's video on Doubles facts: https://youtu.be/mqi4qmciCQA
Doubles Rap 1-5:
https://www.youtube.com/watch?v=Ik_-OAgzD-8
Doubles Rap 1-10:
https://www.youtube.com/watch?v=8jOzhiACB68
Umigo:
https://www.youtube.com/watch?v=R__VKQRYcDg

Mr R's Songs for Teaching, Tens Frames - Double Numbers 1-5: https://youtu.be/4mzn6X2-tqs
Mr R's Songs for Teaching, Double Number Zoo: https://youtu.be/e-KTHfrFit0
Rocking Dan Teaching Man, Doubles Doubles Dancing Doubles: https://youtu.be/4U2QLjqripY

FIGURE 4.10   Videos

Online Games

Online Games about Doubles
https://www.topmarks.co.uk/maths-games/hit-the-button https://www.mathgames.com/skill/1.68-adding-doubles

FIGURE 4.11 Online Games

Anchor Chart

Anchor charts support the teaching and learning of doubles. Here are a few examples of what they might look like. It is important that the teacher makes the charts with the students, but also that that students have an opportunity to make their own charts. Students should keep their charts in their math journal under the Math Strategy Section.

Doubles Pictorial Activities	
Teacher Made	Student Made to store in toolkits

Doubles poster	
1 + 1	
2 + 2	
3 + 3	
4 + 4	
5 + 5	
6 + 6	
7 + 7	
8 + 8	
9 + 9	
10 + 10	

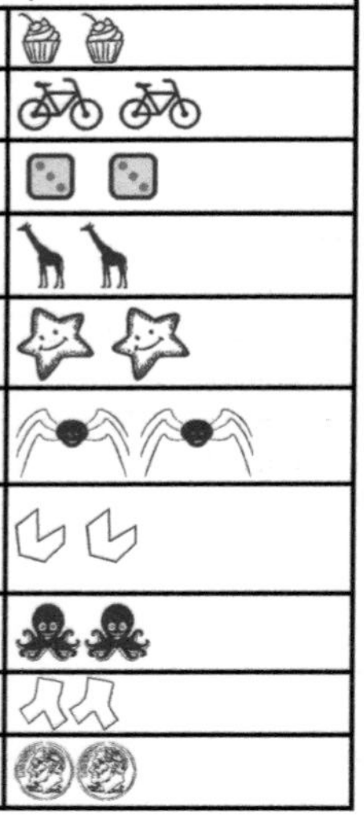

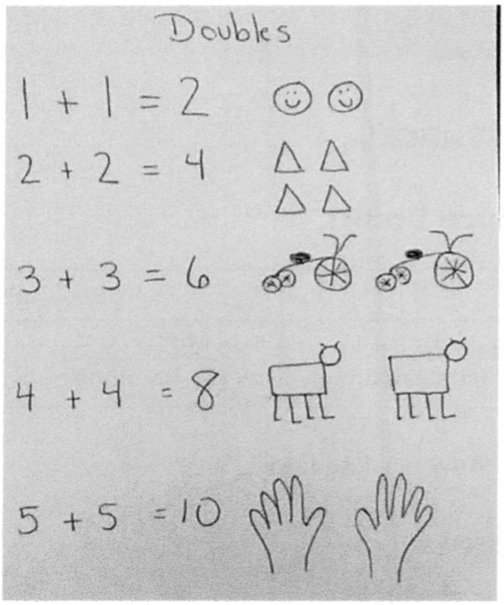

FIGURE 4.12 Anchor Chart

Quiz

Doubles Quiz

Name: Date:

| 2 + 2 =
 Model with a drawing. | 7 + 7 =
 Model on the double ten frame. | Solve.
 Cheryl walked 4 miles on Saturday and 4 miles on Sunday. How many miles did she walk?

 Write the equation:

 Answer: _____ |

| Solve.
 Lisa gave gifts to her friends. If Molly received 6 gifts and Callie received 6 gifts, how many gifts were there in all?

 Write the equation:

 Answer: _____ | Solve.

 6 + _____ = 12

 _____ + 9 = 18

 20 = 10 + _____

 _____ = 8 + 8 | Solve

 _____ + _____ = 0

 _____ + _____ = 2 |

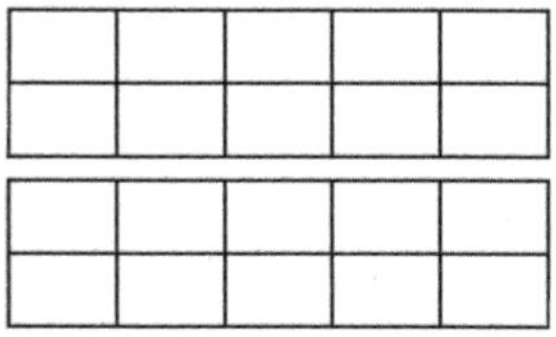

5 + 5 =

Model on the number line.

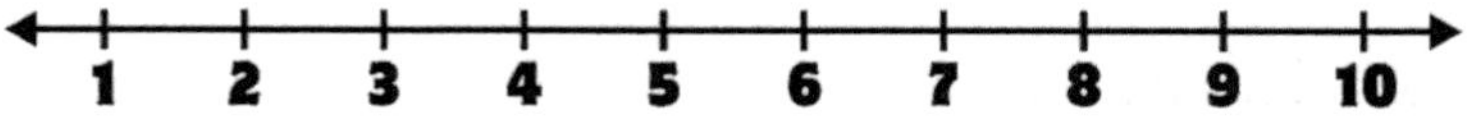

```
<---+----+----+----+----+----+----+----+----+----+--->
    1    2    3    4    5    6    7    8    9    10
```

What are doubles? Explain with numbers, words and pictures.

Circle how good you think you are at doing Doubles facts!

Great   Good    OK, still thinking

FIGURE 4.13 Quiz

TEACHING AND LEARNING DOUBLES PLUS 1 FACTS

The Doubles Plus 1 strategy is the next step in the progression of learning. Once students demonstrate a solid understanding of their doubles facts, it is easy to make a connection to the Doubles Plus 1 facts. There are some great songs, poems, and videos about Doubles Plus 1 facts and it is great to engage students in predictions about these sums. It is also powerful to highlight the decomposition of the addend where the "+1" is hiding so that the double fact becomes clearly visible to the students. Be sure to model the Doubles Plus 1 facts on a variety of concrete and digital tools. These experiences will once again empower students to discover patterns in this collection of facts that will allow them to make important connections. Automaticity will develop after lots of practice and exposure to the patterns within these sums. (See Figures 4.20–4.30.)

WHOLE CLASS ACTIVITIES

Routines

Use the virtual rekenrek or ten frame to introduce and discuss Doubles Plus 1. Later on in the week, after students have learned the strategy, play Doubles Plus 1 Bingo with the whole class. Students can either have their own boards or they can play with partners. Also play Doubles Plus 1 Tic-Tac-Toe as a whole class game. The class divides up into two teams and they take turns picking a square and stating the answer. Also do the routine What Doesn't Belong? (See Figure 4.14.) In this routine students have to find an expression that doesn't belong and support their reasoning for why it doesn't belong. One possibility is 2 + 5 because it is not a Doubles Plus 1 fact. Some students might also say 9 + 11 because it is the only one with a 2 digit number. There is no one right answer.

6 + 7	5 + 4
9 + 11	2 + 5

FIGURE 4.14 What Doesn't Belong?

WHOLE CLASS MINI-LESSON: DOUBLES PLUS 1

Introduction

Teacher Launch: *Today we are going to look at something called Doubles Plus 1 Facts.*
Teacher: *I want you all to look at the ten frame and tell me what you see. (See Figure 4.15.)*

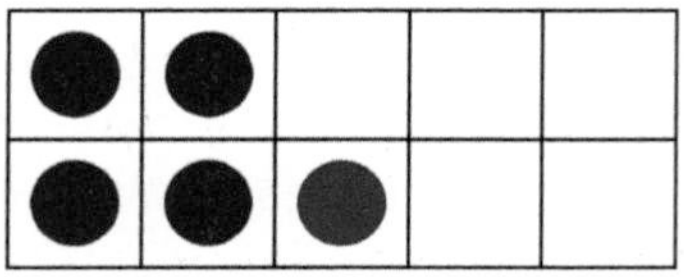

FIGURE 4.15 Ten Frame Doubles Plus 1 Example 1

Kelly:	*I see 5. There is a double 2 facts and then 1 more.*
Teacher:	*Does everybody see what she is talking about? Ted, can you come up and circle that double 2 fact that Kelly was talking about.*
	Let's look at another model. (See Figure 4.16.)

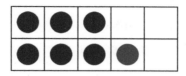

FIGURE 4.16 Ten Frame Doubles Plus 1 Example 2

Teacher:	*What do you notice now?*
Kimi:	*I notice double 3s and 1 more.*
Teacher:	*Marta can you come up and circle that double 3 fact that Kimi is talking about.*

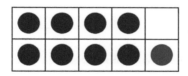

FIGURE 4.17 Ten Frame Doubles Plus 1 Example 3

Teacher:	*Let's look at one more (see Figure 4.17). Tell your partner what you notice.*
Jamal:	*I notice 4 + 4 makes 8 and then 1 more.*
Teacher:	*Taylor, come up and circle that double 4 fact. (Taylor does it.)*
Teacher:	*We are going to be studying these types of facts. You know how we have been studying doubles. Well, now we are going to look at the next set of facts. And they are called doubles, plus 1. Just like you have been saying them. Who could tell me why we might call them doubles plus 1 facts?*
Mike:	*Because it is a doubles and then 1 more.*
Teacher:	*Yes. That's it. Let look at the number line to see where these numbers sit. (See Figure 4.18.)*

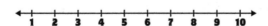

FIGURE 4.18 Number line

Teacher:	*Let's look at 2 + 3. What do you notice?*
Sam:	*They are next to each other.*
Teacher:	*Let's look at 3 + 4. What do you notice?*
Luke:	*They sit next to each other on the number line.*
Teacher:	*Wow! So, do all the numbers that sit next to each other on the number line make a doubles plus 1 fact? I want you to explore that in the workstations this week. That is something I want us to think about more deeply.*

SPOTLIGHT ACTIVITY

Have the students explore if all the numbers that sit side by side on the number line ("neighbor numbers") are Doubles Plus 1 facts and then have them discuss why (see Figure 4.19). Give the students a double ten frame and a number line.

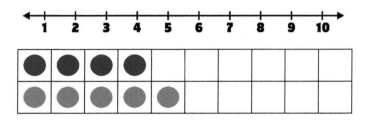

FIGURE 4.19 Number Line and Ten Frame

MATH WORKSTATIONS

	Workstations to Explore Doubles Plus 1	
Concrete	**Pictorial**	**Abstract**
Roll or Pull and Build a Double Plus 1 fact on a Double Ten Frame	Draw on Double Ten Frame Template	Doubles Plus 1 Face Off
Roll and Build a Double Plus 1 fact on a Rekenrek	Draw on Rekenrek Template	Doubles Plus 1 Board Games
Roll and Build a Double Plus 1 fact with the Cubes	Doubles Plus 1 Domino Sort & Record	Doubles Plus 1 Bingo
Roll and Build a Double Plus 1 fact in a Part-Part Whole Mat	Draw on Cube Template	Doubles Plus 1 Tic-Tac-Toe
Roll and Show a Double Plus 1 fact in a Number Bond	Draw in a Part-Part Whole Mat	Doubles Plus 1 Four in a Row
Pull and build a Double Plus 1 fact with Play-Doh©	Draw and Show in a Number Bond	Doubles Plus 1 Flashcards
Pull and show Double Plus 1 facts with Cuisenaire© rods	Doubles Plus 1 Flashcards	Doubles Plus 1 Clip Cards
	Doubles Plus 1 Booklet	Bump
	Doubles Plus 1 draw Cuisenaire© rods on 1 cm grid	Interactive Number Line

FIGURE 4.20 Math Workstations

CONCRETE ACTIVITIES

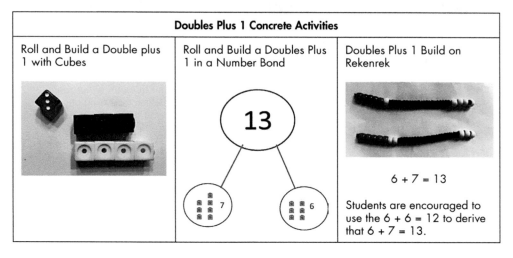

FIGURE 4.21 Concrete Activities

PICTORIAL ACTIVITIES

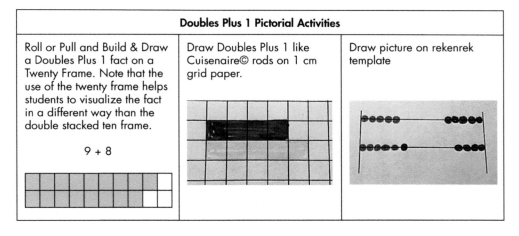

FIGURE 4.22 Pictorial Activities

ABSTRACT ACTIVITIES

Doubles Plus 1 Abstract Activities		
Doubles +1 Four in a Row  Pull and Double the card and add 1 and Cover the Sum. 4 in a row wins.	Doubles Plus 1 Sort Students sort popsicle sticks, number cards or dominos. They decide which ones are doubles, doubles plus 1, or other.	Doubles Plus 1 Tic-Tac-Toe Students play Tic-Tac-Toe as usual but they have to answer the question in the space before they can put an x or an o. Whoever gets 3 in a row first wins.

Doubles +1 Four in a Row table			
5	13	19	17
3	15	5	11
19	9	7	5
7	19	11	9
11	17	3	19

Doubles Plus 1 Tic-Tac-Toe		
2 + 3	3 + 4	4 + 5
7 + 6	5 + 6	1 + 2
8 + 9	6 + 7	10 + 9

FIGURE 4.23 Abstract Activities

STRATEGY FLASHCARDS

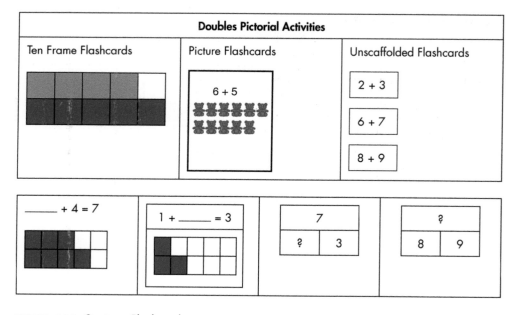

Doubles Pictorial Activities		
Ten Frame Flashcards	Picture Flashcards	Unscaffolded Flashcards
	6 + 5	2 + 3
		6 + 7
		8 + 9

_____ + 4 = 7

1 + _____ = 3

7	
?	3

?	
8	9

FIGURE 4.24 Strategy Flashcards

WORD PROBLEMS

In every fluency module there should be a focus on word problems. Here are a few examples of the types of word problems for doubles +1.			
My Doubles Plus 1 Story Problems Booklet	**Emily had 4 grape lollipops and 5 strawberry ones. How many lollipops did she have?** **Write the set-up equation:** **Show your thinking with a model.** **Write the solution equation.**	**Joanne had 7 coins in her collection. Pamela had 1 more than she did. How many did they have altogether?** **Write the set-up equation:** **Show your thinking with a model.** **Write the solution equation.**	**Nick had 8 watches. He got some more. Now he has 17. How many did he get?** **Write the set-up equation:** **Show your thinking with a model.** **Write the solution equation.**

FIGURE 4.25 Word Problems

RESOURCES

Picture Books and More

Books about Doubles Plus 1				
Videos	Teaching Ideas	Doubles Resources	Power Point	Practice
https://www.youtube.com/watch?v=W7-hnKA0ALE	http://boymamateachermama.com/2017/01/01/teacher-mama-6-games-for-teaching-doubles/	https://www.pinterest.com/drnicki7/doubles/	https://es.slideshare.net/dhedg5/doubles-plus-1	https://www.tes.com/teaching-resource/doubles-plus-one-addition-game-doubles-1-jump-a-math-game-freebie-11483472

FIGURE 4.26 Picture Books and More

Videos

 Video Songs about Doubles Plus 1

Ann Elise's video on Doubles Plus 1: https://youtu.be/F1rS6NsTED4
PISD Mathematics, Fact Fluency Video Doubles & Near Doubles: https://youtu.be/zXkfwQgliio
PISD Mathematics, Doubles & Near Doubles (with math tools): https://youtu.be/orbLOtehPQ0

FIGURE 4.27 Videos

Online Games

Online Games about Doubles Plus 1

https://www.ixl.com/math/grade-1/add-using-doubles-plus-one

FIGURE 4.28 Online Games

Anchor Charts

Anchor Charts support the teaching and learning of Doubles Plus 1. Here are a few examples of what they might look like. It is important that the teacher makes the charts with the students, but also that the students have an opportunity to make their own charts. Students should keep their charts in their math journal under the Math Strategy Section.

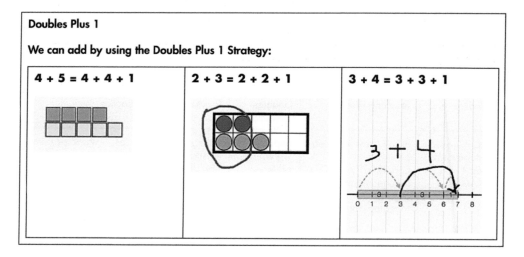

Doubles Plus 1

We can add by using the Doubles Plus 1 Strategy:

4 + 5 = 4 + 4 + 1

2 + 3 = 2 + 2 + 1

3 + 4 = 3 + 3 + 1

FIGURE 4.29 Anchor Chart

Quiz

Doubles Plus 1 Quiz

Name: Date:

---

2 + 3 =

Model with a drawing.

| 7 + 8 =
Model on the twenty frame.

| Solve.
Dana had 4 stickers. She got 5 more. How many does she have now?

Write the equation:

Answer: _____

Solve.
Derrik has 3 striped shirts and 4 solid color ones. How many shirts does he have?

Write the equation:

Answer: _____

| Solve.

6 + _____ = 13

_____ + 9 = 19

_____ = 8 + 9

| Marilyn had 2 rings. She got 3 more. How many does she have now?

Draw a model.

Answer: _____

---

5 + 6 =

Model on the number line.

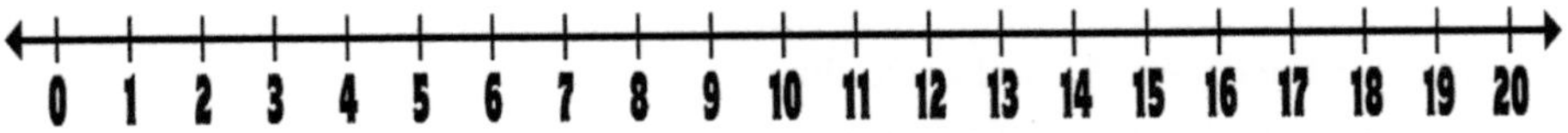

0 1 2 3 4 5 6 7 8 9 10 11 12 13 14 15 16 17 18 19 20

What are Doubles Plus 1 facts? Explain with numbers, words and pictures.

Circle how good you think you are at doing Doubles Plus 1 facts!

Great   Good   OK, still thinking

FIGURE 4.30 Quiz

EXPLORING AND LEARNING DOUBLES PLUS 2

Doubles Plus 2 is one of the last strategies that students learn. In order for students to acquire facts using this strategy, they have to possess a strong foundation in Doubles and Doubles Plus 1. If they have that foundation, then learning Doubles Plus 2 is not difficult. It is important to teach Doubles Plus 2 with many different models. Students should see it modeled on the twenty frame, the rekenrek, with cubes, in part-part whole mats, in number bonds, and on number lines. Anchor charts should be done in order to reinforce these models. Again, students should be encouraged to make discoveries in the patterns of this collection of facts and make connections to prior learning. It is fascinating for students to discover that Doubles Plus 2 facts are the same as the double fact of the number that lies between the two addends on the number example. For example 3 + 5 is the same as 4 + 4 and 6 + 8 is the same as 7 + 7. These discoveries make math exciting and wonderous for students so we should be cognizant of making time for that exploration. (See Figures 4.36–4.47.)

WHOLE CLASS ACTIVITIES

Routines

Use virtual dice to roll a number and have students double that number and then add 2 more. Use jumbo cards and have students double that number and add 2 more. Play Doubles Plus 2 Bingo with the whole class. Students can either have their own boards or they can play with partners. Also play Doubles Plus 2 Tic-Tac-Toe as a whole class game. The class divides up into two teams and they take turns picking a square and stating the answer.

Virtual Dice

www.curriculumbits.com/prodimages/details/maths/mat0005.html

Also do number strings with the students. Number strings is where the teacher gives the students a variety of expressions that deal with a certain concept and students use that concept and discuss the expressions. For instance a set of number strings for these facts would be: 2 + 4, 3 + 5, 4 + 6, 6 + 8, 7 + 9. These can be written on the board or done in a PowerPoint. Students should talk out what they see and a strategy that helps them to solve the problems. Number strings are usually centered around a strategy that you want to practice with the students.

WHOLE CLASS MINI-LESSON: DOUBLES PLUS 2

Introduction

Launch: *Teacher shows the students a big ten frame.*

Teacher: *We have been studying doubles facts and doubles plus 1 facts. Today, I want us to talk about another kind of doubles fact. This is called doubles plus 2 facts. (See Figures 4.31–4.35.)*

Teacher: *Let's take a look.*

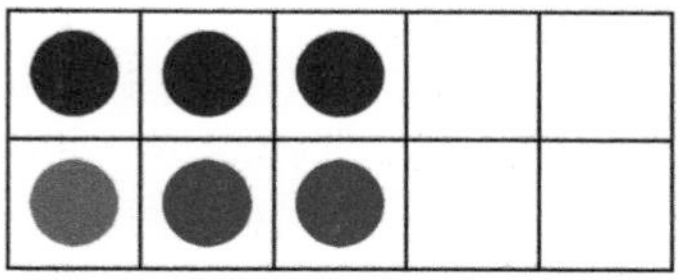

FIGURE 4.31   Ten Frame Doubles

Teacher: *This was a doubles.*

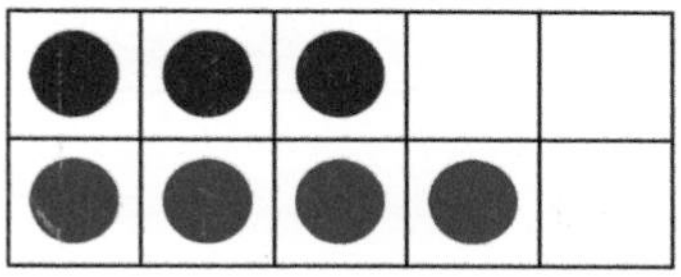

FIGURE 4.32   Ten Frame Doubles Plus 1

Teacher: *This was a doubles plus 1.*

Teacher: *Who can tell me what a doubles plus 2 might look like?*

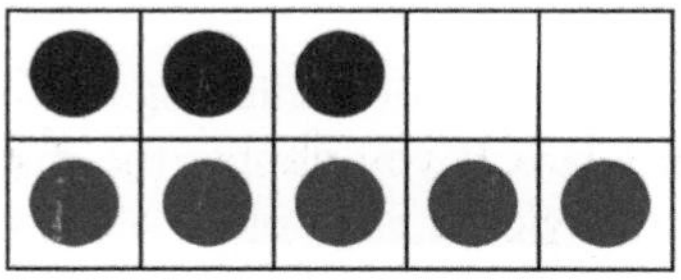

FIGURE 4.33   Ten Frame

Tom: *You would put 1 more red one.*

Teacher: *Ok, tell me more. Why would that make it doubles plus?*

Katie: *Because there is a double 3 and then 2 more.*

Teacher: *Who can come up and circle that double?*

Mike: *I can. (He circles the double 3s.)*

Tami: *And then there are 2 more so it is 6 + 2.*

Teacher: *Well, it is 6 plus 2 … another way to look at it is 3 + 5 … Do you all see that …? Who can explain it?*

Tami: *I see it. There is a group of 3 on top and 5 on the bottom.*

Joe: *3 and 5 make 8.*
Teacher: *Let's look at another one.*

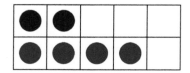

FIGURE 4.34 Ten Frame

Teacher: *Tell me what you see?*
Kimi: *I see 2 + 4 and that makes 6.*
Jon: **2 + 2 and then 2 more.**
Ted: *It's a doubles and then 2 more.*
Teacher: *Let's look at another one.*

FIGURE 4.35 Ten Frame

Debbie: *I see 5 and 7. That makes 12.*
Teacher: *Ok, so when we see these facts we can use our doubles to add those and then just add 2 more. We are going to be working on modeling these and talking about them for the next few days.*

 SPOTLIGHT ACTIVITY

Monkey in the Middle is a friendly way of reminding students a fact about consecutive sums. When 3 numbers are in a row, if you double the middle number, it is always the sum of the numbers on either side. So for example, 3 + 5 is 4 doubled; 5 + 7 is 6 doubled. In order to reinforce this strategy, students work with Monkey in the Middle strategy flashcards that have a monkey on them with a number line. For example, with 4 + 6, 5 is in the middle on the number line and 5 doubled is 10.

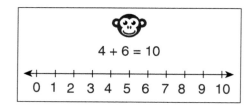

FIGURE 4.36 Monkey in the Middle Strategy Flashcard

MATH WORKSTATIONS

 Workstations to Explore Doubles Plus 2

Concrete	Pictorial	Abstract
Roll or Pull and Build a Double Plus 2 fact on a Twenty Frame	Draw on Twenty Frame Model	Doubles Plus 2 Face Off
Roll and Build a Double Plus 2 fact on a Rekenrek	Draw on Rekenrek Model	Doubles Plus 2 Board Game 1
Roll and Build a Double Plus 2 fact with the Cubes	Draw on Cube Template	Doubles Plus 2 War
Roll and Build a Double Plus 2 fact in a Part-Part Whole Mat	Draw in a Part-Part Whole Mat	Doubles Plus 2 Tic-Tac-Toe
Roll and Show a Double Plus 2 fact in a Number Bond	Draw and Show in a Number Bond	Doubles Plus 2 Four in a Row
Double it Plus 2 with Play-Doh©	Doubles Plus 2 Flashcards	Doubles Plus 2 Slides and Ladders
Spin and Double Plus 2 to 5	Doubles Plus 2 Booklet	Spin and Double Plus 2
Spin and Double Plus 2 to 10	Doubles Plus 2 Domino Sort & Record	Doubles Board Game 2
Show with Cuisenaire© rods	Doubles Plus 2 Poster	Doubles Plus 2 Bingo
		Roll & Double Plus 2
		Doubles Plus 2 Bump
		Doubles Plus 2 PPW
		Missing Number Flashcards
		Power Towers
		Interactive Number Line

FIGURE 4.37 Math Workstations

CONCRETE ACTIVITIES

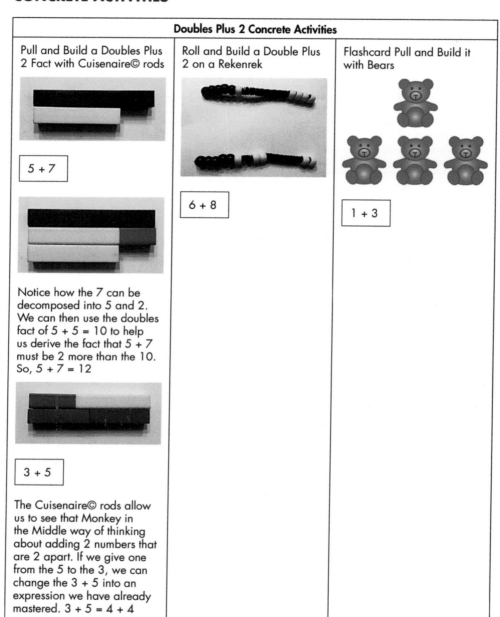

Doubles Plus 2 Concrete Activities		
Pull and Build a Doubles Plus 2 Fact with Cuisenaire© rods	Roll and Build a Double Plus 2 on a Rekenrek	Flashcard Pull and Build it with Bears

5 + 7

6 + 8

1 + 3

Notice how the 7 can be decomposed into 5 and 2. We can then use the doubles fact of 5 + 5 = 10 to help us derive the fact that 5 + 7 must be 2 more than the 10. So, 5 + 7 = 12

3 + 5

The Cuisenaire© rods allow us to see that Monkey in the Middle way of thinking about adding 2 numbers that are 2 apart. If we give one from the 5 to the 3, we can change the 3 + 5 into an expression we have already mastered. 3 + 5 = 4 + 4

FIGURE 4.38 Concrete Activities

PICTORIAL ACTIVITIES

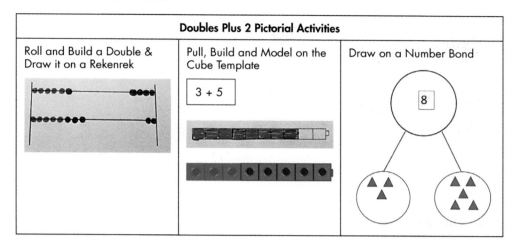

FIGURE 4.39   Pictorial Activities

ABSTRACT ACTIVITIES

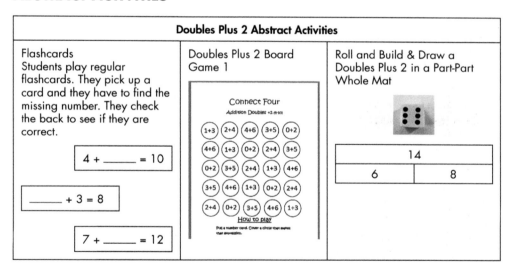

FIGURE 4.40   Abstract Activities

STRATEGY FLASHCARDS

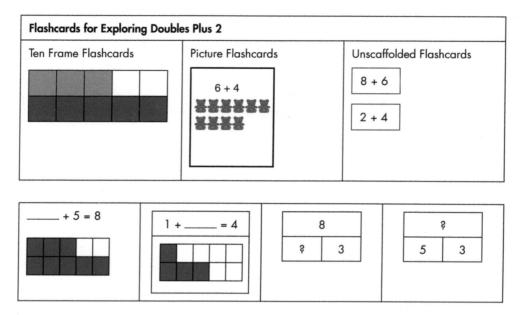

FIGURE 4.41 Strategy Flashcards

WORD PROBLEMS

In every fluency module there should be a focus on word problems. Here are a few examples of the types of word problems for doubles plus 2.

My Doubles Plus 2 Story Problems Booklet	Kylie scored 4 goals in her soccer game on Saturday and 6 goals on Sunday. How many goals did she score?	There were 12 books. 5 were fiction and the rest were non-fiction. How many were non-fiction?	Brody had 3 toy trucks. His brother had 2 more than he did. How many did they have altogether?
	Write the set-up equation:	Write the set-up equation:	Write the set-up equation:
	Show your thinking with a model.	Show your thinking with a model.	Show your thinking with a model.
	Write the solution equation.	Write the solution equation.	Write the solution equation.

FIGURE 4.42 Word Problems

RESOURCES

Videos

 Videos about Doubles Plus 2

Ann Elise's video on Doubles Plus 2: https://youtu.be/hlx1dPqbqiU
PISD Mathematics Doubles & Near Doubles (with math tools):
https://youtu.be/orbLOtehPQ0

FIGURE 4.43   Videos

ANCHOR CHARTS

Anchor charts support the teaching and learning of Doubles Plus 2. Here are a few examples of what they might look like. It is important that the teacher makes the charts with the students, but also that students have an opportunity to make their own charts. Students should keep their charts in their math journal under the Math Strategy Section.

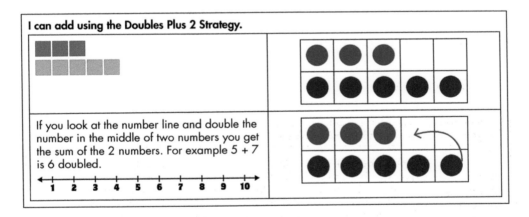

I can add using the Doubles Plus 2 Strategy.

If you look at the number line and double the number in the middle of two numbers you get the sum of the 2 numbers. For example 5 + 7 is 6 doubled.

FIGURE 4.44   Anchor Chart

Anchor Charts About Exploring Doubles Plus 2	
Teacher Made Charts	**Student Made Charts**
Doubles +2 are facts that are doubles facts plus 2 more. 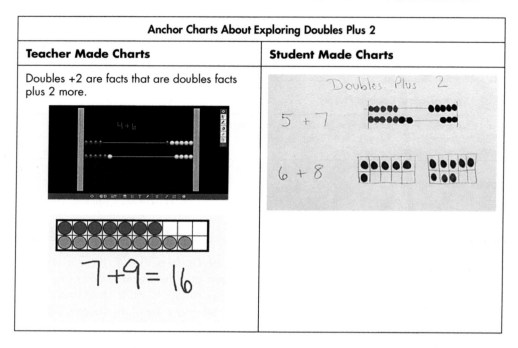	

FIGURE 4.45 Anchor Charts

Quiz

Doubles Plus 2 Quiz

Name: Date:

2 + 4 = Model with a drawing.	7 + 9 = Model on the twenty frame. 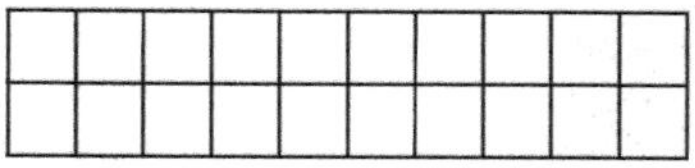 (twenty frame grid)	Solve. Ashton scored 5 points in his ultimate frisbee game on Tuesday. He scored 7 more points in his game on Thursday. How many points did he score? Write the equation: Answer: _____
Solve. Addison picked 3 blueberries. Then she picked 5 more. How many does she have now? Write the equation: Answer: _____	Solve. 7 + ____ = 12 ____ + 9 = 20 18 = 8 + _____ ____ = 6 + 4	Solve as a doubles plus 2 facts. ____ + ____ = 14 ____ + ____ = 8

2 + 4 =

Model on the number line.

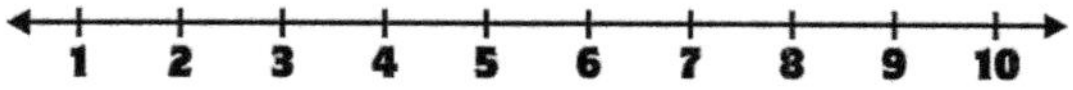

$\xleftarrow{\qquad}$ 1 2 3 4 5 6 7 8 9 10 $\xrightarrow{\qquad}$

What are Doubles Plus 2 facts? Explain with numbers, words and pictures.

Circle how good you think you are at doing Doubles Plus 2 facts!

Great   Good   OK, still thinking

FIGURE 4.46 Quiz

EXPLORING AND LEARNING ADD 10

Add 10 is actually a pretty easy concept for many students as they recognize the composition of teen numbers as a 10 and some 1s. Many students see the pattern and are able to answer the problems very quickly. It is important for us to check and be sure this understanding is in place, though, so that we can provide the appropriate experiences to those students who do not understand this concept (see Figures 4.51–4.60).

WHOLE CLASS ACTIVITIES

Routines

Use virtual dice to roll a number and have students add 10 to that number. Use jumbo cards and have students add 10 to that number. Play Bingo and Tic-Tac-Toe with the class.

Virtual Dice

www.curriculumbits.com/prodimages/details/maths/mat0005.html

WHOLE CLASS MINI-LESSON: ADD 10

Introduction

Launch: *Teacher shows the students a big ten frame.*
Teacher: *We have been looking at various strategies. Today, we are going to look at what happens when you add 10 to a single digit number. Let's take a look at some problems.*
Teacher: *If I have 10 and I add 2, what do I get? (See Figure 4.47.)*

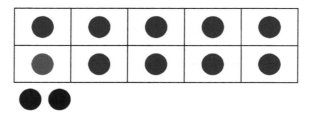

FIGURE 4.47 Ten Frame Add 10

Tracie: *You get 12.*
Teacher: *Let's take a look at that on the number line. (See Figure 4.48.)*

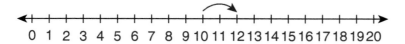

0 1 2 3 4 5 6 7 8 9 10 11 12 13 14 15 16 17 18 19 20

FIGURE 4.48 Number Line

Teacher:　Let's look at another one. (See Figure 4.49.)

FIGURE 4.49　Ten Frame Add 10

Teacher:　*What do you notice?*
Lucy:　*I see 14. I see a 10 and a 4.*
Teacher:　*Do you all agree with her or not? Show me with your hands. Who can come up and point out what she means? (Josh comes up and circles the 10.) Ok, let's take a look at this problem on the number line. (See Figure 4.50.)*

FIGURE 4.50　Number Line Add 10

SPOTLIGHT ACTIVITY

Add 10 Bingo

Students take turns pulling a card and calling that sum. Each player checks to see where it is on their board and they cover that space. Whoever gets 4 in a row horizontally or vertically or 4 corners gets bingo (see Figure 4.51).

2 + 10	10 + 5	10 + 6	10 + 2
8 + 10	10 + 1	10 + 8	9 + 10
10 + 7	10 + 9	10 + 5	10 + 7
10 + 2	10 + 4	8 + 10	10 + 3

3 + 10	10 + 7	10 + 8	10 + 4
6 + 10	10 + 1	10 + 9	9 + 10
1 + 10	9 + 10	10 + 5	10 + 7
10 + 2	4 + 10	8 + 10	10 + 2

FIGURE 4.51　Bingo Cards

MATH WORKSTATIONS

 Workstations to Explore Add 10

Concrete	Pictorial	Abstract
Roll or Pull and Build an Add 10 fact on a Double Ten Frame	Draw on Double Ten Frame Model	Add 10 Face Off
Roll and Build an Add 10 fact on a Rekenrek	Draw on Rekenrek Model	Add 10 Board Game
Roll and Build an Add 10 fact with the Cubes	Draw on Cube Template	Add 10 War
Roll and Build an Add 10 fact in a Part-Part Whole Mat	Draw in a Part-Part Whole Mat	Add 10 Tic-Tac-Toe
Roll and Show an Add 10 fact in a Number Bond	Draw and Show in a Number Bond	Add 10 Four in a Row
Add 10 with Play-Doh©	Add 10 Flashcards	Add 10 Slides and Ladders
Spin and Add 10 to 5	Add 10 Booklet	Spin and Add 10
Spin and Add 10 to 10	Draw Cuisenaire© rods on 1 cm grid paper	Add 10 Bingo
Show with Cuisenaire© rods		Roll & Add 10
		Add 10 Bump
		Power Towers
		Record on Number Path
		Record on Number Line

FIGURE 4.52 Math Workstations

CONCRETE ACTIVITIES

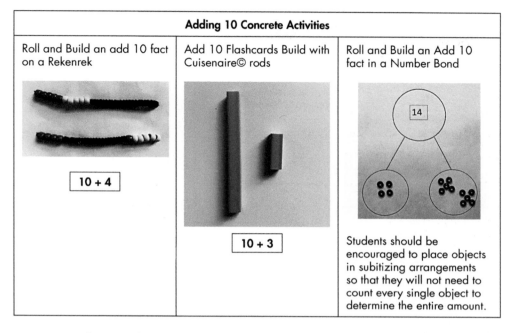

Adding 10 Concrete Activities		
Roll and Build an add 10 fact on a Rekenrek	Add 10 Flashcards Build with Cuisenaire© rods	Roll and Build an Add 10 fact in a Number Bond
10 + 4	10 + 3	Students should be encouraged to place objects in subitizing arrangements so that they will not need to count every single object to determine the entire amount.

FIGURE 4.53 Concrete Activities

PICTORIAL ACTIVITIES

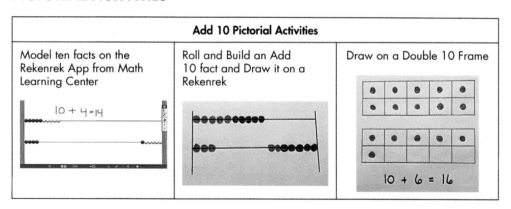

Add 10 Pictorial Activities		
Model ten facts on the Rekenrek App from Math Learning Center	Roll and Build an Add 10 fact and Draw it on a Rekenrek	Draw on a Double 10 Frame
10 + 4 = 14		10 + 6 = 16

FIGURE 4.54 Pictorial Activities

ABSTRACT ACTIVITIES

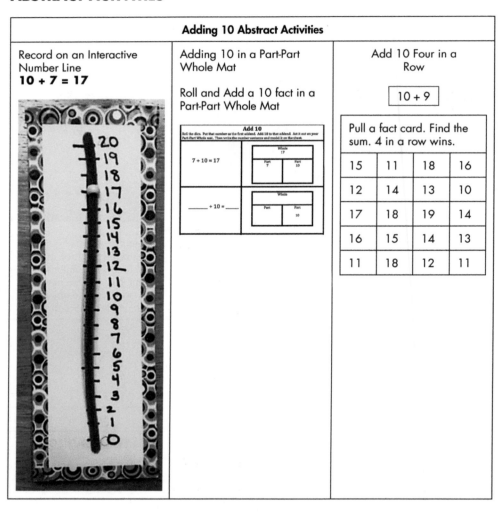

Adding 10 Abstract Activities

| Record on an Interactive Number Line | Adding 10 in a Part-Part Whole Mat | Add 10 Four in a Row |

Record on an Interactive Number Line
10 + 7 = 17

Adding 10 in a Part-Part Whole Mat

Roll and Add a 10 fact in a Part-Part Whole Mat

Add 10 Four in a Row

$$10 + 9$$

Pull a fact card. Find the sum. 4 in a row wins.

15	11	18	16
12	14	13	10
17	18	19	14
16	15	14	13
11	18	12	11

FIGURE 4.55 Abstract Activities

STRATEGY FLASHCARDS

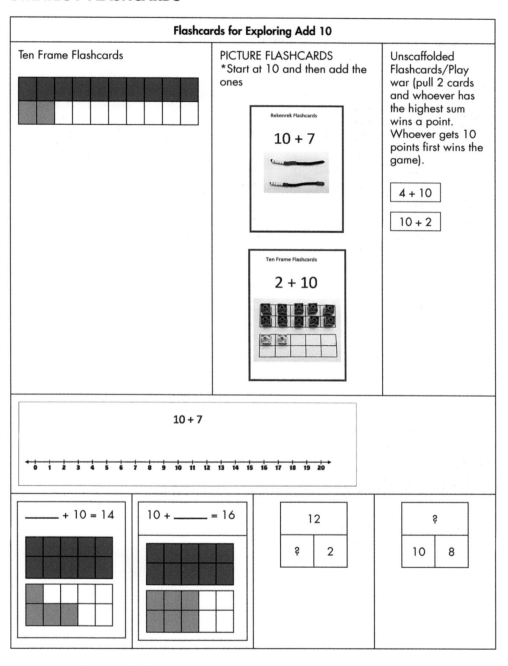

FIGURE 4.56 Strategy Flashcards

WORD PROBLEMS

In every fluency module there should be a focus on word problems. Here are a few examples of the types of word problems for Add 10.			
My Add 10 Story Problems Booklet	**Hannah had 4 bracelets. She got 10 more for her birthday. How many does she have now?** **Write the set-up equation:** **Show your thinking with a model.** **Write the solution equation.**	**There were 12 flowers in a pot. 2 were daisies and the rest were violets. How many were violets?** **Write the set-up equation:** **Show your thinking with a model.** **Write the solution equation.**	**Amy had 8 stuffed animals. She got some more. Now she has 18. How many did she get?** **Write the set-up equation:** **Show your thinking with a model.** **Write the solution equation.**

FIGURE 4.57 Word Problems

RESOURCES

Videos

Video Songs about Add 10
Ann Elise's Video on Adding 10: https://youtu.be/wd13Yk00Fco Mr R's Songs for Teaching, 20s Frame Song (Double Tens Frame) Add to Numbers Greater than Ten: https://youtu.be/rG-lJ0yzYis

FIGURE 4.58 Videos

Anchor Chart

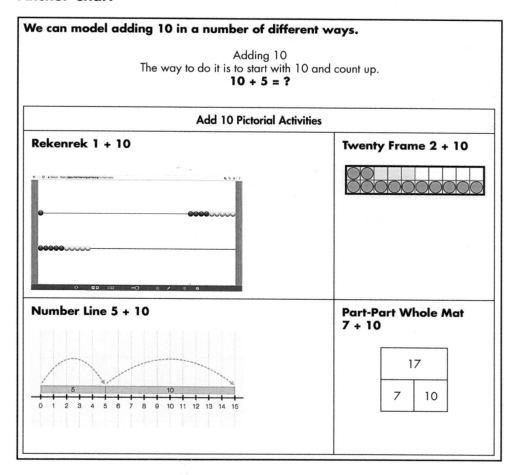

We can model adding 10 in a number of different ways.

Adding 10
The way to do it is to start with 10 and count up.
10 + 5 = ?

Add 10 Pictorial Activities

Rekenrek 1 + 10

Twenty Frame 2 + 10

Number Line 5 + 10

Part-Part Whole Mat 7 + 10

FIGURE 4.59 Anchor Chart

Quiz

Add 10 to a Number Quiz

Name: Date:

10 + 4 = Model with a drawing.	10 + 7 = Model on the twenty frame.	Solve. Merida had 2 beads. She got 10 more. How many does she have now? Write the equation: Answer: _____
Solve. Sue had 10 marbles. She got 5 more. How many does she have now? Write the equation: Answer: _____	Solve. 10 + _____ = 12 _____ + 9 = 19 11 = 10 + _____ _____ = 8 + 10	Solve. _____ + 3 = 13 10 + _____ = 14

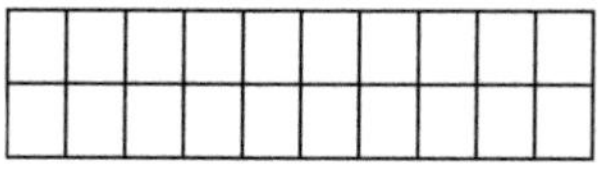

10 + 8 =   Model on the number line.

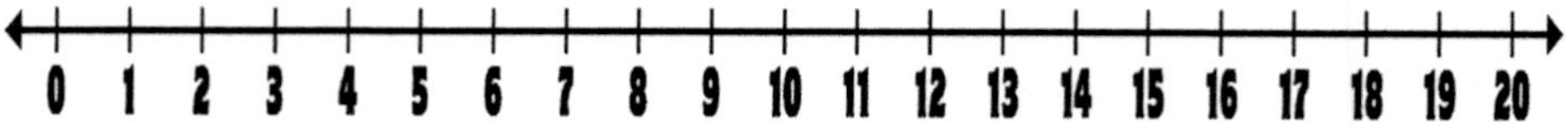

0 1 2 3 4 5 6 7 8 9 10 11 12 13 14 15 16 17 18 19 20

What are adding 10 facts? Explain with numbers, words and pictures.

Circle how good you think you are doing Add 10 facts!

Great   Good    OK, still thinking

FIGURE 4.60 Quiz

EXPLORING AND LEARNING BRIDGING 10 WITH 7, 8, OR 9

Teaching Bridging 10 is one of the last addition strategies that students learn. Many top performing math countries put an emphasis on Bridging 10 (Henry & Brown, 2008). The idea is that whenever you see 7, 8, or 9 you make it into a 10 to add. This strategy is reliant upon the ability of students to flexibly decompose and recompose numbers. For example, if the equation was 5 + 8, students could choose to decompose the 8 to 5 + 3 and combine the 5s to make a 10. This leaves them with the simple problem of 10 + 3, and makes what could be a challenging fact accessible without finger counting! Also students could just count up to 10 and then add the rest. This would look like 8 + 2 = 10, 10 + 3 = 13. Bridge to 10 is a strategy that can greatly improve student efficiency, however students need a great deal of practice manipulating the addends concretely, pictorially and, finally, abstractly (see Figures 4.61–4.71). Bridge to 10 is especially important since it will generalize easily to computation involving larger numbers and make operations simpler for students.

WHOLE CLASS ACTIVITIES

Routines

Use virtual dice to roll a number and have students add 7, 8, or 9 to that number. Use jumbo cards and have students add 7, 8, or 9 to that number. Play Bridging 10 Bingo and Tic-Tac-Toe with the whole class. Do number strings around this strategy with the class as well. Here is an example: 3 + 8, 4 + 8, 5 + 8, 6 + 8, 7 + 8.

WHOLE CLASS MINI-LESSON

Introduction

Teacher:	*Today we are going to talk about what it means to add 8 to a number. Yesterday, we were talking about what happens when you have a 7 and you are adding a number greater than 3. Who can tell me what we discussed and what we practiced yesterday?*
Joe:	*When you see 7 you know that if it is 4 or more you are going to bridge 10.*
Teacher:	*Why would we want to bridge 10?*
Jena:	*Because it makes it easier.*
Teacher:	*Who can come up to the board and use a model to explain?*
Mark:	*Ok (uses the virtual ten frame), if we have 7 and we add 5 we just fill in these 3 spaces and then we count 2 more on from 10.*
Teacher:	*Does everybody see that? Ok, how do you think we can use this same idea with 8.*
Kelly:	*I know. Let me show you (uses the virtual ten frame) … see if we have 8 and there are 2 spaces … are going to add 4 so we fill in those spaces and make a 10 and then count on 2 more.*
Teacher:	*Does everybody see that? Does anybody have any questions? I know, let's try it out in the big ten frame. Ok, everybody sit. I am going to count out 8 kids. (Teacher pulls 8 popsicle stick names and then 5 more.) Ok, come stand in the ten frame. Now we are going to add 5 more. Oh, I see you 2 went and filled in the ten frame first … now we have 3 kids more to count. Let's do another one … Let's see … let's do 9 + 2 … you all sit down and I'm going to call 9 more (teacher pulls 9 more popsicle sticks and then 2 more … students come up and act out problem again).*

Explicit Instruction/Teacher Facilitating

Teacher: *I want us to look at what was happening? What does it really mean to bridge 10? Why would we do that?*

Timothy: *It means you make a 10 first and then count on.*

Teacher: *So, we are saying that bridging 10 is a way to add bigger numbers. We are using the ten frame to model it.*

Teacher: *What do we notice?*

Marta: *We notice that with numbers like 7, 8, and 9 you can make 10 and then count on.*

Teacher: *Who agrees? (Many students agree with Marta.)*

Guided Practice/Interactive Modeling

Teacher: *Ok, let's see if you all can show me that on your whiteboard ten frames. I am going to say a fact and I want you to show me the bridge 10 strategy on your boards. I want you all to model 8 + 3 with the make 10 strategy.*

Teacher: *Ok, who can explain what they did?*

Susana: *Yes, I can show it here … 8 + 3 is 11 … there were 2 spaces and then I filled them in and counted 1 more.*

Teacher: *Ok, today we have looked at the Bridging 10 strategy. We will be looking at modeling this in different ways over the next few days. Ok, get ready to go to workstations and guided math.*

 SPOTLIGHT ACTIVITY

These are just some poems that Dr. Nicki made up years ago to reinforce the Make 10 or Bridging 10 strategy. They should be taught after the students have had plenty of opportunities to act out the strategy and work with it on the ten frame and the rekenrek. (See Figure 4.61.)

Poem

A Poem About 8 and 9	
Lucky 8 You're So Great! When I see you I know what to do Go to the other number And take two!	**Lucky 9** You're So Fine! Glad to see you every time It's just too much fun To go to the other number And take one!

FIGURE 4.61 Poem

MATH WORKSTATIONS

 Workstations to Explore Bridge 10 with 7, 8 and 9

Concrete	Pictorial	Abstract
Roll and Build a Bridging 10 Fact on a Double Ten Frame	Draw on Ten Frame Model	Bridging 10 spin to win
Roll and Build a Bridging 10 Fact on a Rekenrek	Draw on Rekenrek Model	Bridging 10 War
Spin and Build a Bridging 10 Fact using cubes	Bridging 10 Booklet	Bridging 10 clip cards
Build using Cuisenaire© rods	Draw Bridging 10 Cuisenaire© rods on cm paper	Bridging 10 Tic-Tac-Toe
Bridging 10 flashcards build	Bridging 10 with cubes and recording	Bridging 10 Bingo
Build a Bridging 10 Beaded Number Line	Bridging 10 domino sort	Bridging 10 card sort
		Bridging 10 flashcards
		Record Bridging 10 on a Number Line or Open Number Line
		Record Bridging 10 on a Numberpath
		Power Towers
		Bridge 10 Bump
		Interactive Number Line

FIGURE 4.62 Math Workstations

CONCRETE ACTIVITIES

Bridging 10 Concrete Activities		
Roll or Pull and Build Bridge 10 on a Beaded Number Line 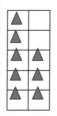 $8 + 5$ Using the beaded number line, students can see that 8 + 5 can be renamed to 10 + 3 to make it easier.	Bridge 10 Fact Flashcards Build on Double 10 Frame  Encourage students to move some from the 2nd addend so that the top 10 frame can be filled.  $7 + 4$	Build with Cuisenaire© rods  $9 + 5$ Students can see that 9 + 5 can be renamed 10 + 4.

FIGURE 4.63 Concrete Activities

PICTORIAL ACTIVITIES

Bridge 10 Pictorial Activities		
Students can draw shapes on a double 10 frame by putting each addend on its own 10 frame to reinforce the benchmark of 5 within the addends of higher doubles facts.  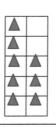	Bridge 10 Domino Sort 	Draw a Bridge 10 on a Cube Template 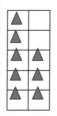 $8 + 4 = 10 + 2 = 12$

FIGURE 4.64 Pictorial Activities

ABSTRACT ACTIVITIES

Bridge 10 Abstract Activities

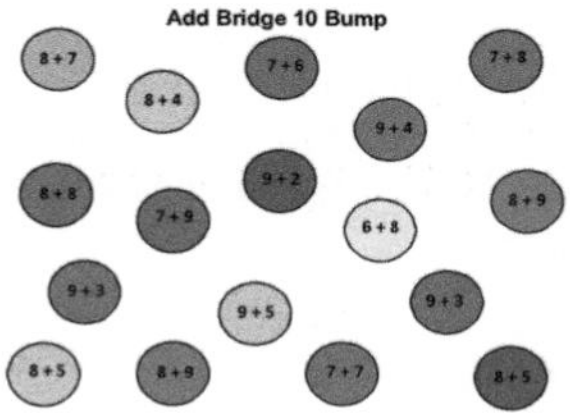
Add Bridge 10 Bump
8 + 7
7 + 6
7 + 8
8 + 4
9 + 4
8 + 8
9 + 2
8 + 9
7 + 9
6 + 8
9 + 3
9 + 5
9 + 3
8 + 5
8 + 9
7 + 7
8 + 5

Interactive Number Line

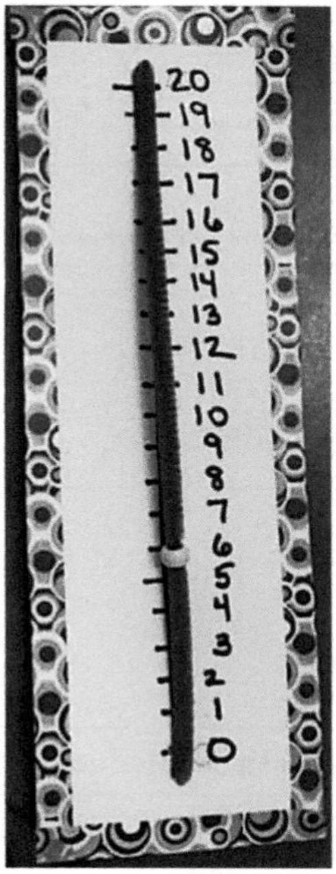
20
19
18
17
16
15
14
13
12
11
10
9
8
7
6
5
4
3
2
1
0

Spin to Win

Students spin the spinner and compare sums. They have to write the expression on a recording sheet. Whoever gets 5 points first wins the game.

Player 1	<>=	Player 2
7 + 9	>	8 + 5

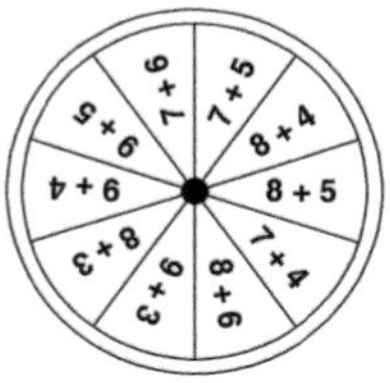
7 + 5
8 + 4
8 + 5
7 + 4

FIGURE 4.65 Abstract Activities

STRATEGY FLASHCARDS

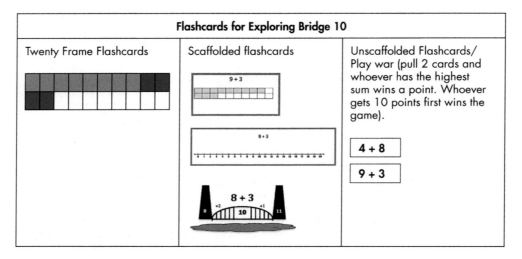

FIGURE 4.66 Strategy Flashcards

MORE STRATEGY FLASHCARDS

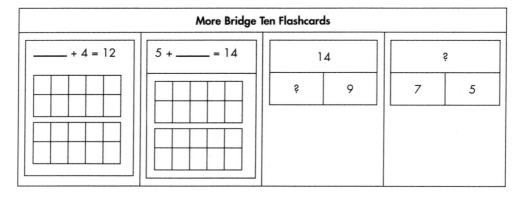

FIGURE 4.67 More Strategy Flashcards

WORD PROBLEMS

In every fluency module there should be a focus on word problems. Here are a few examples of the types of word problems for Bridge 10.			
My Bridge 10 Story Problems Booklet	**There were 7 boys and 4 girls playing on the playground. How many children were there altogether?** **Write the set-up equation:** **Show your thinking with a model.** **Write the solution equation.**	**Liza had 9 avocados. She got some more. Now she has 12. How many did she get?** **Write the set-up equation:** **Show your thinking with a model.** **Write the solution equation.**	**Alison had some cookies. She got 8 more. Now she has 14. How many did she get?** **Write the set-up equation:** **Show your thinking with a model.** **Write the solution equation.**

FIGURE 4.68 Word Problems

RESOURCES

Videos

Videos about Bridge 10
Ann Elise's video on Bridge 10 when adding with a 9: https://youtu.be/xLCMvzJFoU4 Ann Elise video on Bridge 10 when adding with 7 or 8: https://youtu.be/hnXF2szfg2k Origo One, Teaching the Bridge 10 Strategy for Addition: https://www.youtube.com/watch?v=SZy2abGiCpQ
Ronit Bird, Bridging Through 10: https://www.youtube.com/watch?v=BUXpV2Wjb-U&t=1s
WSKG Public Media, Mental Math: Make 10: https://www.youtube.com/watch?v=ftST1Uzcpr4
Danielle the Tutor, Make a Ten: https://www.youtube.com/watch?v=ltSQfA_fT1g
PISD Mathematics, Fact Fluency Video Make 10 & More, Build Up Thru 10, Back Down Thru 10: https://youtu.be/7BT8Kf3YvHg
PISD Mathematics, +/− 7, 8, 9 facts on Double Ten Frame: https://youtu.be/afO2a3SKEqk
Susan Burke, Bridging to 10 - Addition: https://youtu.be/x3hIOBCKwL0
Tori Ricker, Make 10 Strategy for Addition: https://youtu.be/q9h4skGoWJ8

FIGURE 4.69 Videos

Anchor Chart

Anchor charts support the teaching and learning of Bridge 10. Here are a few examples of what they might look like. It is important that the teacher makes the charts with the students, but also that the students have an opportunity to make their own charts. Students should keep their charts in their math journal under the Math Strategy Section.

We can bridge ten. It means we walk through ten to add numbers together. Ten is a bridge that makes adding easy.

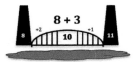

FIGURE 4.70 Anchor Chart

Quiz

Bridge 10 Quiz		
Name:		Date:
9 + 2 = Model with a drawing.	7 + 4 = Model on the twenty frame.	Solve. Harry had 8 baseball cards. Sally gave him 4 more. How many does he have now? Write the equation: Answer: _____
Solve. There were 3 baby elephants and 9 adult elephants. How many elephants were there in all? Write the equation: Answer: _____	Solve. 7 + _____ = 12 _____ + 8 = 14 13 = 6 + _____ _____ = 9 + 7	Solve as a bridging fact. 9 + 4
8 + 5 = Model on the number line. 0 1 2 3 4 5 6 7 8 9 10 11 12 13 14 15 16 17 18 19 20		

What is the bridging 10 strategy? Explain with numbers, words and pictures.

Circle how good you think you are at doing Bridge 10 facts!

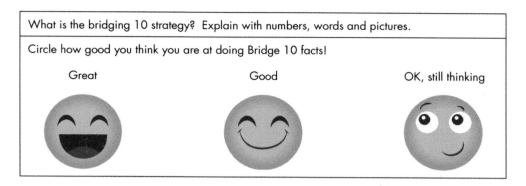

| Great | Good | OK, still thinking |

FIGURE 4.71 Quiz

Special Note: There should be a constant reflection on ways to make 20 when working with the higher facts. Students should build on what they know about their make 10 facts to do this.

KEY POINTS

- doubles
- doubles + 1
- doubles + 2
- adding 10 to a number
- Bridge 10.

SUMMARY

We need to give students adequate time to work with number combinations within 20. There should be plenty of opportunities to work with activities at the concrete, pictorial, and abstract level. The research clearly states that although there are many different strategies for adding higher numbers, there should be a strong emphasis on Bridging 10 (Henry & Brown, 2008). 10 is like a superhighway to numbers. This is the very foundation that students will need when working with multi-digit numbers. We would like to reemphasize that it is important that the school develop and employ consistent names for these strategies so that everyone in every grade is on the same page in regard to naming and describing their thinking.

REFLECTION QUESTIONS

1. What did you learn in this chapter?
2. Do you currently teach all of these strategies? How do you keep track of who knows them? How do you scaffold the progression of teaching and learning the strategies?
3. Name one or two things that you will do differently based on this chapter.

REFERENCES

Henry, V. J., & Brown, R. S. (2008). First-grade basic facts: An investigation into teaching and learning of an accelerated, high-demand memorization standard. *Journal for Research in Mathematics Education*, 39(2), 153–183.

LeFevre, J. A., Smith-Chant, B. L., Hiscock, K., Daley, K. E., & Morris, J. (2003). Young adults' strategic choices in simple arithmetic: Implications for the development of mathematical representations. In A. J. Baroody, & A. K. Erlbaum, *The development of arithmetic concepts and skills: Constructive adaptive expertise* (pp. 203–228). Mahwah, NJ: Lawrence Erlbaum Associates.

Steinberg, R. M. (1985). Instruction on derived facts strategies in addition and subtraction. *Journal for Research in Mathematics Education*, 16(5), 337–355.

Willingham, D. T. (2009). *Why don't students like school?: A cognitive scientist answers questions about how the mind works and what it means for the classroom.* Hoboken, NJ: John Wiley & Sons.

PART III

Introduction to Exploring and Learning Subtraction Strategies

CHAPTER 5

Exploring and Learning Subtraction within 10

Before we embark on the journey of exploring subtraction strategies for basic math facts, it bears repeating that we cannot just "teach" these strategies. Instead, we must provide a classroom full of rich experiences to help students develop number sense. This includes experiences that highlight the inverse relationships of addition and subtraction and the meaning of equality. It is by providing experiences using concrete materials with interesting and engaging real-life situations, showing these same situations using pictures, and then recording these situations using numbers, that we will provide the conditions necessary for young mathematicians to set the foundation for their learning.

The more we can expose students to all three representations in the C-P-A progression and connect them, the better (see Figures 5.1–5.11). *Too often we rush to numbers before students fully understand the relationships inherent in the strategies*. To build this understanding, students need lots and lots of practice using concrete materials and visuals, preferably in the context of real-world problems. As students begin exploring the early subtraction strategies, they can use real-life objects like bears or toy dinosaurs to mimic the story until they demonstrate proficiency modeling the situation and accurately figuring out how many are left. From there, they can substitute cubes or other items that can represent these objects. This eventually leads to pictures and, finally, number sentences.

As noted by Carpenter et al. (2015), there are three basic types of subtraction problems: separate, part-whole, and comparison or difference. An important foundational understanding relating to subtraction is that subtraction problems can be thought of as missing addend problems. This reinforces the importance of the relationship to addition and allows students to leverage what they already know to access the unknown. Thus, if a student is presented with 10 - 5, they can think about what can be added to 5 to get 10. Addition skills are typically stronger than subtraction skills, so students can build their proficiency with subtraction by relying on their strength with addition.

Fluency with basic facts is multifaceted, including accuracy, flexibility, efficiency, and automaticity. Subtraction is where the skill of being flexible in our thinking comes to the forefront because it is the numbers that lead us towards using one strategy over another. For example, if asked 8 - 6, thinking about what can be added to 6 to make 8 is more efficient than thinking about taking away the 6 from the 8. If asked 8 - 2, though, counting back the 2 is the most efficient. This thinking extends to larger numbers as well as with our work on fractions and decimals down the road. In our experience, subtraction math facts is the biggest weakness for students of all ages. At times, it truly feels like there is an epidemic of inefficient subtraction strategies. Students need to fully understand all of the meanings of subtraction so that they can choose which method will work for them in each situation. The only way this will happen is if we give subtraction equal instructional time.

EXPLORING AND LEARNING HOW TO SUBTRACT 0

The Subtract 0 strategy is exploring what happens when we do not take away a quantity from a group of items. We want students to generalize that when we take 0 away from any number we are left with the same amount since nothing was taken away. While it is tempting to gloss over this, it is a very important concept that causes confusion for students. We need to be sure we are giving the appropriate instructional time dedicated to exploring what it means. We have found success working on both the Subtract 0 and Subtract 1 strategy at the same time when working with students. A great way to introduce the Subtract 0 strategy is through poems, songs, and picture books. Be sure to model the Subtract 0 facts on a variety of concrete and digital tools within the contexts of real-life situations. We want students to develop automaticity with their Subtract 0 facts as well as generalize what will happen when we Subtract 0 from any number. We will only be giving a few examples of teaching this through the cycle of engagement. Many people argue that Subtract 1 should be taught first because it is an easier strategy than Subtract 0. We think this is a strong argument.

WHOLE CLASS ACTIVITIES

Routines

Use virtual dice to roll a number and have students take 0 away from that number. Use jumbo cards and have students take 0 away from that number. Play Subtract 0 Bingo with the whole class. Students can either have their own boards or they can play with partners. Also play subtract Tic-Tac-Toe as a whole class game. The class divides up into two teams and they take turns picking a square and stating the answer. The whole team helps the person who is at the board to decide what is the correct answer.

WHOLE CLASS MINI-LESSON

Teacher:	*Today we are going to work on what happens when you take 0 from a number. I want 5 students to come and stand in the five frame.*
	Ok, now nobody leave. How many are left?
Stevie:	*5.*
Teacher:	*Ok, let's do another problem. Let's have 4 kids come up. Now, nobody leave. How many kids are left?*
Tami:	*4.*
Teacher:	*Ok, let's do another problem. Let's have 3 kids come up. Now, nobody leave. We are not going to take away any. How many kids are left?*
Jamal:	*3.*
Teacher:	*So, who can tell me what happens when we take 0 away from a number?*
Lucy:	*Nothing. The number stays the same.*
Teacher:	*Is that always true? Let's try a few more. Who wants to give us a problem?*
Kiyana:	*7 kids go up. Nobody leaves.*
Teacher:	*Ok, so we are going to take away 0, which means we are taking away nothing. How many kids are left?*
David:	*7.*

Teacher: *Ok, so what happens when we take away 0 from a number?*
Harry: *Nothing. The number stays the same.*

Guided Practice/Interactive Modeling: In this lesson, the guided practice and the interactive modeling was with the whole group as the students acted out the problem.

SPOTLIGHT ACTIVITY

Zero, zero, zero makes a number stay the same, If you take away zero the number doesn't change Zero, zero, zero makes a number stay the same, If you take away zero the number doesn't change. 1 – 0 = 1 2 – 0 = 2 3 – 0 = 3 4 – 0 = 4 5 – 0 = 5	Resources and Lesson Plans Teach the students the chant Have them act out it on their fingers, with counters and by acting it out in the 5 frame with students.

FIGURE 5.1 Spotlight Activity

MATH WORKSTATIONS

 Workstations to Explore the Subtract 0 Strategy

Concrete	Pictorial	Abstract
Roll or Pull and Build a Subtract 0 fact on a Ten Frame	Roll, Build and Draw it on a Ten Frame model	Subtract 0 Clip Flashcards
Roll or Pull and Build a Subtract 0 fact on a Rekenrek	Roll, Build and Draw it on a Rekenrek	Spin and Subtract 0 to 5
Roll or Pull and Build a Subtract 0 fact with Cubes	Roll, Build and Model it on the Cube Template	Spin and Subtract 0 to 10
Roll or Pull and Build a Subtract 0 fact in a Part-Part Whole Mat	Roll, Build and Draw in a Part-Part Whole Mat	Subtract 0 Board Game
Roll or Pull and Show a Subtract 0 fact in a Number Bond	Roll, Build and Draw in a Number Bond	Subtract 0 War
Subtract 0 with Play-Doh©	Subtract 0 Domino Sort, Draw and Record	Subtract 0 Tic-Tac-Toe
Spin, Build and Subtract 0 to 5	Subtract 0 Booklet	Pull and Subtract 0

Spin, Build and Subtract 0 to 10	Build and Draw Cuisenaire© rods on 1cm paper	Subtract 0 Four in a Row
Roll or Pull and Build Subtract 0 with Cuisenaire© rods	Subtract 0 Poster	Missing Number Flashcards
		Record on a Number Path
		Record on a Number Line

FIGURE 5.2 Math Workstations

CONCRETE ACTIVITIES

Subtract 0 Concrete Activities		
Roll and Build a Subtract 0 on a 1 row Rekenrek	Roll and Build a Subtract 0 in a Part-Part Whole Mat	Spin, Build and Subtract 0 from numbers 1 to 10
4 – 0	2 – 0	___ - ___ = ___	___ - ___ = ___ ___ - ___ = ___	___ - ___ = ___

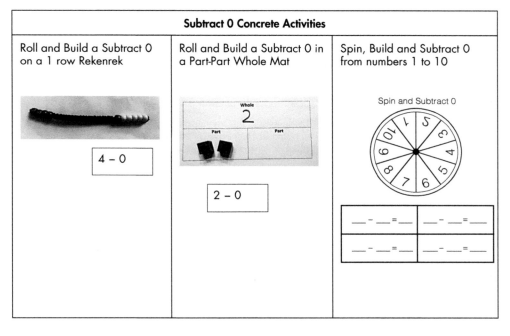

FIGURE 5.3 Concrete Activities

PICTORIAL ACTIVITIES

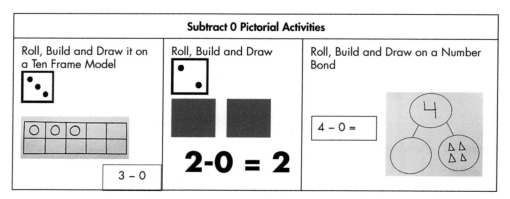

FIGURE 5.4 Pictorial Activities

ABSTRACT ACTIVITIES

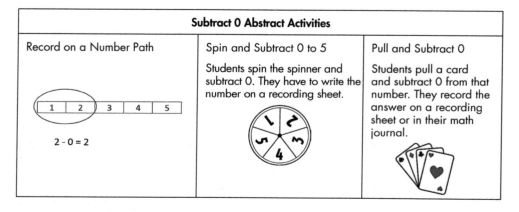

FIGURE 5.5 Abstract Activities

STRATEGY FLASHCARDS

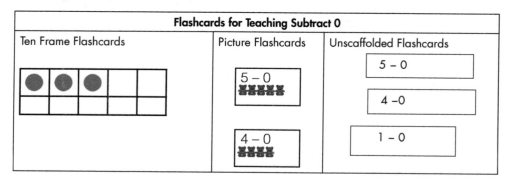

FIGURE 5.6 Strategy Flashcards

MORE STRATEGY FLASHCARDS

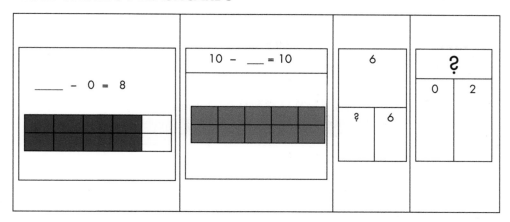

FIGURE 5.7 More Strategy Flashcards

WORD PROBLEMS

In every fluency module there should be a focus on word problems. Here are a few examples of the types of word problems for Subtract 0.

My Subtract 0 Story Problems Booklet	There were 4 kites in the sky. None of them fell down. How many are in the sky now? Write the set-up equation: Show your thinking with a model. Write the solution equation.	There were 5 toy cars. 5 of them were blue and the rest were green. How many were green? Write the set-up equation: Show your thinking with a model. Write the solution equation.	There were 3 birds sitting on a fence. None of them flew away. How many are on the fence now? Write the set-up equation: Show your thinking with a model. Write the solution equation.

FIGURE 5.8 Word Problems

RESOURCES

Videos

 Video Songs about subtracting 0

Ann Elise's video on Subtraction 0 or 1: https://youtu.be/tJp4GcL3XW0
My Growing Brain, Subtracting Zero: https://www.youtube.com/watch?v=1qqRfewfAjk
PISD Mathematics, +/− 0 Facts Part Part Whole Mat: https://youtu.be/rNyKFP8WEag

FIGURE 5.9 Videos

ANCHOR CHART

When you subtract 0 from a number, the number stays the same!

$$4 - 0 = 4$$
$$5 - 0 = 5$$

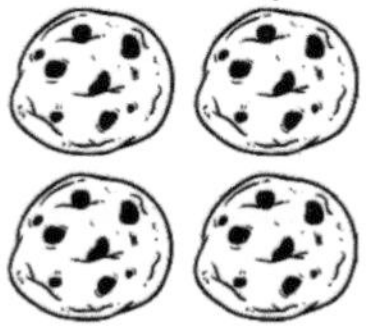

FIGURE 5.10 Anchor Chart

Quiz

Subtract 0 Quiz

Name:

Date:

2 – 0 = Model with a drawing.	6 – 0 = Model on the ten frame. 	Solve. Ann had 4 dance outfits. She did not give any of them away. How many outfits does she have now? Write the equation: Answer: _____
Solve. Jen had 5 cookies. She ate none of them. How many does she have now? Write the equation: Answer: _____	Solve. 6 – ____ = 6 ____ – 0 = 7 3 = 3 – _____	Tell a story about the picture:

5 – 0 =

Model on the number path.

1	2	3	4	5

What are Subtract 0 facts? Explain with numbers, words and pictures.

Circle how good you think you are at doing Subtract 0 facts!

Great   Good    OK, still thinking

FIGURE 5.11 Quiz

EXPLORING AND LEARNING HOW TO SUBTRACT 1

When working on the Subtract 1 strategy we are exploring that the resulting difference is always the previous counting number. Similar to learning our ABCs, students are able to recite the counting numbers long before they understand that the words for the numbers represent a quantity. We need to assist them as they attach the word for a number to the quantity associated with it and then the written numeral. It is especially important that we have kids counting forward and backward from their earliest years. A great way to introduce Subtract 1 is through poems, songs, and picture books. Be sure to model the Subtract 1 facts on a variety of concrete and digital tools within the context of real-life situations. We want students to develop automaticity with their Subtract 1 facts and generalize what will happen when we Subtract 1 from any number. After students are comfortable with the idea of just knowing that it is the number that precedes the one that is being taken away from, then we can move on to counting back with 2 and 3. We felt that it was important to work on 1 first, and build this understanding through a variety of activities, rather than just lump everything together and rush through (see Figures 5.12–5.25).

WHOLE CLASS ACTIVITIES

Routines

Use the virtual rekenrek or ten frame to introduce and discuss taking away 1. After students have learned the strategy, play Subtract 1 Bingo with the whole class. Students can either have their own boards or they can play with partners. Also play Subtract 1 Tic-Tac-Toe as a whole class game. The class divides up into two teams and they take turns picking a square and stating the answer.

WHOLE CLASS MINI-LESSON: SUBTRACT 1

Introduction

Launch: *Today, we are going to look at something called Subtract 1 facts on the number line. Remember that yesterday we acted them out on the walkable number line. Who can tell me what you remember?*

Joleyn: *You just take 1 away.*

Tim: *You just have to step back 1.*

Teacher: *If I am on the number line and I am at 4 and I take 1 away where do I land? Everybody take out your number lines and tell me.*

Tiffany: *You land on 3.*

Teacher: *Come up and show that on the virtual number line.*

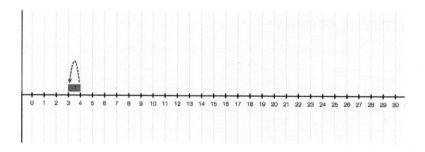

FIGURE 5.12 Virtual Number line *(Math Learning Center)*

Teacher: Who agrees that that is correct? Ok ... everybody does. Who can come up and do
             another take away 1 fact?
Joel: I can ... 6 - 1 is 5.

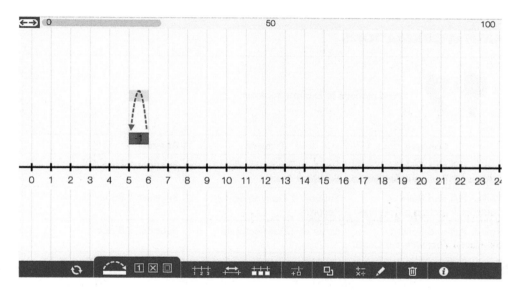

FIGURE 5.13 Virtual Number Line

Teacher: Ok, so what happens when we take away 1 from a number?
Harry: You just hop back 1.
Teacher: I have a question ... do we really even need to count or can we just think about
             the number that come before the number we are subtracting 1 from?
Ted: You don't need to count. It's just the number before the number you are on.

*Guided Practice/Interactive Modeling: In this lesson, the guided practice and the interactive
modeling is with the whole group as the students have acted out the problem the day before and
in today's lesson it is the students following along on their number lines.*

SPOTLIGHT ACTIVITY

Make a variety of activities based on the book *Monster Musical Chairs* (Stuart Murphy).

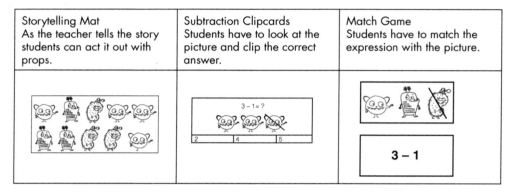

Storytelling Mat	Subtraction Clipcards	Match Game
As the teacher tells the story students can act it out with props.	Students have to look at the picture and clip the correct answer.	Students have to match the expression with the picture.

FIGURE 5.14 Spotlight Activity

MATH WORKSTATIONS

Workstations to Explore Subtract 1

Concrete	Pictorial	Abstract
Roll or Pull and Build a Subtract 1 fact on a Ten Frame	Draw on Ten Frame & Rekenrek Model	Subtract 1 Face Off
Roll or Pull and Build a Subtract 1 fact on a Rekenrek	Subtract 1 Domino Sort & Record	Subtract 1 Board Games
Roll or Pull and Build a Subtract 1 Fact with the Cubes	Draw on Cube Template	Subtract 1 Bingo
Roll or Pull and Build a Subtract 1 Fact in a Part-Part Whole Mat	Draw on a Part-Part Whole Mat	Subtract 1 Tic-Tac-Toe
Roll or Pull and Show a Subtract 1 Fact in a Number Bond	Draw and Show in a Number Bond	Subtract 1 Four in a Row
Roll or Pull and Build a Subtract 1 Fact with Play-Doh©	Subtract 1 Flashcards	Subtract 1 Flashcards
Roll or Pull and Show Subtract 1 facts with Cuisenaire© rods	Subtract 1 Booklet	Subtract 1 Clip Cards
Roll or Pull and Show on a Number Bracelet	Build and Draw Cuisenaire© rods on 1cm paper	Subtract 1 War
	Savvy Subitizing Subtract 1	

FIGURE 5.15 Math Workstations

CONCRETE ACTIVITIES

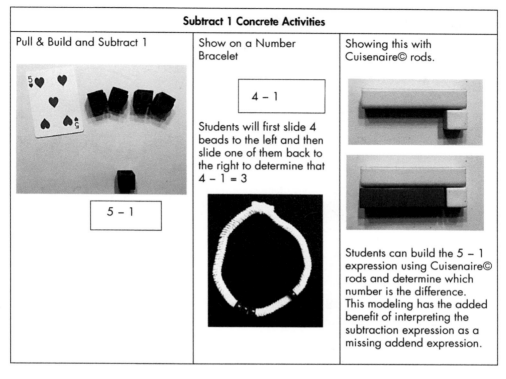

FIGURE 5.16 Concrete Activities

PICTORIAL ACTIVITIES

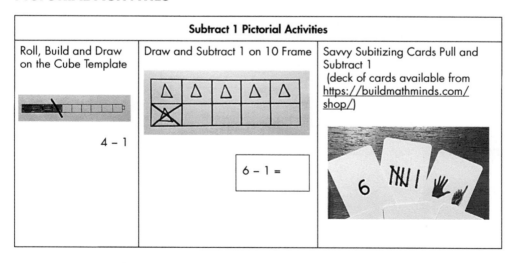

FIGURE 5.17 Pictorial Activities

ABSTRACT ACTIVITIES

Subtract 1 Abstract Activities

Subtract 1 4 in a Row

Pull and Subtract 1 and cover the difference. 4 in a row wins.			
5	3	9	7
2	4	5	1
9	8	6	5
6	7	1	9
2	4	5	8

Subtract 1 War
Pull 2 flashcards and whoever has the largest difference wins that hand and gets the 2 cards. Whoever has the most cards at the end of the game is the winner.

5 – 1

7 – 1

Spin and Subtract 1

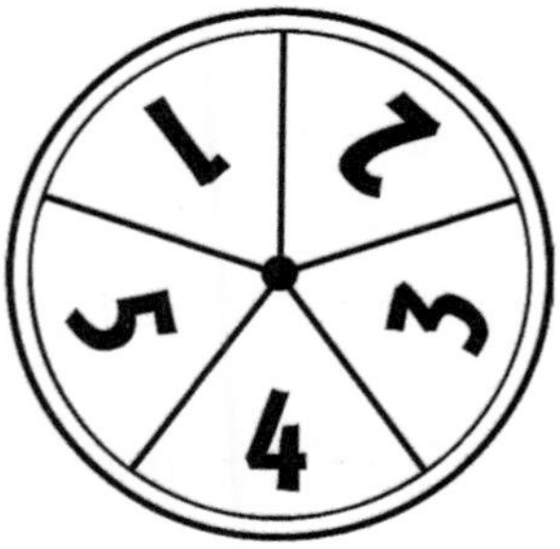

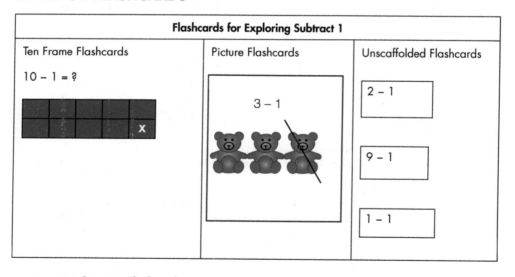

FIGURE 5.18 Abstract Activities

STRATEGY FLASHCARDS

Flashcards for Exploring Subtract 1

Ten Frame Flashcards

10 – 1 = ?

Picture Flashcards

3 – 1

Unscaffolded Flashcards

2 – 1

9 – 1

1 – 1

FIGURE 5.19 Strategy Flashcards

MORE STRATEGY FLASHCARDS

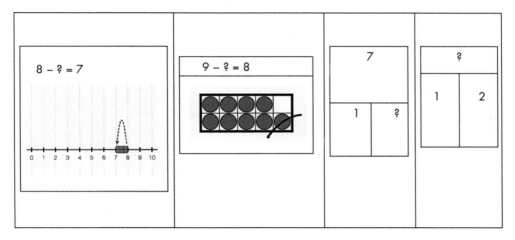

FIGURE 5.20 More Strategy Flashcards

WORD PROBLEMS

In every fluency module there should be a focus on word problems. Here are a few examples of the types of word problems for Subtract 1.			
My Subtract 1 Story Problems Booklet	**Heidi had 5 cupcakes. She gave one to Meg. How many cupcakes does she have now?** **Write the set-up equation:** **Show your thinking with a model.** **Write the solution equation.**	**Julie made 7 snowballs. She threw 1 of them. How many snowballs does she have left?** **Write the set-up equation:** **Show your thinking with a model.** **Write the solution equation.**	**There were 7 flowers. 1 of them was a rose. The rest were daisies. How many daisies were there?** **Write the set-up equation:** **Show your thinking with a model.** **Write the solution equation.**

FIGURE 5.21 Word Problems

RESOURCES

Picture Books

Books about Subtract 1				
One Less Fish by Kim Michelle Toft and Allan Sheather	Ten, Nine, Eight by Molly Bang	Monster Musical Chairs by Stuart Murphy	Ten Sly Piranhas: A Counting Story in Reverse by William Wise	Famous Poems: Five Little Ducks, Five Little Frogs, Five Little Monkeys etc.

FIGURE 5.22 Picture Books

Videos

Videos about Subtract 1
Ann Elise's video on Subtraction 0 or 1: https://youtu.be/tJp4GcL3XW0 PISD Mathematics, Fact Fluency Video Count On & Count Back: https://youtu.be/N36t_sSZPww Harry Kindergarten Music, One Less (shows number path): https://youtu.be/D3b-kcK3Eg8 Periwinkle, One Less Than a Number 0–9: https://youtu.be/-ClMW-bqR4 Jack Hartmann, One Less Number Game Open Answer (with numbers 0-10): https://youtu.be/5Dd4tt-lCxl Jack Hartmann, One Less Number Game Open Answer (with numbers up to 100): https://youtu.be/iflh1gg4O58

FIGURE 5.23 Videos

Anchor Chart

When you take 1 from a number, you hop back to the number before it!

9 − 1 = 8

10 − 1 = 9

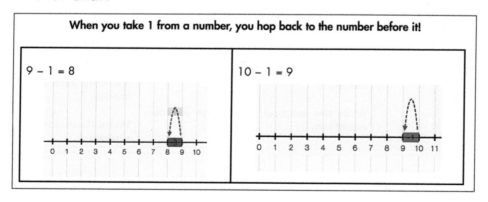

FIGURE 5.24 Anchor Chart

Quiz

Subtract 1 Quiz		
Name: Date:		
3 – 1 = Model with a drawing.	6 – 1 = Model on the ten frame. 	Solve. Daven had 5 baseball cards. He lost one. How many does he have now? Write the equation: Answer: _____
Solve. Daemon made 6 towers. His sister knocked one down. How many are still standing? Write the equation: Answer: _____	Solve. _____ – 1 = 5 _____ – 1 = 8 _____ = 6 – 1	7 kids were on the playground. 1 was a boy and the rest were girls. How many girls are on the playground? Draw a model: Answer: _____

4 – 1 =   Model on the number line.

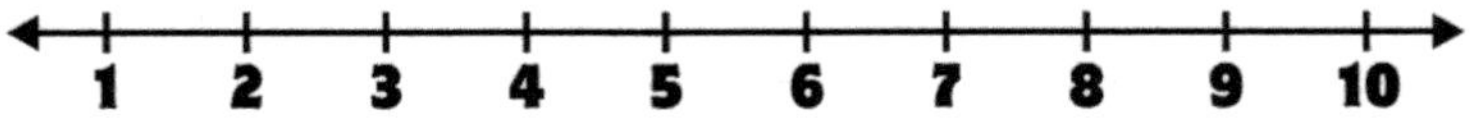

```
◄——┼——┼——┼——┼——┼——┼——┼——┼——┼——►
   1   2   3   4   5   6   7   8   9   10
```

What are Subtract 1 facts? Explain with numbers, words and pictures.

Circle how good you think you are at doing Subtract 1 facts!

Great	Good	OK, still thinking

FIGURE 5.25 Quiz

EXPLORING AND LEARNING SUBTRACT A NUMBER FROM ITSELF

Teaching students how to subtract a number from itself can be tricky. In this strategy we are exploring what happens when we take away everything from a group of items. We want students to generalize that when we take a number away from itself, we are left with 0. Students should get to do this with counters, on the number line, with pictures and, especially, by coming up and acting it out in a variety of ways. Be sure to use lots of stories, poems, and real-life situations (see Figures 5.26–5.36).

WHOLE CLASS ACTIVITIES

Routines

Use virtual dice to roll a number and have students take the same amount away from that number. Use jumbo cards and have students take the same amount away from that number. Play subtract a number from itself Bingo with the whole class. Students can either have their own boards or they can play with partners. Also play subtract Tic-Tac-Toe as a whole class game. The class divides up into two teams and they take turns picking a square and stating the answer. The whole team helps the person who is at the board to decide what is the correct answer.

WHOLE CLASS MINI-LESSON

Teacher: *Today we are going to look at what happens when you take a number from itself. Let's say there were 4 children on the playground. (Teacher calls up 4 children to stand in the ten frame.) Then, they all went inside. (Students go and sit down.) How many are left on the playground?*

Students: *0.*

Teacher: *Let's do another one. Let's say there were 10 kids on the playground. (Teacher calls up 10 children to stand in the ten frame.) Then, they all went inside. (Students go and sit down.) How many are left on the playground?*

Students: *0.*

Teacher: *Who wants to tell a story like this?*

Samantha: *There were 5 kids on the playground. (Teacher calls up 5 children to stand in the ten frame.) Then, they all went inside. (Students go and sit down.) How many are left on the playground?*

Students: *0.*

Teacher: *Tell me what you notice is happening when we take a number from itself. Teacher writes 4 - 4, 10 - 10, and 5 - 5 on the board.*

Students: *The answer is always 0.*

Teacher: *Are you sure?*

Students: *Yes.*

Teacher: *Do you think it always works? Who can give me some more examples?*

Mateo: *7 take away 7 is 0 too!*

Teacher: *Can you prove it?*

Mateo: Yes ... (holds up 7 fingers and then puts them down) ... see it's 0.

Teacher: Well, we will be looking at this for the next few days and trying to prove it with different models. Now, let's get ready for our workstations.

 ## SPOTLIGHT ACTIVITY

Act out the concept of taking a number from itself by telling stories with the children. After acting it out several times, teach the children the song.

(sung to the tune of If You're Happy and You Know it)

If you take a number from itself it's zero
If you take a number from itself it's zero
If you take a number from itself
It's really easy peasy to see
What the answer will always be!

FIGURE 5.26 Spotlight Activity

MATH WORKSTATIONS

 Workstations to Explore the Subtract a Number from Itself Strategy

Concrete	Pictorial	Abstract
Roll or Pull and Build & Draw a Subtract a Number From Itself fact on a Ten Frame	Roll, Build and Draw it on a ten frame model	Subtract a Number From Itself Clip Flashcards
Roll and Build a Subtract a Number From Itself fact on a Rekenrek	Roll, Build and Draw it on a Rekenrek	Spin and Subtract a Number From Itself 0 to 5
Roll and Build a Subtract a Number From Itself fact with Cubes	Roll, Build and Model it on the Cube Template	Spin and Subtract a Number From Itself 0 to 10
Roll and Build a Subtract a Number From Itself fact in a Part-Part Whole Mat	Roll, Build and Draw in a Part-Part Whole Mat	Subtract a Number From Itself Board Game 1
Roll and Show a Subtract a Number From Itself fact in a Number Bond	Roll, Show, and Draw in a Number Bond	Subtract a Number From Itself War
Subtract a Number From Itself fact with Play-Doh©	Subtract a Number From Itself Domino Sort Draw and Record	Subtract a Number From Itself Tic-Tac-Toe
Spin, Build and Subtract 0 to 5	Subtract a Number From Itself Booklet	Pull and Subtract a Number From Itself Flashcards
Spin, Build and Subtract 0 to 10	Build and Draw on 1cm paper with Cuisenaire© rods	Subtract a Number From Itself Four in a Row
Pull and Show a Subtract a Number From Itself fact with Cuisenaire© rods	Subtract a Number From Itself Poster	Missing Number Flashcards
		Subtract a Number from Itself on a Number Line

FIGURE 5.27 Math Workstations

CONCRETE ACTIVITIES

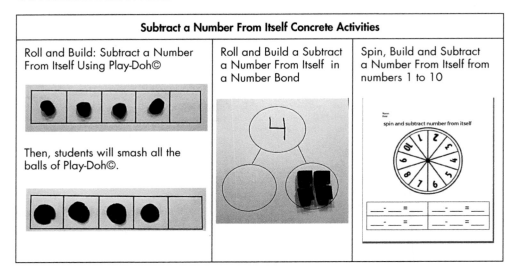

FIGURE 5.28 Concrete Activities

PICTORIAL ACTIVITIES

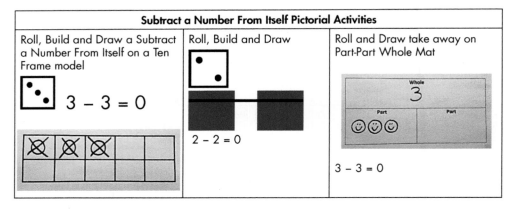

FIGURE 5.29 Pictorial Activities

ABSTRACT ACTIVITIES

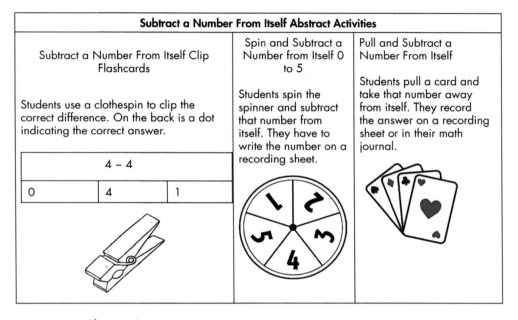

Subtract a Number From Itself Abstract Activities		
Subtract a Number From Itself Clip Flashcards Students use a clothespin to clip the correct difference. On the back is a dot indicating the correct answer.	Spin and Subtract a Number from Itself 0 to 5 Students spin the spinner and subtract that number from itself. They have to write the number on a recording sheet.	Pull and Subtract a Number From Itself Students pull a card and take that number away from itself. They record the answer on a recording sheet or in their math journal.

FIGURE 5.30 Abstract Activities

STRATEGY FLASHCARDS

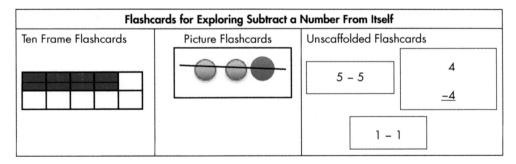

Flashcards for Exploring Subtract a Number From Itself		
Ten Frame Flashcards	Picture Flashcards	Unscaffolded Flashcards

FIGURE 5.31 Strategy Flashcards

MORE STRATEGY FLASHCARDS

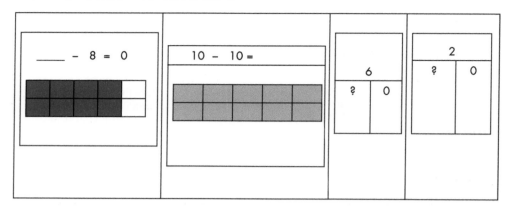

FIGURE 5.32 More Strategy Flashcards

WORD PROBLEMS

In every fluency module there should be a focus on word problems. Here are a few examples of the types of word problems for subtract a number from itself.

My Subtract a Number From Itself Story Problems Booklet	Randall had 4 jelly beans. He ate 4 of them. How many does he have now? Write the set-up equation: Show your thinking with a model. Write the solution equation.	There were 3 cats. 3 of them were black and white and the rest were orange. How many were orange? Write the set-up equation: Show your thinking with a model. Write the solution equation.	Kate had 3 balloons and Kevin had 3 balloons. How many more balloons did Kate have than Kevin? Write the set-up equation: Show your thinking with a model. Write the solution equation.

FIGURE 5.33 Word Problems

RESOURCES
Videos

 Videos about Subtract Self

Ann Elise's video on Subtraction 0 or 1: https://youtu.be/W6RNKktb1Gs

FIGURE 5.34 Videos

Anchor Chart

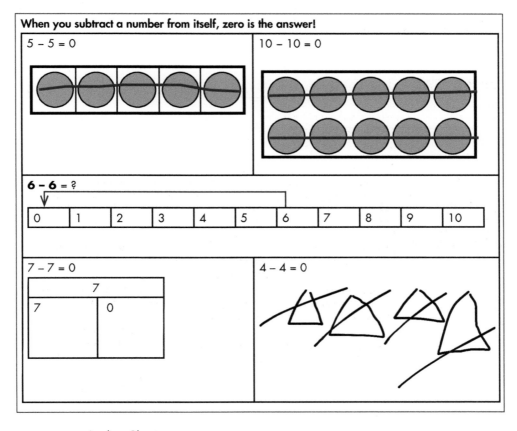

FIGURE 5.35 Anchor Chart

QUIZ

Subtract a Number From Itself Quiz

Name:
Date:

$3 - 3 =$ Model with a drawing.	$8 - 8 =$ Model on the ten frame. (ten frame)	Solve. Zuki had 5 apples. He used 5 of them to make a pie. How many apples did he have left? Write the equation: Answer: _____
Solve. Jack had 6 orange slices. He ate 6 of them. How many orange slices did he have left? Write the equation: Answer: _____	Solve. $6 - $ ____ $= 0$ ____ $- 3 = 0$ $0 = 4 - $ _____	Tell a story about this picture: (giraffes)

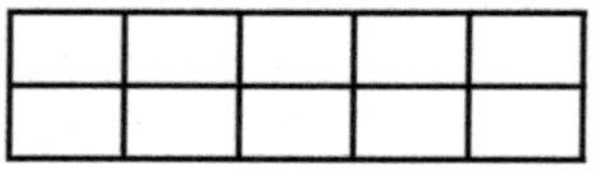

$5 - 5 = ?$ Model on the number line.

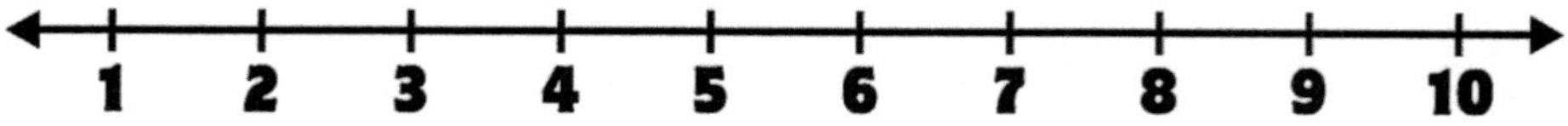

(number line marked 1 2 3 4 5 6 7 8 9 10)

What are Subtract a Number From Itself facts? Explain with numbers, words and pictures.

Circle how good you think you are at doing Subtract a Number From Itself facts!

    Great   Good    OK, still thinking

FIGURE 5.36 Quiz

EXPLORING AND LEARNING SUBTRACT WITHIN 5

At this point in our progression of strategies, we want to ensure that the math facts within 5 are fluent, meaning that there is accuracy, flexibility, efficiency, and automaticity. Students will be reviewing Subtract 0 and Subtract 1 but will also be able to extend these into counting up or back 2 or 3. Students should see these modeled on the ten frame, the rekenrek, with cubes, in part-part whole mats, in number bonds, and on number line (see Figures 5.37–5.51). Anchor charts should be done in order to reinforce these models. Students should be acting out the stories on human-size ten frames, part-part whole mats, number bonds, and number paths.

WHOLE CLASS ACTIVITIES

Routines

Use virtual dice to roll a number and have students subtract 2 or 3 from that number. Use jumbo cards and have students subtract 2 or 3. Play Subtract within 5 Bingo with the whole class. Students can either have their own boards or they can play with partners. Also play Subtract within 5 Tic-Tac-Toe as a whole class game. The class divides up into two teams and they take turns picking a square and stating the answer.

WHOLE CLASS MINI-LESSON: SUBTRACT WITHIN 5

Introduction

Teacher: *Today we are going to continue talking about subtraction. Let's see. I am going to show you a picture and I want you to tell me the story.*

Joel: *There were 5 frogs and 2 hopped off the log.*

Teacher: *Who agrees? (Everyone agrees.) So who can come and write the number sentence.*

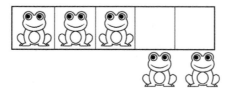

FIGURE 5.37 Frogs

Kelly: 5 - 2 = 3.

Teacher: *Here's another one.*

Teacher: *Who can tell me a story?*

Mike: *3 frogs take away 1.*

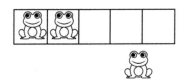

FIGURE 5.38 More Frogs

Teacher: *Who can come and write the number sentence? As that person writes the number sentence on the board, I want you all to write it on your whiteboards.*
Lucy: *I can … (she writes 3 - 1.)*
Teacher: *Who wants to come up to the board and show a frog story?*
(Timothy comes up.)
Timothy: *I want to use the five frame. (He shows this:)*

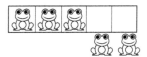

FIGURE 5.39 Blue frogs

Teacher: *Everybody write the correct equation that matches this story on your number board. I have a question. What is important about matching the story problem with the equation?*

Explicit Instruction/Teacher Facilitating

Teacher: *So today we have been looking at matching story models with number sentences.*
Ted: *The numbers have to match.*
Teacher: *What do you mean?*
Ted: *You have to use the numbers in the story. Like if there are 5 frogs you can't say 7.*
Teacher: *Yes, it is really important that when writing the equation (or number sentence) we use the numbers in the problem. Ok, we are going to get ready to go to work stations.*

*Guided Practice/Interactive Modeling: In this lesson, the guided practice is when the students are coming up and are doing problems and the rest of the class is interacting with their whiteboards.

 SPOTLIGHT ACTIVITY

Pete the Cat is a great book to practice subtracting 1 from a number. In this activity, I make storytelling ropes, with buttons on them, and as we read the story we act it out on the ropes or pipe cleaners. There are so many activities online now about Pete the Cat. Here are a few resources:

Activities: www.pinterest.com/drnicki7/pete-the-cat-math/
Video: www.youtube.com/watch?v=dkQ4d_fff3E

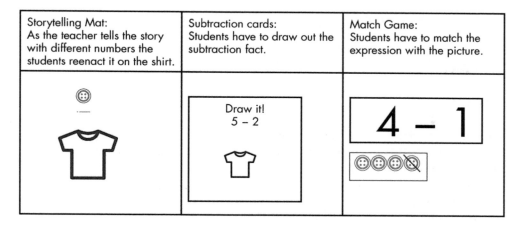

Storytelling Mat: As the teacher tells the story with different numbers the students reenact it on the shirt.	Subtraction cards: Students have to draw out the subtraction fact.	Match Game: Students have to match the expression with the picture.

FIGURE 5.40 Buttons

MATH WORKSTATIONS

Workstations to Explore Subtraction within 5

Concrete	Pictorial	Abstract
Roll or Pull and Build Subtract within 5 fact on a Five Frame	Draw on Five Frame Model	Subtract within 5 Face Off
Roll or Pull and Build a Subtract within 5 fact on a Rekenrek	Draw on Rekenrek Model	Subtract within 5 Board Game 1
Roll or Pull and Build a Subtract within 5 fact with the Cubes	Draw on Cube Template	Subtract within 5 War
Roll or Pull and Build a Subtract within 5 fact on a Part-Part Whole Mat	Draw in a Part-Part Whole Mat	Subtract within 5 Tic-Tac-Toe
Roll or Pull and Show a Subtract within 5 fact on a Number Bond	Draw and Show in a Number Bond	Subtract within 5 Four in a Row
Subtract within 5 with Play-Doh©	Subtract within 5 Flashcards	Subtract within 5 Slides and Ladders
Spin and Subtract within 5	Subtract within 5 Booklet	Spin and Subtract within 5
Roll or Pull and Subtract on a Number Bracelet	Subtract within 5 Domino Sort & Record	Subtract within 5 Game 2
Show with Cuisenaire© rods	Subtract within 5 Poster	Subtract within 5 Bingo
Flashcard Build	Build and Draw Subtract within 5 Cuisenaire© rods on 1cm paper	Roll & Subtract within 5
		Clip Flashcards

FIGURE 5.41 Math Workstations

CONCRETE ACTIVITIES

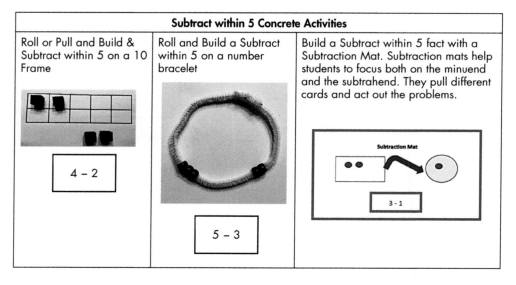

FIGURE 5.42 Concrete Activities

PICTORIAL ACTIVITIES

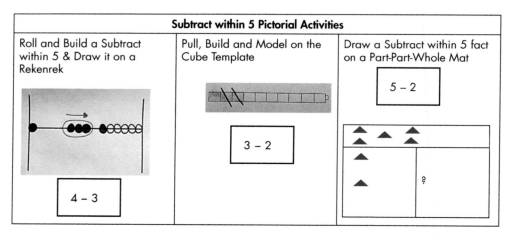

FIGURE 5.43 Pictorial Activities

ABSTRACT ACTIVITIES

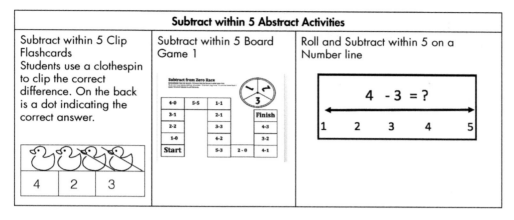

FIGURE 5.44   Abstract Activities

STRATEGY FLASHCARDS

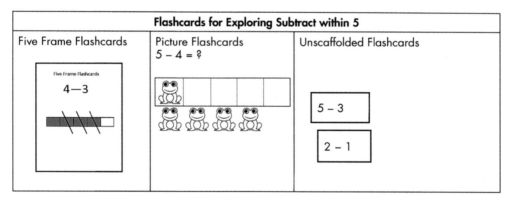

FIGURE 5.45   Strategy Flashcards

WORD PROBLEMS

In every fluency module there should be a focus on word problems. Here are a few examples of the types of word problems for subtract within 5.

My Subtract within 5 Story Problems Booklet	Maria had 5 marbles. She gave her sister 2. How many does she have left? Write the set-up equation: Show your thinking with a model. Write the solution equation.
There were 5 marbles. 3 were red and the rest were blue. How many were blue? Write the set-up equation: Show your thinking with a model. Write the solution equation.	Joe had 3 toy trucks. He gave 1 to his brother. How many does he have left? Write the set-up equation: Show your thinking with a model. Write the solution equation.

FIGURE 5.46 Word Problems

RESOURCES
Picture Books

Books about Subtract within 5				
Five Little Speckled Frogs by Make Believe Ideas Ltd.	Five Little Ducks by Raffi and Jose Aruego	5 Little Monkeys Jumping on the Bed by Eileen Christelow	5 Little Pumpkins by Dan Yaccarino	Five Little Monkeys Play Hide and Seek by Eileen Chistelow

FIGURE 5.47 Picture Books

Videos

 Video Songs about Subtract within 5

Harry Kindergarten Music, When You Subtract with a Pirate: https://youtu.be/QkPa9V2wtZs
Mr. R's Songs for Teaching, Subtraction Cat: https://youtu.be/UccMY5_YN4

FIGURE 5.48 Videos

Online Games

Online Games about Subtract within 5
https://www.nctm.org/Classroom-Resources/Illuminations/Interactives/Five-Frame/

FIGURE 5.49 Online Games

Anchor Chart

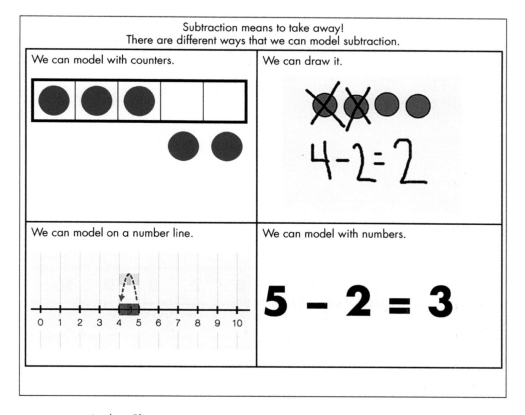

FIGURE 5.50 Anchor Chart

Quiz

<table>
<tr><td colspan="3" align="center">**Subtract within 5 Quiz**
Name:
Date:</td></tr>
<tr>
<td>5 – 3 =

Model with a drawing.</td>
<td>4 – 2 =
Model on the five frame.

□□□□□</td>
<td>Solve.
Tim had 5 marbles. He gave 2 of them to Vanessa. How many does he have now?

Write the equation:

Answer: _____</td>
</tr>
<tr>
<td>Solve.
Zachary had 4 cookies. He ate 3 of them. How many does he have now?

Write the equation:

Answer: _____</td>
<td>Solve.

3 – ____ = 1

____ – 4 = 0

3 = 5 – _____

____ = 4 – 3</td>
<td>Tell a story about this picture:</td>
</tr>
<tr>
<td colspan="3">4 – 4 =
Model on the number line.

← 1 2 3 4 5 6 7 8 9 10 →</td>
</tr>
<tr><td colspan="3">What are subtracting within 5 facts? Explain with numbers, words and pictures.</td></tr>
<tr><td colspan="3">Circle how good you think you are at doing Subtract within 5 facts!

Great   Good   OK, still thinking</td></tr>
</table>

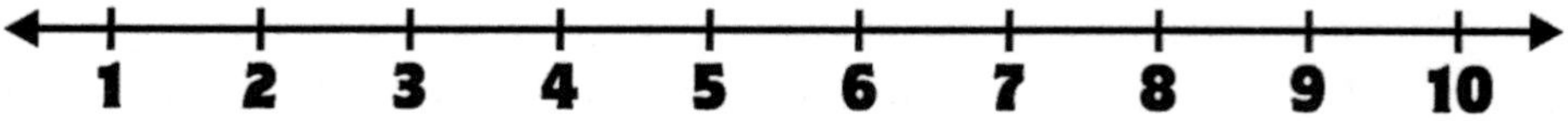

FIGURE 5.51 Quiz

EXPLORING AND LEARNING SUBTRACT FROM 5

5 is a benchmark fact. We need students to be able to know and understand the numbers that combine to make 5 fluently. There should be lots of work decomposing the number 5 so that students can visualize all the combinations of numbers that make 5. Exploring the decomposing with Cuisenaire© rods, ten frames, dot patterns, and on rekenreks is important (see Figures 5.52–5.62). We also want to relate these decomposition possibilities to the inverse relationship between addition and subtraction and more abstractly with the equations that correspond to them. If we know that 5 can be decomposed into a 3 and a 2, then we know not only that 3 + 2 = 5, but also that 5 – 3 = 2 and 5 – 2 = 3. Fluency with these math facts is expected, within state standards, to be in place by the end of kindergarten.

WHOLE CLASS ACTIVITIES

Routines

Use virtual dice to roll a number and have students take it away from 5. Use jumbo cards and have students take the number away from 5. Play Bingo and Tic-Tac-Toe with the class.

WHOLE CLASS MINI-LESSON: SUBTRACT FROM 5

Introduction

Teacher: *Today we are going to look at subtracting from 5. Remember we looked at the video about the 5 little monkeys yesterday. Well, today we are going to act it out on our five frames. Let's see. (Teacher pulls 5 sticks with students, names and they come up and stand in the five frame.)*

Teacher: *Ok, you guys are going to be jumping on the bed … (so the students jump up and down.) And we, the class, are going to be the doctor. What do we say? "No more monkeys jumping on the bed."*

Teacher: *Ok, here we go: 5 little monkeys jumping on the bed, 1 fell off and bumped his head (everybody show me that on your fingers). Momma called the doctor and the doctor said...*

Everybody: *No more monkeys jumping on the bed!*

Teacher: *Ok, we need a new monkey so we can start with 5 again. (Teacher pulls a stick.) Jen'ai come up. 5 little monkeys jumping on the bed, 2 fell off and bumped their heads … Momma called the doctor and the doctor said...*

Everybody: *No more monkeys jumping on the bed!*

*Guided Practice: This lesson continues with the students acting out various subtraction facts from 5.

Explicit Instruction/Teacher Facilitating

Teacher: Who can tell me what we have been practicing today?
Lara: We have been talking about taking away from 5.
Teacher: So we have been modeling it by acting it out. We are going to continue to work on taking from 5 using different models. Does anybody have any questions before we go to workstations?

 SPOTLIGHT ACTIVITY

Use one of the many five books about animals (five little monkeys, five little ducks, five little frogs). I love to spotlight the five little monkeys. You can make monkey puppets, retelling sticks, and glove puppets.

Monkey Finger Puppet Students can use these to act out the story as a class and then tell transformations of the story by changing the numbers.	Monkey Popsicle Stick Puppets	Monkey Story Telling Sticks	Monkey Glove
	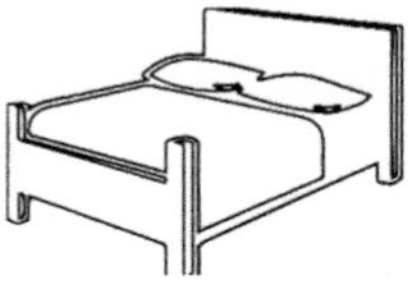 See the link for activities. http://www. makinglearningfun. com/themepages/ FiveLittleMonkeys. htm		

FIGURE 5.52 Spotlight Activity

WORKSTATION ACTIVITIES

 Workstations to Explore Subtraction from 5

Concrete	Pictorial	Abstract
Roll or Pull and Build Subtract from 5 fact on a Five Frame	Draw on Five Frame Model	Subtract from 5 Face Off
Roll and Build a Subtract from 5 fact on a Rekenrek	Draw on Rekenrek Model	Subtract from 5 Board Game 1
Roll and Build a Subtract from 5 fact with the Cubes	Draw on Cube Template	Subtract from 5 War
Roll and Build a Subtract from 5 fact on a Part-Part Whole Mat	Draw in a Part-Part Whole Mat	Subtract from 5 Tic-Tac-Toe
Roll and Show a Subtract from 5 fact on a Number Bond	Draw and Show in a Number Bond	Subtract from 5 Four in a Row
Subtract from 5 with Play-Doh©	Subtract from 5 Flashcards	Subtract from 5 Slides and Ladders
Spin and Subtract from 5	Subtract from 5 Booklet	Spin and Subtract from 5
Subtraction Mat	Subtract from 5 Domino Sort & Record	Subtract from 5 Game 2
Show with Cuisenaire© rods	Subtract from 5 Poster	Subtract from 5 Bingo
Build on a Number Wand	Build and Draw Subtract from 5 Cuisenaire© rods on 1cm paper	Power Towers
Split Machine	Math Learning Center app	Interactive Number Line
	Flashcard & picture matchup	
	Savvy Subitizing Subtract	

FIGURE 5.53 Workstation Activities

CONCRETE ACTIVITIES

Subtract from 5 Concrete Activities		
Roll 5 playdoh balls. Roll the dice and smash that amount. Say the number sentence. Keep playing. 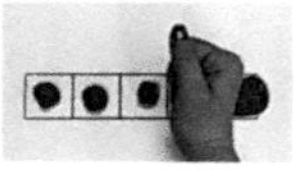 5 – 3	Students use the subtraction mat to act out stories.  Addition Story Mat 5 – 2	Build a fact on a number wand. 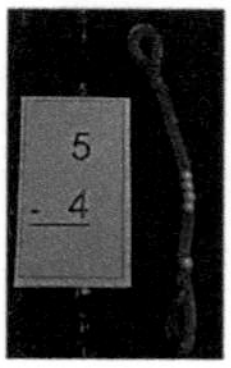 5 - 4

FIGURE 5.54 Concrete Activities

PICTORIAL ACTIVITIES

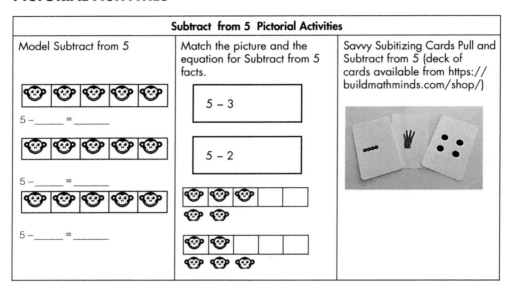

FIGURE 5.55 Pictorial Activities

ABSTRACT ACTIVITIES

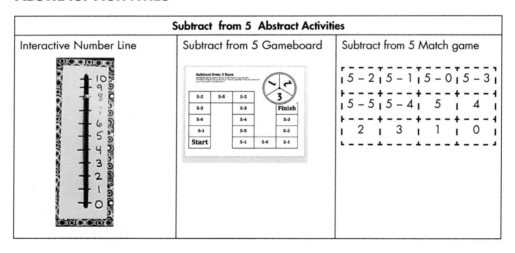

FIGURE 5.56 Abstract Activities

STRATEGY FLASHCARDS

Flashcards for Teaching Subtract from 5		
Five Frame Flashcards	Picture Flashcards	Unscaffolded Flashcards

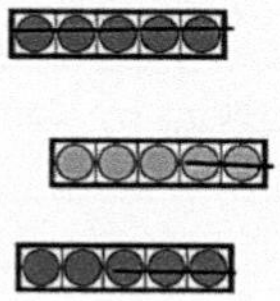

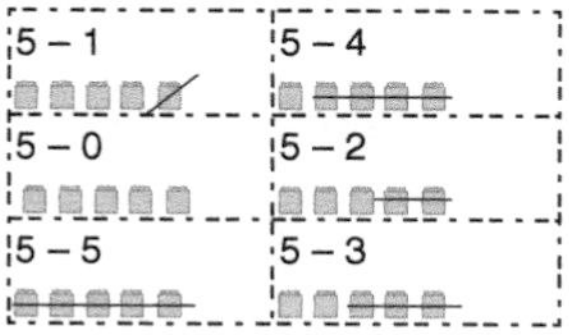

FIGURE 5.57 Strategy Flashcards

WORD PROBLEMS

In every fluency module there should be a focus on word problems. Here are a few examples of the types of word problems for subtract from 5.

My Subtract from 5 Story Problems Booklet	There were 5 flowers in a vase. 3 of them were red, the rest were yellow. How many were yellow? Write the set-up equation: Show your thinking with a model. Write the solution equation.	There were 5 bluebirds in a tree. 4 of them flew away. How many bluebirds are still in the tree? Write the set-up equation: Show your thinking with a model. Write the solution equation.	Adrienne had 5 cookies. John had 2. How many more cookies did Adrienne have than John? Write the set-up equation: Show your thinking with a model. Write the solution equation.

FIGURE 5.58 Word Problems

RESOURCES

Picture Books

Books And Poems about Subtracting from 5		
Five Little Ducks by Rafi and Jose Aruego	Five Little Monkeys Jumping on the Bed by Eileen Christelow	Five Little Pumpkins by Dan Yaccarino

FIGURE 5.59 Picture Books

Videos

Video Songs about Subtracting from 5
Ann Elise's Video on Subtract from 5 – Decomposition of 5: https://youtu.be/pxreCrHuqwg The Five Little Leaves: https://www.youtube.com/watch?v=enj02EUG-0 https://www.youtube.com/watch?v=mTr7EQ4KwrE

FIGURE 5.60 Videos

Anchor Chart

There are many ways to model our thinking!			
We can use the five frame.	We can use our fingers.	We can use different tools to help us subtract from 5! We can use our number lines.	We can use our counters.

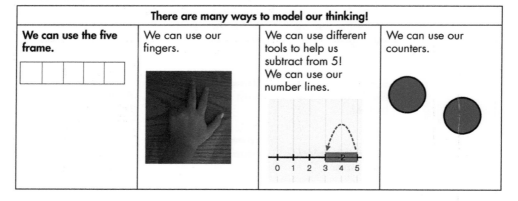

FIGURE 5.61 Anchor Chart

Quiz

Subtract from 5 Quiz Name: Date:		
5 – 3 = Model with a drawing.	5 – 1 = Model on the five frame. ⬚⬚⬚⬚⬚	Solve. Donna had 5 jelly beans. She ate 2 of them. How many jelly beans does she have left? Write the equation: Answer: _____
Solve. Darcy has 5 pencils. Christine has 1. How many fewer pencils does Christine have than Darcy? Write the equation: Answer: _____	Solve. 5 – _____ = 4 _____ – 3 = 2 4 = 5 – _____ _____ = 5 – 0	Tell a story about this picture:

5 – 3 = ?   Model on the number path.

1	2	3	4	5

What are subtracting from 5 facts? Explain with numbers, words and pictures.

Circle how good you think you are at doing Subtract From 5 facts!

Great   Good   OK, still thinking

FIGURE 5.62 Quiz

EXPLORING AND LEARNING SUBTRACT WITHIN 10

Once students have developed fluency subtracting within and from 5, then we can progress them to working on their math facts within 10 and review all of the strategies already introduced just with the numbers within 10. Within this set of facts are the beginning half facts as well, which will be introduced later on in the progression. Once again, we will use the concrete, pictorial, and abstract progression to explore these facts on the way to automaticity. A big emphasis in exploring how to subtract within 10 should be students working with composing and decomposing numbers within 10 (see Figures 5.63–5.75). If students can flexibly compose and decompose numbers, then they will easily be able to work with subtraction. We want to be sure we are making connections between the decompositions of the numbers and how we can use those decompositions to work on the inverse relationship between addition and subtraction.

WHOLE CLASS ACTIVITIES

Routines

Use virtual dice to roll a number and have students subtract 0–10 from that number. Use jumbo cards and have students subtract 0–10 from that number. Play Subtract within 10 Bingo and Tic-Tac-Toe with the whole class.

WHOLE CLASS MINI-LESSON

Introduction

Launch: Teacher and students have read If You Were a Minus Sign by Shaskan, 2008.
Teacher: We are going to talk about subtracting from different numbers today. Look what I have, a cookie jar! We are going to take turns pulling number sentences and acting them out! So, as we get started, who can tell me, what is subtraction?
Carla: It is when you take stuff away.
Teacher: Who can give me an example?
Maria: Like if I have 5 cookies and I give you 2.
Teacher: Yes, that is an example. Remember, we have been working with subtraction with numbers within 5. Now we are going to look at even bigger numbers. Let's say I have 6 people in the playground. (Teacher points to 6 students and they come and stand in the ten frame.
There is a student who is designated to pull the number sentence. They pull 6 - 4. 4 people step outside the ten frame.)

Teacher:	*Ok, so we had 6 and we took away 4. How many are left? Yes, 2. So we can see 4 and 2 make 6 and 6 take away 4 is 2.*
Teacher:	*Ok, let's have 7 people on the playground. Our number sentence says 7 - 5. So, 5 people are going to step out of the ten frame. How many are left? 2. Wow! And notice that 5 and 2 make 7. Those numbers are all related. Ok, let's have 8 people on the playground. Let's see. Our number sentence is 8 - 0. What happens anytime we take away 0 from a number?*
Students chant:	*The number stays the same!*

*Guided Practice/Interactive Modeling: Teacher continues having students come up and stand in the ten frame and act out a subtraction problem.

Explicit Instruction/Teacher Facilitating

Teacher:	*Ok, who can tell me what we were practicing today?*
Timothy:	*Subtraction.*
Teacher:	*Who can give me an example?*
Lara:	*When you take stuff away. Like we had 8 people in the ten frame and then we took away 8. Nobody was left.*
Teacher:	*So when we subtract we are taking things away. Today we looked at some subtraction problems with numbers bigger than 5. We are going to continue looking at different ways to model subtraction problems. Are there any questions before we go off to workstations?*

 SPOTLIGHT ACTIVITY

Get off my boat: https://www.youtube.com/watch?v=QtEiO_YBbKg&t=25s

It is really important to have students act out stories. In this video we see Greg Smedley-Warren does a great job of acting out problems with students. He draws a boat and then has the students out act subtraction problems. This is a great activity and once students act it out they can then go and act it out on templates.

FIGURE 5.63 Spotlight Activity

MATH WORKSTATIONS

 Workstations to Explore Subtracting within 10

Concrete	Pictorial	Abstract
Show a Subtract within 10 Fact on the Ten Frame	Draw on Ten Frame Model	Subtract within 10 spin to win
Show a Subtract within 10 Fact on a Rekenrek	Draw on Rekenrek Model	Subtract within 10 War
Spin and Subtract within 10 Fact	Draw in Part-Part Whole Mat	Subtract within 10 clip cards
Roll and Build a Subtract within 10 Fact with cubes	Draw in Number Bond	Subtract within 10 Tic-Tac-Toe
Roll and Build a Subtract within fact on Part-Part Whole Mat	Subtract within 10 Booklet	Subtract within 10 Bingo
Pull and Build a Subtract within 10 Fact in a Number Bond	Subtract within 10 on cm paper	Subtract within 10 card sort
Pull and Build a Subtract within 10 fact with Play-Doh©	Subtract within with cubes and recording	Subtract within 10 flashcards
Subtract within 10 flashcards	Build and Draw Subtract within 10 Cuisenaire© rods on 1cm paper	
Pull and Build a Subtract within 10 with Cuisenaire© rods	Subtract within 10 Domino sort	
Stamp Subtraction	Sticker Subtraction	
Monster Mat Subtraction	Story Problem Subtraction	

FIGURE 5.64 Math Workstations

CONCRETE ACTIVITIES

Subtract within Ten Concrete Activities
As students work on these activities, be sure to discuss that they can count back if it is 1, 2 or 3 as well as count up. We want all students to develop the flexibility to count back and up. Remember that Van de Walle (2007) notes that counting up is much easier than counting back.

Subtract within 10 Fact Flashcards	Pull a flashcard and solve on the subtraction monster board.

Subtract within 10 Fact Flashcards

7 – 4

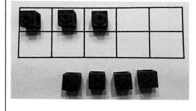

Pull a flashcard and solve on the subtraction monster board.

Feed the Monster!
Put 10 counters in the 10 frame.

Roll the dice.
Feed the Monster that many counters.

Subtract on a rekenrek

Students pick a card and subtract the problem on the rekenrek.

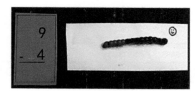

FIGURE 5.65 Concrete Activities

PICTORIAL ACTIVITIES

Subtract within 10 Pictorial Activities		
Make up a subtraction story online with different items.  *Math Learning Center Apps are great for this!	Sticker Subtraction Stories Students pick different sticker circles and then build a story and cross it out. 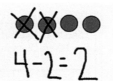 4−2=2	Subtract within 10 Booklet – Students illustrate their facts in a booklet. Be sure to have the students give examples of counting up and counting back. I know my subtract within 10 facts!  8—5

FIGURE 5.66 Pictorial Activities

ABSTRACT ACTIVITIES

Subtract within 10 Abstract Activities		
Subtract within 10 Clip Flashcards Students use a clothespin to clip the correct difference. On the back is a dot indicating the correct answer. Clip the correct difference. 7 – 5 | 1 | 2 | 3	Subtract within 10 Tic-Tac-Toe Students play Tic-Tac-Toe as usual but they have to answer the question in the space before they can put an x or an o. Whoever gets 3 in a row first wins.	Subtract within 10 War Pull 2 flashcards and whoever has the largest difference wins that hand and gets the 2 cards. Whoever has the most cards at the end of the game is the winner. Or you could roll a die that just has "greater difference" and "smaller difference" written on it to determine the winner.

Subtract within 10 Tic Tac Toe

8 - 2	7 -1	6 - 3
9 - 7	5 - 5	10 - 9
7 – 4	8 - 4	9 - 6

9 – 4

7 – 2

FIGURE 5.67 Abstract Activities

STRATEGY FLASHCARDS

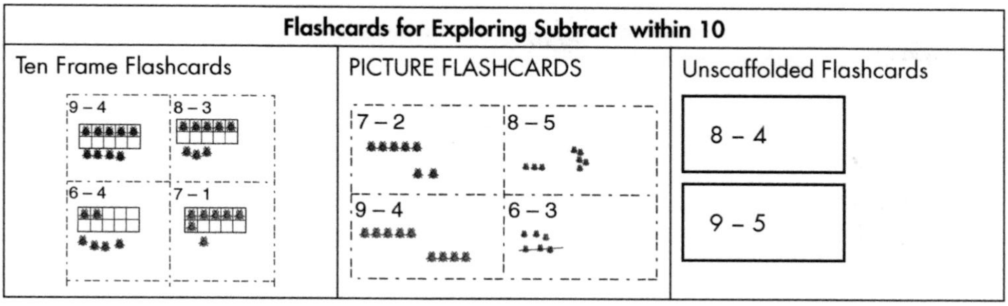

Flashcards for Exploring Subtract within 10
Ten Frame Flashcards
9 – 4
8 – 3
6 – 4
7 – 1
PICTURE FLASHCARDS
7 – 2
8 – 5
9 – 4
6 – 3
Unscaffolded Flashcards
8 – 4
9 – 5

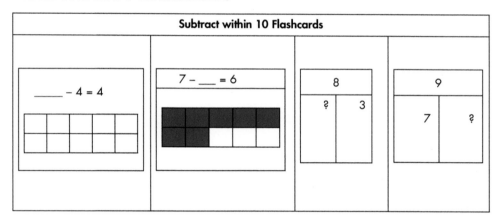

FIGURE 5.68 Strategy Flashcards

MORE STRATEGY FLASHCARDS

Subtract within 10 Flashcards
____ – 4 = 4
7 – ___ = 6
8
?
3
9
7
?

FIGURE 5.69 More Strategy Flashcards

WORD PROBLEMS

In every fluency module there should be a focus on word problems. Here are a few examples of the types of word problems for subtract within 10.

| **My Subtract within 10 Story Problems Booklet** | Jonna had 8 princess dolls. 2 of them wore tiaras. How many of her princess dolls did not wear a tiara?

Write the set-up equation:

Show your thinking with a model.

Write the solution equation. | Beckham had 6 dinosaur toys that walked on four legs. He had 2 dinosaurs that walked on two legs. How many fewer dinosaurs did he have that walked on two legs than four legs?

Write the set-up equation:
Show your thinking with a model.
Write the solution equation. | Tate had 7 trucks on the rug. He put 3 of them into his toy box. How many trucks were still left on the rug?

Write the set-up equation:

Show your thinking with a model.

Write the solution equation. |

FIGURE 5.70 Word Problems

RESOURCES

Picture Books

Books about Subtract within 10				
Subtraction Action by Loreen Leedy	Elevator Magic by Stuart J. Murphy and G. Brian Karas	The Action of Subtraction by Brian P Cleary and Brian Gable	If You Were a Minus Sign by Trisha Speed Shaskan and Francesca Carabelli	Hershey's Kisses Subtraction Book by Jerry Pallotta and Rob Bolster

FIGURE 5.71 Picture Books

Videos

 Video Songs about Subtract within 10

Ann Elise's Video on Subtracting within 10: https://youtu.be/D4dXVXQqF0M
Harry Kindergarten Music, When You Subtract with a Pirate: https://youtu.be/QkPa9V2wtZs
Jack Hartmann, Subtraction Songs for Kids, https://youtu.be/pwQKugrFmJQ
Mr R's Songs for Teaching, My Dog Subtraction: https://youtu.be/fW14jOElUrl
PISD Mathematics, Fact Fluency Video Count On & Count Back: https://youtu.be/N36t_sSZPww
PISD Mathematics, + 0 1 2 3 on a Number Line: https://youtu.be/x87vvAXjEyw

https://www.youtube.com/watch?v=bnBeGmjWnK4

https://www.youtube.com/watch?v=7oiLU3jQH-E

FIGURE 5.72 Videos

Online Games

Online Games about Subtract within 10
https://www.multiplication.com/games/subtraction-games
http://www.abcya.com/subtraction_game.htm

FIGURE 5.73 Online Games

Anchor Chart

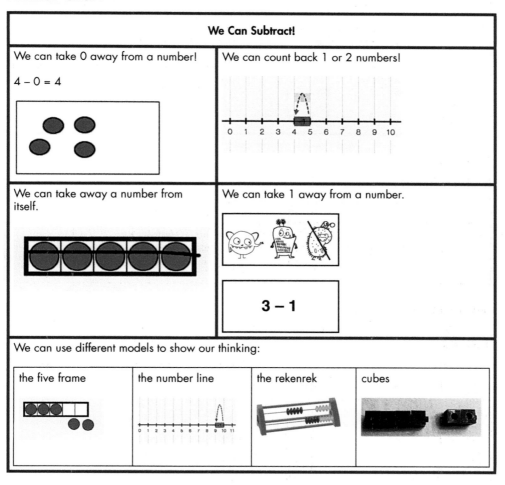

FIGURE 5.74 Anchor Chart

Quiz

Subtract within 10 Quiz		
Name: Date:		
9 – 2 = Model with a drawing.	7 – 3 = Model on the ten frame. <table><tr><td> </td><td> </td><td> </td><td> </td><td> </td></tr><tr><td> </td><td> </td><td> </td><td> </td><td> </td></tr></table>	Solve. Pam had 7 cupcakes. She gave 3 of them to her friends. How many cupcakes did she have left? Write the equation: Answer: _____
Solve. Hamilton played with 4 cat toys. He knocked 2 of them under the couch. How many cat toys could he still play with? Write the equation: Answer: _____	Solve. 8 – ____ = 5 ____ – 2 = 3 4 = 8 – _____	Tell a story about the picture:
6 – 3 = ? Model on the number path. <table><tr><td>1</td><td>2</td><td>3</td><td>4</td><td>5</td><td>6</td><td>7</td><td>8</td><td>9</td><td>10</td></tr></table>		
What is the Subtract within 10 strategy? Explain with numbers, words and pictures.		
Circle how good you think you are at doing Subtract within 10 facts! Great Good OK, still thinking		

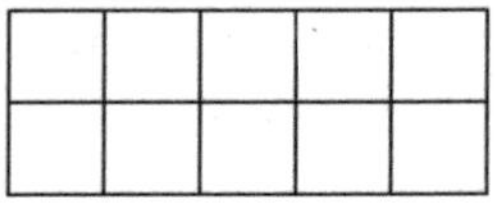

FIGURE 5.75 Quiz

EXPLORING AND LEARNING SUBTRACT FROM 10

The Subtract from 10 strategy is an especially important strategy because it will be used further down the math journey when students are subtracting from decade numbers. At this point in the progression, students should have their pairs of numbers that make 10 automatized. Now we want to connect that understanding to the inverse relationship between addition and subtraction. If we know that 6 + 4 = 10, then we also know that 10 – 6 = 4, as well as 10 – 4 = 6. Students need to have a lot of practice using concrete objects and visually seeing this connection. (See Figures 5.76–5.88.)

WHOLE CLASS ACTIVITIES

Routines

Use virtual dice to roll a number and have students subtract that number from 10. Use jumbo cards and have students subtract that number from 10. Play Subtract from 10 Bingo and Tic-Tac-Toe with the whole class.

WHOLE CLASS MINI-LESSON

Introduction

Launch: *Let's talk about bowling today. How many people know what bowling is? (Some students raise their hands.) Ok, well we are going to look at how bowling can help us with our make 10 facts. When you bowl, there are 10 pins. They are set up like this.*

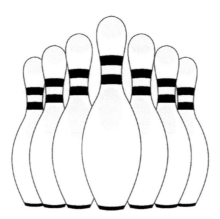

FIGURE 5.76 Bowling Pins

Teacher:	*The goal is to knock the pins down. So, we are going to be playing different versions of bowling. Some people are going to play bowling games on the computer. Some people are going to play bowling in our "bowling alley." Some people are going to play bowling on paper. We are going to have so much fun learning how to take away from 10. We will each get to practice all of these things before we go and work on them in the workstation.*

Teacher puts the template under the Elmo and calls a student up. Juan comes up and rolls the dice and gets a 9. He then crosses out 9 pins and writes the equation.

Teacher:	*Does everybody agree with him? Why is that correct, who can explain?*
Tami:	*(Holding up her fingers.) If you have 10 and you take away 9 then you only have 1 left.*
Ned:	*And 9 and 1 is 10.*
Teacher:	*Ohhh, so you used your addition fact to think about it.*

*Guided Practice/Interactive Modeling: Teacher calls up a few more students and the class discusses the correctness of their model and equation.

Explicit Instruction/Teacher Facilitating

Teacher:	*So, we are looking at what happens when you subtract from 10. We are seeing and talking about lots of ways to check your thinking. Good mathematicians can always solve one way and check it another. I like the thinking that I am seeing and hearing. We are going to keep thinking about this taking away from 10 strategy. Are there any questions before we go to workstations?*

Teacher then dismisses everyone to workstations. She takes a group in the back to the "bowling alley" where the students can roll a toy bowling ball and knock down a set of pins and record their thinking.

 SPOTLIGHT ACTIVITY

Ten Frame Subtraction Song and Game

Ten Frame Subtraction: https://www.youtube.com/watch?v=HvxSdytKqgg
This is a great song to teach the students. It is subtracting on the ten frame. After you teach the students the song, they can practice taking off different amounts from the ten frame and discussing how many were taken off based on what is left. This is a catchy little song that is fun to sing and gets the students to focus on subtracting from ten.

FIGURE 5.77 Ten Frame Song

MATH WORKSTATIONS

Workstations to Explore Subtracting from 10

Concrete	Pictorial	Abstract
Roll or Pull and Build a Subtract from 10 Fact on the Ten Frame	Draw on Ten Frame Model	Subtract from 10 Spin to Win
Roll or Pull and Build a Subtract from 10 Fact on a Rekenrek	Draw on Rekenrek Model	Subtract from 10 War
Spin and Subtract from 10 Fact	Subtract from 10 Booklet	Subtract from 10 clip cards
Roll or Pull and Build a Subtract from 10 Fact with Cubes	Draw in a Number Bond	Subtract from 10 Tic-Tac-Toe
Roll or Pull and Build a Subtract from 10 Fact on Part-Part whole mat	Subtract from 10 with Cubes and recording	Subtract from 10 Bingo
Roll or Pull and Build a Subtract from 10 in a Number Bond	Draw on Part-Part-Whole Mat	Subtract from 10 card sort
Pull and Build a subtract from 10 using Play-Doh©	Build and Draw Subtract from 10 Cuisenaire© rods on 1cm paper	Subtract from 10 flashcards
Subtract from 10 flashcards	Subtract from 10 domino sort	Power Towers
Split Machine	10 frame picture matchup	
Build with Cuisenaire© rods		

FIGURE 5.78 Math Workstations

CONCRETE ACTIVITIES

Subtract from 10 Concrete Activities		
Roll and subtract that number from 10. Use two-sided counters to model the problem. Students can turn over the amount on the dice. They draw a pictorial model of their problem on a ten frame and also the number sentence.  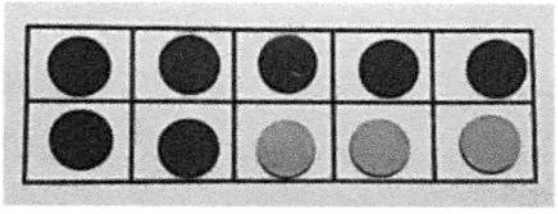	Roll and Build Subtract from 10. Students choose the math tool they use. 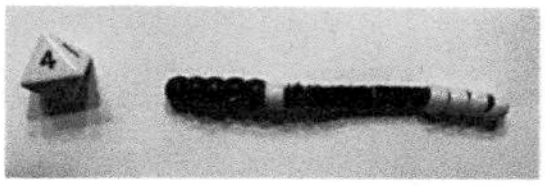	Cuisenaire© rods Build Combinations that Make 10 

FIGURE 5.79 Concrete Activities

PICTORIAL ACTIVITIES

Subtract from 10 Pictorial Activities		
10 Frame Flashcards Show 10 frame Flashcard as a quick image and then hide from students. Then, students will determine how many dots were on the flashcard and how many more are needed to make 10. 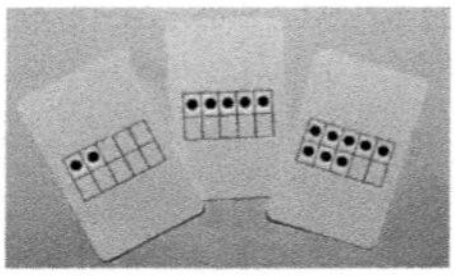	Students match a 10 frame with pictures to the expression that represents the situation. 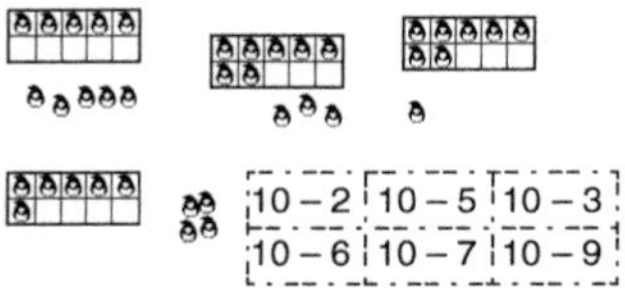 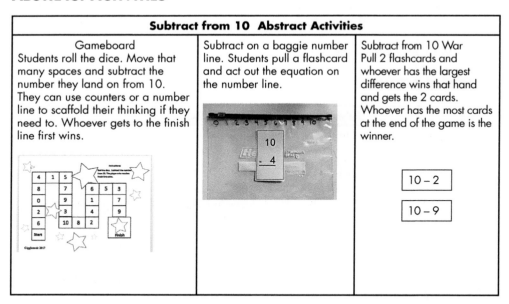	Cuisenaire© rod Draw 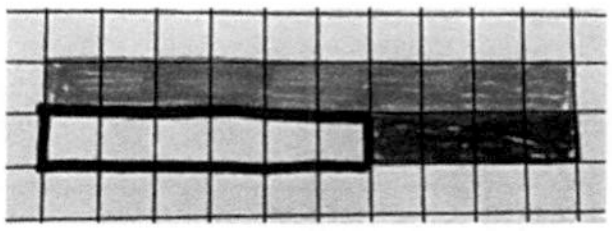 $10 - 4 = 6$

FIGURE 5.80 Pictorial Activities

ABSTRACT ACTIVITIES

Subtract from 10 Abstract Activities		
Gameboard Students roll the dice. Move that many spaces and subtract the number they land on from 10. They can use counters or a number line to scaffold their thinking if they need to. Whoever gets to the finish line first wins.	Subtract on a baggie number line. Students pull a flashcard and act out the equation on the number line.	Subtract from 10 War Pull 2 flashcards and whoever has the largest difference wins that hand and gets the 2 cards. Whoever has the most cards at the end of the game is the winner. $10 - 2$ $10 - 9$

FIGURE 5.81 Abstract Activities

STRATEGY FLASHCARDS

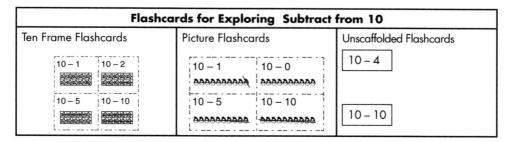

Flashcards for Exploring Subtract from 10		
Ten Frame Flashcards	Picture Flashcards	Unscaffolded Flashcards

FIGURE 5.82 Strategy Flashcards

MORE STRATEGY FLASHCARDS

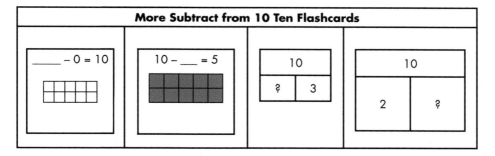

More Subtract from 10 Ten Flashcards

FIGURE 5.83 More Strategy Flashcards

WORD PROBLEMS

In every fluency module there should be a focus on word problems. Here are a few examples of the types of word problems for subtract from 10.			
My Subtract from 10 Story Problems Booklet	There were 10 pieces of fruit on the table. 6 were apples and the rest were oranges. How many oranges were there? Write the set-up equation: Show your thinking with a model. Write the solution equation.	There were 10 horses in a field. 3 of them went into the barn. How many were still out in the field? Write the set-up equation: Show your thinking with a model. Write the solution equation.	Karen had 10 gumballs and Tom had 8. How many more gumballs did Karen have than Tom? Write the set-up equation: Show your thinking with a model. Write the solution equation.

FIGURE 5.84 Word Problems

RESOURCES
Picture Books

Books about Subtract from 10				
*Ten Flashing Fireflies by Philemon Sturges and Anna Vojtech (This is a great book about subtracting 10 fireflies). There are a ton of resources online to support work with this book.	Ten Little Monkeys Jumping on the Bed by Annie Kubler and Tina Freeman	Ten Little Elephants by Ashley Brayden	Ten Little Rubber Ducks by Eric Carle	Ten on the Sled by Kim Norman and Liza Woodruff https://www.youtube.com/watch?v=XBdKHAFvte0
Ten Sly Piranhas by William Wise and Victoria Chess				

FIGURE 5.85 Picture Books

Videos

Video Songs about Subtract from 10
Ann Elise's video on Subtraction from 10 – Decomposing 10: https://youtu.be/vlEm-JLOXhs 10 Little Honeybees: https://www.youtube.com/watch?v=7oiLU3jQH-E Mr R's Songs for Teaching, Ten Frame Subtraction: https://youtu.be/HvxSdytKqgg

FIGURE 5.86 Videos

Anchor Chart

SUBTRACTING FROM TEN

WHEN WE SUBTRACT FROM TEN,
WE SHOULD THINK OF OUR TEN FRIENDS.

10 – 7 THINK 7 + ? = 10   7 + 3 MAKES 10

10 – 9 THINK 9 + ? = 10   9 + 1 MAKES 10
10 – 4 THINK 4 + ? MAKES 10 4 + 6 MAKES 10

TEN FRIENDS CAN HELP US KNOW OUR
SUBTRACTION FACTS!

FIGURE 5.87 Anchor Chart

Quiz

Subtracting from 10 Quiz		
Name:		Date:
10 − 2 = Model with a drawing.	10 − 6 = Model on the ten frame. [ten frame grid]	Solve. Kate had 10 cookies. She gave 3 of them to her friends. How many cookies did she have left? Write the equation: Answer: _____
Solve. There were 10 balloons. 4 of them popped. How many balloons were left? Write the equation: Answer: _____	Solve. 10 − ____ = 5 ____ − 2 = 8 3 = 10 − _____ ____ = 10 − 9	Which addition problem can help you solve 10 − 5? a. 10 + 4 b. 10 + 5 c. 5 + 5 d. none of these

10 − 4 =
Model on the number path.

1	2	3	4	5	6	7	8	9	10

What is the Subtract from 10 strategy? Explain with numbers, words and pictures.

Circle how good you think you are at doing Subtract from 10 facts!

Great   Good    OK, still thinking

FIGURE 5.88 Quiz

KEY POINTS

Subtraction continuum:
- take away 0
- take away 1
- subtract within 5/count back
- subtract from 5
- subtract within 10/count back
- subtract from 10
- cycle of engagement: concrete, pictorial, and abstract.

SUMMARY

Subtraction within 10 is a foundational set of skills. Students need several opportunities to work with these number combinations. Exploring them in the research-based continuum helps students to work and practice with one set of ideas before moving on to a more advanced set of ideas. Scaffolding the activities and allowing for student independent practice allows everyone to work in their zone of proximal development so that they can all get to where they need to be by the end of the year. Activities should be designed so that students can build conceptual understanding through work with concrete materials, then continue the work using pictorial representations and, finally, work on abstract practice.

REFLECTION QUESTIONS

1. Do you teach with reference to the subtraction continuum? Do you make sure that your students understand and are secure with all the subtraction facts within 10 and from 10 before you go on to the higher facts?
2. What have you learned in this chapter?
3. In what ways is this chapter going to influence the way you think about teaching and learning subtraction?

REFERENCES

Carpenter, T. P., Fennema, E., Franke, M. L., Levi, L., & Empson, S. B. (2015). *Children's mathematics: Cognitively guided instruction.* Portsmouth, NH: Heinemann.

CHAPTER 6

Exploring and Learning Subtraction within 20

We are now entering the last phase of the progression of working on our addition and subtraction math facts. This final stage includes working on subtraction from teen numbers, which tends to be the biggest weakness among our upper elementary and middle school students. Within the context of division of multi-digit numbers, students can be seen counting back a math fact using their fingers because they never developed efficient strategies for these math facts. It is particularly imperative, then, that we give these strategies plenty of instructional time so that students are not held up within work on complex math computations by the basic math facts.

We continue to work on accuracy, flexibility, efficiency, and automaticity. There are three main strategies that we focus on when working with subtraction with larger numbers. The first strategy is getting students to bridge back through 10 (Henry & Brown, 2008). In this strategy students will count back from the minuend using larger jumps and use 10 as a bridge. The second strategy is the idea that subtraction includes finding the distance between two numbers. This thinking is related to the inverse relationship between addition and subtraction. An important foundational understanding is that subtraction can be thought of as a missing addend problem. So, for example, if asked what is 15 - 8, students might think to add to 8 to get 15. Addition skills are usually stronger than subtraction skills, so students can build their proficiency with subtraction by relying on their strength with addition (Van de Walle, 2007). At first students may count up by 1s to get to the minuend. This thinking can become more sophisticated as they add up from the subtrahend using larger jumps with 10 as a bridge. The third strategy is if students have an automatic recall of their addition facts they can then know the answer to the related subtraction problem without having to do any jumps at all. For example, if students know their doubles and relate them to their half facts, they can solve the problem automatically (i.e. for 14 - 7, think 7 + 7 = 14 so the answer is 7) (see Figures 6.1–6.15).

EXPLORING SUBTRACT 10 FROM A TEEN NUMBER AND 1 FROM A TEEN NUMBER

At this point in the progression we want to be sure students develop automaticity with decomposing teen numbers into their place values and apply this understanding when given a subtraction expression when either subtracting the 10 or the 1s. We are extending Subtract a Number From Itself to now apply to anytime we are taking the amount in the 1s place value from itself. Students need some time to explore these concepts using a variety of concrete tools, but one especially good tool for this concept is Cuisenaire© rods. Students can see that the teen number is made up of a 10 and then a group of 1s. The Cuisenaire© rods for the 1s digit lend themselves to students seeing them existing as a group rather than a collection of 1s. Oftentimes, when students see a collection of 1s, they are tempted to count them.

FIGURE 6.1 Rods

This is the number 13 using Cuisenaire© rods. You can see how it is decomposed into the 10 and 3. If we remove the 10 rod we are left with 3, and if we remove the 3 we are left with the 10.

WHOLE CLASS ACTIVITIES

Routines

Use the virtual rekenrek or ten frame to introduce and discuss taking 10 or 1s from a teen number. After students have learned the strategy, play Subtract 10 or 1s from a teen number Bingo with the whole class. Students can either have their own boards or they can play with partners. Also play Subtract a 10 or 1s from a teen number Tic-Tac-Toe as a whole class game. The class divides up into two teams and they take turns picking a square and stating the answer.

WHOLE CLASS MINI-LESSON: SUBTRACT 10 OR 1s FROM A TEEN NUMBER (THESE SHOULD BE SEPARATE LESSONS INITIALLY)

Introduction

Teacher: *Today we are going to look at what happens when we take 10 from a teen number. Let's pull up our twenty frame: 12 – 10 = ?*

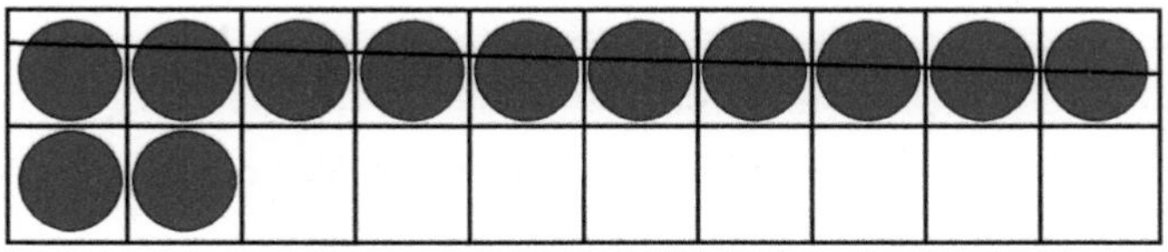

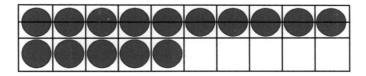

FIGURE 6.2   Twenty Frame

Teacher: *What happened?*
Students: *2 is left.*
Teacher: *15 – 10 = ?*

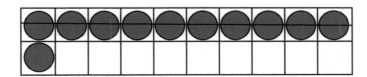

FIGURE 6.3   Twenty frame

Teacher: *What happened?*
Students: *5 is left.*

FIGURE 6.4   Another Twenty Frame

Teacher: *What happened?*
Students: *1 is left.*
Teacher: *What do we notice about taking 10 from a teen number? Turn and tell your math partner what you think. (After students talk, teacher asks them to share their thinking.)*
Maribel: *We noticed that the 10 is gone and only some 1s are left.*
Clark: *Like if you take 9 from 19 you only have 10 left.*
Teacher: *So, what I hear is you all saying that if you take a 10 from a teen number only the 1s are left. That is something that we will be looking for the next couple of days. Tomorrow we will look at it on a number line. Let's get ready for our workstations.*

SPOTLIGHT ACTIVITY

Have students act out taking a 10 from a teen number in a human-size double ten frame. For example, have 11 students come up. Then have 10 sit down. The students can see that only 1 is left. Do this several times so that students can see the pattern.

MATH WORKSTATIONS

	Workstations to Explore Subtract 10 or 1s from a Teen		
Concrete	**Pictorial**	**Abstract**
Roll or Pull and Build a Subtract 10 or 1s from a Teen fact on a Twenty Frame	Draw on Twenty Frame & Rekenrek Model	Subtract 10 or 1s from a Teen Face Off
Roll and Build a Subtract 10 or 1s from a Teen fact on a Rekenrek	Subtract 10 or 1s from a Teen Domino Sort & Record	Subtract 10 or 1s from a Teen Board Games
Roll and Build a Subtract 10 or 1s from a Teen Fact with the Cubes	Draw on Cube Template	Subtract 10 or 1s from a Teen Bingo
Roll and Build a Subtract 10 or 1s from a Teen Fact in a Part-Part Whole Mat	Draw on a Part-Part Whole Mat	Subtract 10 or 1s from a Teen Tic-Tac-Toe
Roll and Show a Subtract 10 or 1s from a Teen Fact in a Number Bond	Draw and Show in a Number Bond	Subtract 10 or 1s from a Teen Four in a Row
Pull and Build a Subtract 10 or 1s from a Teen Fact with Play-Doh©	Subtract 10 or 1s from a Teen Flashcards	Subtract 10 or 1s from a Teen Flashcards War
Roll and Build a Subtract 10 or 1s from a Teen Fact on 20 Beaded Number Line	Subtract 10 or 1s from a Teen Booklet	Subtract 10 or 1s from a Teen on a Number Line
Number Line Pull and show Subtract 10 or 1s from a Teen facts with Cuisenaire© rods	Draw on 1cm paper with Cuisenaire© rods	Subtract 10 or 1s from a Teen Clip Cards
		Subtract 10 or 1s from a Teen on a Number path

FIGURE 6.5 Math Workstations

CONCRETE ACTIVITIES

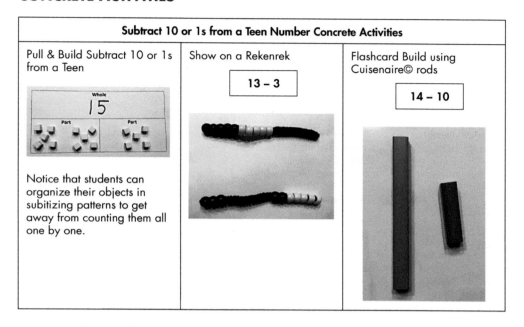

FIGURE 6.6 Concrete Activities

PICTORIAL ACTIVITIES

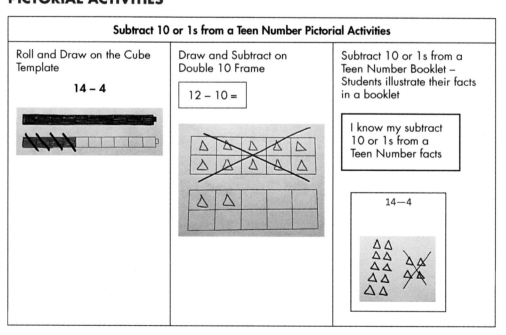

FIGURE 6.7 Pictorial Activities

ABSTRACT ACTIVITIES

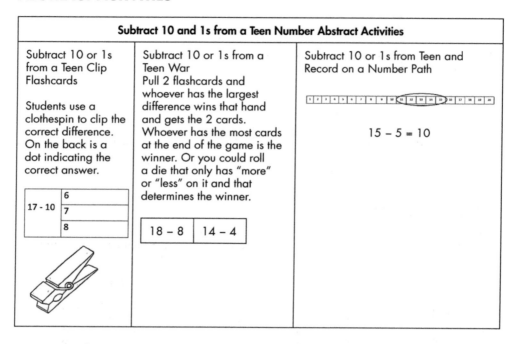

FIGURE 6.8 Abstract Activities

STRATEGY FLASHCARDS

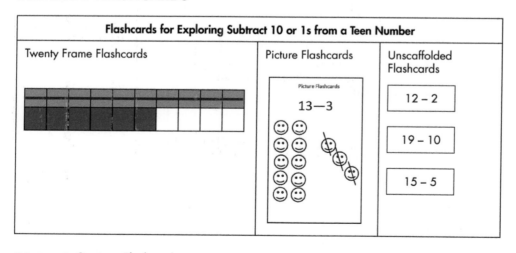

FIGURE 6.9 Strategy Flashcards

MORE STRATEGY FLASHCARDS

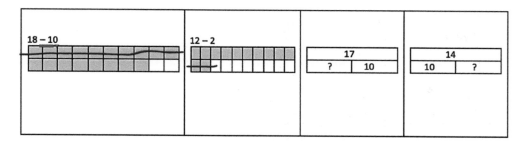

FIGURE 6.10 More Strategy Flashcards

WORD PROBLEMS

In every fluency module there should be a focus on word problems. Here are a few examples of the types of word problems for Subtract 10 or 1s from a Teen Number.			
My Subtract Ten from a Teen/ Ones from a Teen Number Story Problems Booklet	**Fran had 15 lollipops. She gave away 10 of them to her friends. How many did she have left?** **Write the set-up equation:** **Show your thinking with a model.** **Write the solution equation.**	**Darcy had 12 marbles. 2 were blue and the rest were green. How many were green?** **Write the set-up equation:** **Show your thinking with a model.** **Write the solution equation.**	**There were 16 brown bunnies and 10 white bunnies in the grass. How many fewer white bunnies were there than brown bunnies?** **Write the set-up equation:** **Show your thinking with a model.** **Write the solution equation.**

FIGURE 6.11 Word Problems

RESOURCES

Videos

 Video Songs about Subtract 10 or 1s from teen

Ann Elise's video on Subtracting 10 or 1s from a teen: https://youtu.be/OLUD1ufHYlI
Dream English Kids Subtraction - 10 Math Song: https://youtu.be/j_w4i1pcf7E

FIGURE 6.12 Videos

Anchor Charts

We can model taking some ones from a teen number in many different ways!

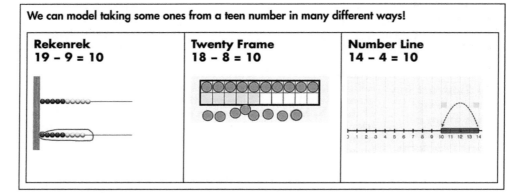

Rekenrek
19 – 9 = 10

Twenty Frame
18 – 8 = 10

Number Line
14 – 4 = 10

FIGURE 6.13 Anchor Chart

It's Easy to Subtract 10 from a Teen Number!
We can model subtracting 10 from a teen number in many ways!

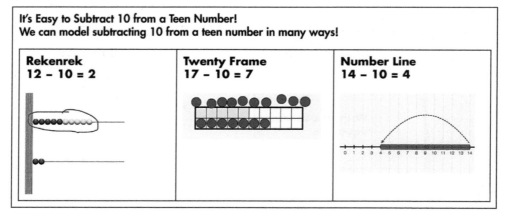

Rekenrek
12 – 10 = 2

Twenty Frame
17 – 10 = 7

Number Line
14 – 10 = 4

FIGURE 6.14 Anchor Chart

QUIZ

Subtract 10 from a Teen and 1s from a Teen Number Quiz

Name: Date:

13 – 3 = Model with a drawing.	18 – 10 = Model on the twenty frame. 	Solve. Eve had 14 brownies. She gave away 10 of them to her friends. How many did she have left? Write the equation: Answer: _____
Solve. Ella made 17 beaded bracelets. She gave away 7 of them. How many does Ella have left? Write the equation: Answer: _____	Solve. _____ – 5 = 10 _____ – 10 = 8 _____ = 16 – 6	There were 18 magazines on a shelf. 10 of them were about animals and the rest were about sports. How many were about sports? Draw a model. Answer: _____

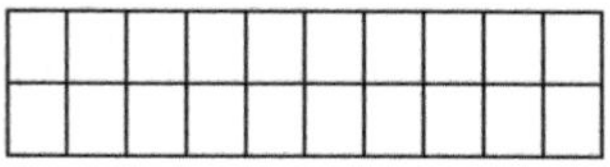

14 – 4 =

Model on the number line.

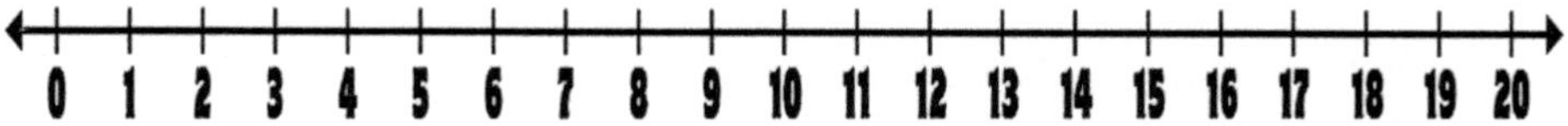

What are 'subtract 10 or 1s from a teen number' facts? Explain with numbers, words and pictures.

Circle how good you think you are at doing Subtract 10 or 1s from a teen number facts!

Great   Good    OK, still thinking

FIGURE 6.15 Quiz

EXPLORING AND LEARNING TO SUBTRACT HALF FACTS

Most students develop automaticity with their doubles facts, so it is a bit surprising to find that students have a difficult time recognizing their half facts. The underlying mathematical principle is the inverse relationship between addition and subtraction. If I know that 6 + 6 = 12, then I also know that 12 − 6 = 6. It is critical that students understand this relationship, beginning at these early stages so that they can continue to see how this concept applies in future math topics. Any time spent on activities that connect the doubles facts to the half facts is time well spent.

WHOLE CLASS ACTIVITIES

Routines

Use jumbo cards and tell the students the amount of that card doubled. Students then need to determine what card you are holding. Play Subtract Half Fact Bingo with the whole class. Students can either have their own boards or they can play with partners. Also play Subtract Half Fact Tic-Tac-Toe as a whole class game. The class divides up into two teams and they take turns picking a square and stating the answer.

WHOLE CLASS MINI-LESSON: SUBTRACT HALF FACTS

Introduction

Teacher: Today we are going to look at half facts. But first, we are going to talk about doubles. Who can tell me what a double fact is?

Maribel: It is like 4 + 4.

Joshua: Or like 5 + 5.

Teddy: Or like 6 + 6.

Teacher: Ok, great. So, we are going to use what we know about doubles to help us solve half facts. Let's take a look. If I have 4 kids come up here and stand in the ten frame, then I double it with 4 more, I will have 8. What do you think will happen if I have 4 sit down?

Tara: 4 will be left because there were 4 at first.

Teacher: Ok, let's have 5 kids come up. Now, let's have 5 more. What's our total? (Class says 10.) What happens if 5 sit down?

Lucy: Then there are 5.

Teacher: Ok, let's have 3 kids come up. Now, let's have 3 more. What's our total? (Class says 6.) What happens if 3 sit down?

Mary: Then there are 3.

Teacher: What do you notice about doubles and half facts?

Raul: It's like if you double the number and take it away then you have the number.

Teacher: Somebody give me an example.

Yesenia: 2 plus 2 makes 4. Then take 2 away and you get 2.

Teacher: Yes, isn't that interesting. We are going to be exploring this concept for the next few days.

SPOTLIGHT ACTIVITY

Build it – Break it. Have the students build a double fact with Unifix® Cubes and then break it in half. Repeat this several times and discuss the relationship (see Figures 6.16–6.45).

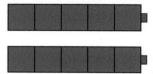

FIGURE 6.16 Spotlight Activity

MATH WORKSTATIONS

 Workstations to Explore Subtract Half Facts

Concrete	Pictorial	Abstract
Roll or Pull and Build Subtract Half Facts on a Twenty Frame	Draw on Twenty Frame Model	Subtract Half Facts Face Off
Roll and Build Subtract Half Facts on a Rekenrek	Draw on Rekenrek Model	Subtract Half Facts Board Game 1
Roll and Build Subtract Half Facts with the Cubes	Draw on Cube Template	Double and Half Card Game
Roll and Build Subtract Half Facts on a Part-Part Whole Mat	Draw in a Part-Part Whole Mat	Subtract Half Facts Tic-Tac-Toe
Roll and Show Subtract Half Facts on a Number Bond	Draw and Show in a Number Bond	Subtract Half Facts Four in a Row
Subtract Half Facts with Play-Doh©	Subtract Half Facts Flashcards	Subtract Half Facts Slides and Ladders
Spin and Subtract Half Facts	Subtract Half Facts Booklet	Spin and Subtract Half Facts
Show Subtract Half Facts with Cuisenaire© rods	Subtract Half Facts Domino Sort & Record	Subtract Half Facts Game 2
	Subtract Half Facts Poster	Subtract Half Facts Bingo
	Draw Subtract Half Facts on 1cm paper using Cuisenaire© rods	Subtract Half Facts on Number Line or Number Path
		Clip Flashcards

FIGURE 6.17 Math Workstations

CONCRETE ACTIVITIES

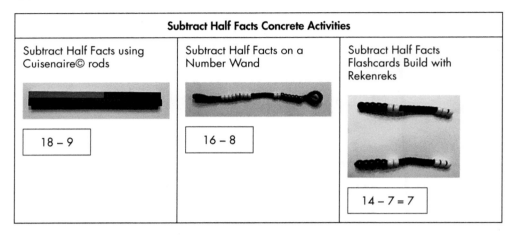

FIGURE 6.18 Concrete Activities

PICTORIAL ACTIVITIES

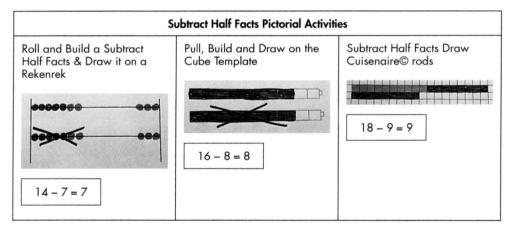

FIGURE 6.19 Pictorial Activities

ABSTRACT ACTIVITIES

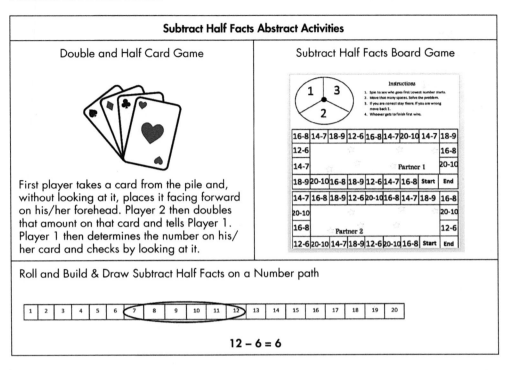

FIGURE 6.20 Abstract Activities

STRATEGY FLASHCARDS

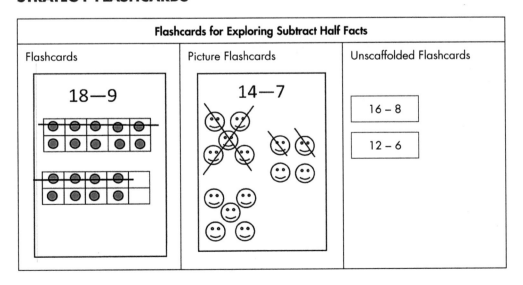

FIGURE 6.21 Strategy Flashcards

WORD PROBLEMS

In every fluency module there should be a focus on word problems. Here are a few examples of the types of word problems for subtract half facts.

| **My Subtract Half Facts Story Problems Booklet** | Olivia had 14 barrettes. She gave 7 of them to her friend Quinn. How many barrettes does Olivia have now?

Write the set-up equation:

Show your thinking with a model.

Write the solution equation. | Benjamin had 16 Lego© sets. 8 of them were Star Wars© themed and the rest were other types. How many of his sets were not Star Wars© themed?

Write the set-up equation:

Show your thinking with a model.

Write the solution equation. | Julie has 18 pairs of earrings. Karen has 9 pairs of earrings. How many more pairs of earrings does Julie have than Karen?

Write the set-up equation:

Show your thinking with a model.

Write the solution equation. |

FIGURE 6.22 Word Problems

RESOURCES

Videos

 Video about Subtract Half Facts

Ann Elise's video on Subtracting Half Facts: https://youtu.be/72FoeoJqnUU
Dream English Kids, Subtraction Halving Numbers Math Song: https://youtu.be/VsyIB2Q6lws

FIGURE 6.23 Videos

Anchor Chart

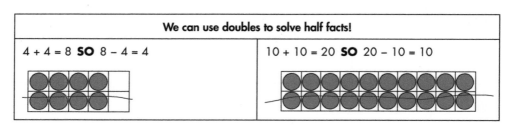

We can use doubles to solve half facts!	
4 + 4 = 8 **SO** 8 – 4 = 4	10 + 10 = 20 **SO** 20 – 10 = 10

FIGURE 6.24 Anchor Chart

Quiz

Subtract Half Facts Quiz

Name: Date:

12 – 6 = Model with a drawing.	16 – 8 = Model on the twenty frame. 	Solve. Colleen collected 18 rocks. She painted 9 of them. How many of her rocks are unpainted? Write the equation: Answer: _____
Solve. Emilio had 14 cookies. He ate 7 of them. How many does he have now? Write the equation: Answer: _____	Solve. 12 – _____ = 6 _____ – 8 = 8 9 = 18 – _____ _____ = 16 - 8	Match the related fact: 20 – 10 8 + 8 18 – 9 6 + 6 16 – 8 7 + 7 14 – 7 5 + 5 12 – 6 10 + 10 10 – 5 9 + 9

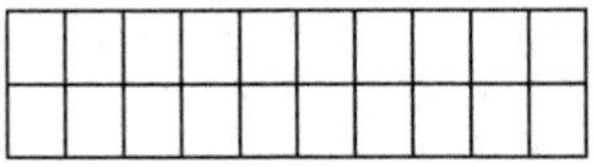

8 – 4 =

Model on the number line.

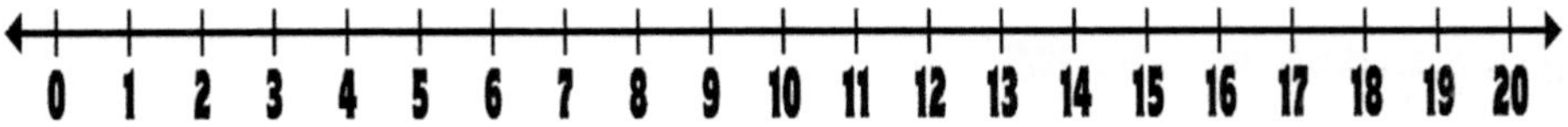

What are half facts? Explain with numbers, words and pictures.

Circle how good you think you are at doing half facts!

Great   Good    OK, still thinking

FIGURE 6.25 Quiz

EXPLORING AND LEARNING HOW TO SUBTRACT BY BRIDGING 10 WITH HIGHER FACTS

We've arrived at one of the most powerful strategies of all – Bridging 10! This strategy sets the foundation for so many other concepts further on in the students' math journeys: it becomes Bridging to the nearest 10 to the nearest 100, and then the nearest whole for fractions and decimals. There are several strategies that must be in place before students can be successful with this one: pairs of numbers that make 10, decomposing of all single-digit numbers, and then the Add Plus 10 strategy. Students can add or subtract, but the key is that they are using 10 as a bridge to add or subtract chunks to get to 10 and then the minuend or subtrahend. For example, if students are asked 12 – 8, there are many ways that they can determine the difference. One student, who prefers to think of subtraction as a take away method, might think 12 - 2 gets me to 10 and then I need to take away 6 more, so 10 – 6 is 4.

Another student might add up. This student might like to interpret subtraction problems as missing addend problems and want to count up from 8 to 12. 8 + 2 makes 10 and then from 10 to 12 is 2, so 2 + 2 is 4. No one way is better than the others. Students need to determine which method works best for their brains. The common thread, though, is that they all are using 10 as that bridge. This is so much more efficient than counting down or up by 1s. Students need lots of time to explore these methods in concrete, pictorial, and abstract ways. Taking the time now though will pay off fantastically later on in their math journey, as computation involving larger numbers, fractions, and decimals will become so much easier and, since students will be developing their number sense, they won't be prone to making conceptual mistakes and not even realizing that their answers are unreasonable.

WHOLE CLASS ACTIVITIES

Routines

Use virtual dice to roll a number and have the class take that number away from a teen number of your choice. Use jumbo cards and have students take the number away from a teen number of your choice. Play Bingo and Tic-Tac-Toe with the class.

WHOLE CLASS MINI-LESSON: SUBTRACT BRIDGE 10

Introduction

Teacher: *Today we are going to look at how 10 can help us subtract higher numbers. Let's look at it on the number line. If I have 12 take away 5, I could hop back 2 to 10 and then 3 more. Let's walk it out. Who wants to be the number line walker today? What if I have 14 and I take away 9? What would the walker do?*

Tim: *She should walk back 4 to get to 10 and then 5 more.*

Teacher: *Ok, we need a new walker. Brian, show us how to solve 17 take away 8. (Brian does it.)*

Teacher: *Who can tell us what he did?*

Kelly:	*He walked back 7 and then took away 1 more.*
Teacher:	*Who could explain what we are doing?*
Maritza:	*We take away some to get to 10 and then the rest.*
Teacher:	*Yes, exactly, with this strategy we are taking away some and then taking away the rest. Who wants to give us another example?*
Jamal:	*Like, if I had 14 and I took away 8, I would hop back 4 to 10 and then 4 more. I would get 6.*
Teacher:	*Yes! We are going to be practicing this for the next few days. Let's get ready to go to our workstations.*

 ## SPOTLIGHT ACTIVITY

Subtraction Strings

This is a great tool to teach Bridging 10. There are 9 strings with the numbers 11 through 19 on them. Start with string 11. There are 10 beads of 1 color and 1 bead of another. With this string we are working on subtracting numbers from 11. Students then work on taking 2 from 11. They see that they jump back 1 to 10 and then 1 more. For taking 3 from 11, they jump back 1 and then 2 more. They always use 10 as a bridge to subtract. Let's say they are working on subtracting from 15. They would have the 15 bead. If they were subtracting 8 from 15, they could take away 5 and then 3 more. I love this tool, and I tell everyone to use it when they are trying to teach Bridging 10 facts.

FIGURE 6.26 Tool

Special Note about subtracting 8 or 9. Students can use the Bridging 10 strategy or they could just take away 10 and add back 1 or 2 depending on the number. It is important to work with students on the take away 10 strategy with concrete materials, drawings, and abstract tools such as the number line.

There is also the Doubles Minus 1 or 2 strategy. Of course, there are other strategies. In the case of 15 − 8, they could think doubles and know that 7 + 7 is 14 so 7 + 8 is 15. Therefore, 15 − 8 would be 7. In this strategy students use what they know about doubles and relate it to subtraction. Another example is, students might say when looking at 14 – 8, "I know that 14 – 7 is 7, so 14 – 8 is 6 because you are taking 1 more away." Some students do use this strategy. One way to get students to practice this strategy is to make flashcards that have a hint on them like this:

14 – 8 think 14 – 7

FIGURE 6.27 Strategy Flashcard

MATH WORKSTATIONS

 Workstations to Explore Subtraction Bridge 10

Concrete	Pictorial	Abstract
Roll or Pull and Build Subtract a Bridge 10 fact on a Double Ten Frame	Draw on Twenty Frame Model	Subtract Bridge 10 Face Off
Roll and Build a Subtract a Bridge 10 fact on a Rekenrek	Draw on Rekenrek Model	Subtract Bridge 10 Board Game 1
Roll and Build a Subtract a Bridge 10 fact with the Cubes	Draw on Cube Template	Subtract Bridge 10 War
Subtract a Bridge 10 fact with Play-Doh©	Subtract Bridge 10 Flashcards	Subtract Bridge 10 Tic-Tac-Toe
Spin and Subtract Bridge 10	Subtract Bridge 10 Booklet	Subtract Bridge 10 Four in a Row
Show with Cuisenaire© rods	Subtract Bridge 10 Domino Sort & Record	Subtract Bridge 10 Slides and Ladders
Build on a 20 beaded Number Line	Subtract Bridge 10 Poster	Spin and Subtract Bridge 10
Build on a Number wand	Subtract Bridge 10 draw Cuisenaire© rods on grid paper	Subtract Bridge 10 Bingo
		Show Subtract Bridge 10 on Number Line or Open Numberline
		Power Towers
		Kaboom Game

FIGURE 6.28 Math Workstations

CONCRETE ACTIVITIES

<table>
<tr><td colspan="2" align="center">**Subtract Bridge 10 Concrete Activities**</td></tr>
<tr>
<td>

Build Bridge 10 fact using Cuisenaire© rods

$$17 - 9 = ?$$

Orienting the Cuisenaire© rods this way allows students to see the removal of 9 from the 17. Removing 7 from the 17 lands us on 10. We then have 2 more to take away, and 10 − 2 = 8. So, 17 − 9 = 8.

Orienting the Cuisenaire© rods this way allows students to think of the subtraction problem as a missing addend problem. So, 17 − 9 can be thought of as something + 9 = 17. 10 can then be used as a bridge while thinking additively. 9 + 1 = 10 and 10 + 7 makes the 17. So, the 1 + 7 = 8.

</td>
<td>

Build a Bridge 10 fact using Beaded Number Line

$$15 - 7 = 8$$

Using the beaded number line allows students to see 20 linearly and with the color change at 10 to additionally visualize the using of the 10 as a bridge. This is a concrete representation of the bridging 10.

This is a concrete representation of interpreting 15 − 7 as 7 + ? = 15. Starting at 7, there are 3 more to get to 10 and then 5 more to get to 15. 3 + 5 = 8, so 15 − 7 = 8.

</td>
</tr>
<tr>
<td colspan="2">

Build Bridge 10 on Double 10 frame

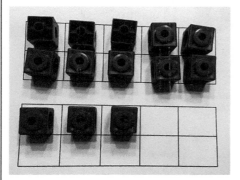

$$13 - 6 = 7$$

By using the structure of the double 10 frame, students can see that 13 − 3 is 10 and that taking away 3 more results in there being 7 cubes left.

</td>
</tr>
</table>

FIGURE 6.29 Concrete Activities

PICTORIAL ACTIVITIES

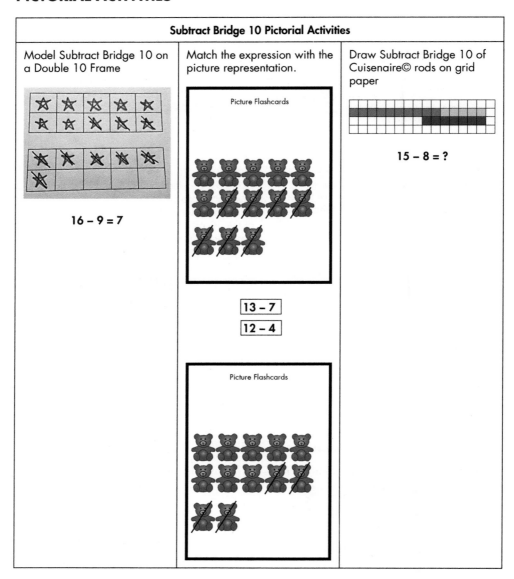

FIGURE 6.30 Pictorial Activities

ABSTRACT ACTIVITIES

Subtract Bridge 10 Abstract Activities	
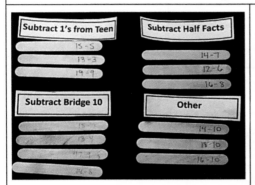	**KABOOM!** Math facts to practice are written on popsicle sticks. Then a few extra have KABOOM written on them. All the sticks go into a cup. Player 1 chooses a stick and answers the math fact. If correct, the stick can be kept. If incorrect, then the stick goes back into the cup. If a KABOOM stick is pulled, the player needs to put all their collected sticks back into the cup. Game continues until all the KABOOM sticks have been pulled. Player with the most sticks is the winner. 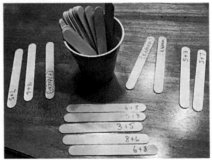
Subtract Bridge 10 using Open Number Line	
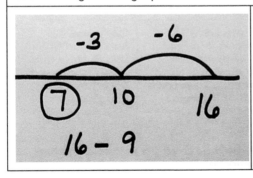	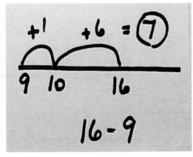

FIGURE 6.31 Abstract Activities

STRATEGY FLASHCARDS

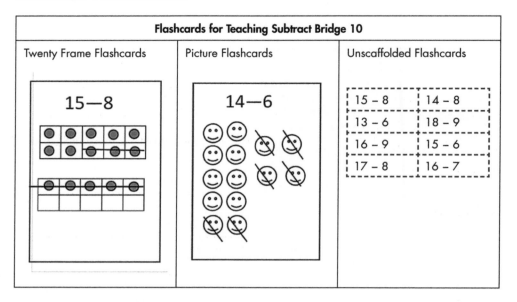

Flashcards for Teaching Subtract Bridge 10		
Twenty Frame Flashcards	Picture Flashcards	Unscaffolded Flashcards
15—8	14—6	15 – 8 14 – 8 13 – 6 18 – 9 16 – 9 15 – 6 17 – 8 16 – 7

FIGURE 6.32 Strategy Flashcards

WORD PROBLEMS

In every fluency module there should be a focus on word problems. Here are a few examples of the types of word problems for Bridge 10 to subtract.

My Subtract Bridge 10 Story Problems Booklet	There were 17 apples in a basket. 8 of them were red, the rest were green. How many were green?	There were 12 horses in a field. 7 of them went in the barn. How many horses were left in the field?	Mary had 16 books and Chris had 9. How many fewer books did Chris have than Mary?
	Write the set-up equation:	Write the set-up equation:	Write the set-up equation:
	Show your thinking with a model.	Show your thinking with a model.	Show your thinking with a model.
	Write the solution equation.	Write the solution equation.	Write the solution equation.

FIGURE 6.35 Word Problems

RESOURCES

Videos

 Videos about Bridge 10 to Subtract

Ann Elise's video on Subtracting Bridge 10: https://youtu.be/YmUzN0jQSiY
PISD Mathematics, Fact Fluency Video Make 10 & More, Build Up Thru 10, Back Down Thru 10:
https://youtu.be/7BT8Kf3YvHg
PISD Mathematics, +/- 7, 8, 9 facts on Double Ten Frame: https://youtu.be/afO2a3SKEqk

FIGURE 6.34 Videos

Anchor Chart

<table>
<tr><td colspan="2" align="center">We can use 10 to subtract!</td></tr>
<tr>
<td>
Twenty frame Model
15 – 9
15 – 5 = 10
10 – 4 = 6
First take away 5 to get to 10.
Then, 10 – 4. These are partial sums! We are taking away a part of the number at a time.

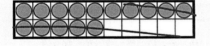
</td>
<td>
Number Line Model
14 – 6
14 – 4 = 10
10 – 2 = 8
First take away 4 to get to 10. Then, take away 2 from 10. The answer is 8. We are taking away a part of the number at a time.

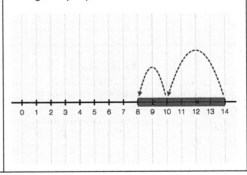
</td>
</tr>
</table>

FIGURE 6.33 Anchor Chart

Quiz

Subtract Bridge 10 Quiz Name:		Date:
14 − 8 = Model with a drawing.	15 − 9 = Model on the twenty frame. (twenty frame grid)	Solve. Mr. Baker had 13 pies. He sold 5 of them. How many pies did he have left? Write the equation: Answer: _____
Solve. Pam made 12 cookies. Angela made 8. How many more cookies did Pam make than Angela? Write the equation: Answer: _____	Solve. 18 − _____ = 9 _____ − 3 = 8 5 = 14 − _____ _____ = 14 − 8	Solve. _____ − 7 = 8 15 − _____ = 9

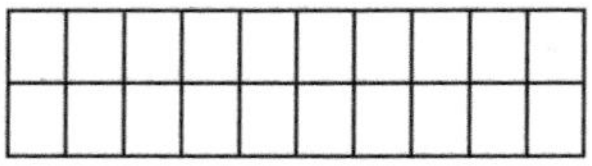

14 − 9 =

Model on the number line.

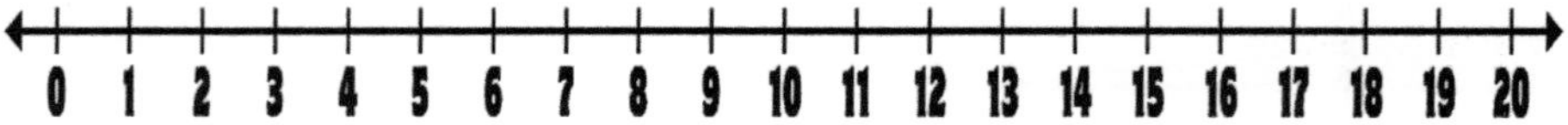

What are Subtracting Bridge 10 facts? Explain with numbers, words and pictures.

Circle how good you think you are at doing Subtract Bridge 10 facts!

Great	Good	OK, still thinking

FIGURE 6.36 Quiz

SUBTRACTING HIGHER FACTS: FACT FAMILIES

There are a variety of ways to think about subtracting higher facts. It is important that students work with fact families as well as using strategies for subtracting 8 and 9. There is also the Double Minus 1 or 2 strategy.

WHOLE CLASS ACTIVITIES

Routines

Do different activities such as "Which one doesn't belong?" in which you would put up different sentences that all belong to a fact family and then one that doesn't.

8 + 6 = 14	8 – 6 = 2	6 + 8 = 14	14 – 8 = 6

FIGURE 6.37 Game 1

Do activities like Two Truths and a Fib, in which you would put up two things that are true and one thing that isn't.

12 – 9 = 3	14 – 9 = 5	15 – 9 = 7

FIGURE 6.38 Game 2

WHOLE CLASS MINI-LESSON

Teacher: *How many of you remember working with fact families for numbers within 10? Today, we are going to look at fact families for higher numbers. Look at my card. What do we see? 5 + 6 = ?, 6 + 5 = ?, 11–5 = ?, 11–6 = ? All these numbers are related. We can use our strategy flashcards to show the relationships.*
(Have the students cover the number that the question mark represents as they are working through that strategy flashcard. The teacher does two or three of these cards with students as an introduction.)

STRATEGY FLASHCARD

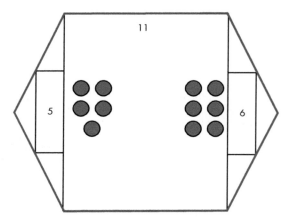

FIGURE 6.39 Strategy Flashcard

 SPOTLIGHT ACTIVITY

It is really important when working with students around fact families to have them experience the math, rather than just hand them a triangle and basically say "go for what you know." This concept of number relationships is really important and should be handled with the utmost care. They will use this foundation for the rest of their mathematical lives. It builds the understanding of inverse operations. So, students should do a lot of work with double ten frames and building facts to understand this relationship. I would have the students build the facts on a double ten frame and then discuss the relationships.

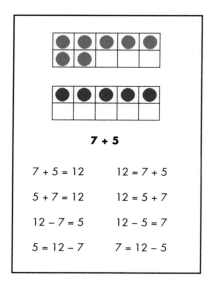

FIGURE 6.40 Fact Families

MATH WORKSTATIONS

 Workstations to Explore Fact Families

Concrete	Pictorial	Abstract
Build Fact Families on Double Ten Frames	Students Make Pictorial Fact Family Cards	Play Fact Family Card Sort Fact Family Clip Cards Fact Family Tic-Tac-Toe

FIGURE 6.41 Math Workstations

Activities for Fact Families		
Concrete	**Pictorial**	**Abstract**
Have students explore fact families with ten frames first and then double ten frames.	Have the students match the fact family cards with the models.	Have students make up their own fact family cards.

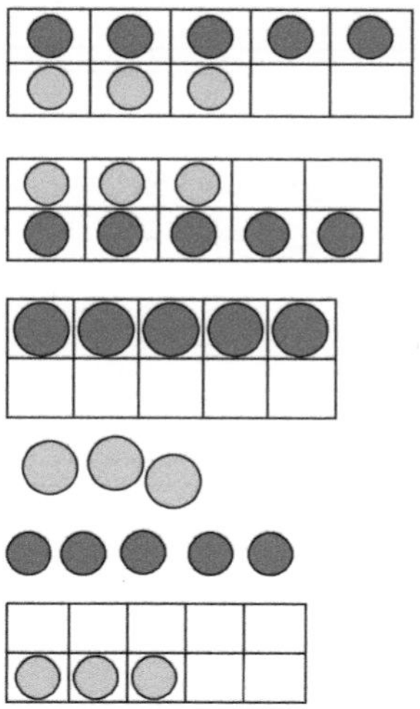

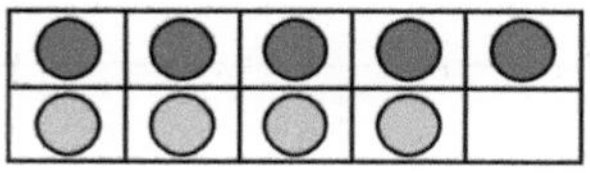

4, 5, 9

4 + 5 =
5 + 4 =
9 − 5 =
9 − 4 =

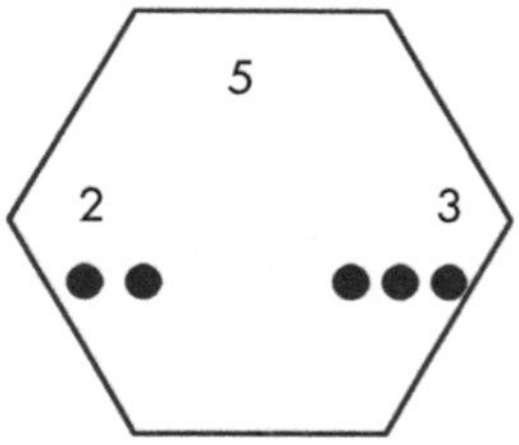

5

2   3

2 + 3 = 5

3 + 2 = 5

5 − 2 = 3

5 − 3 = 2

FIGURE 6.42 Activities

STRATEGY FLASHCARDS

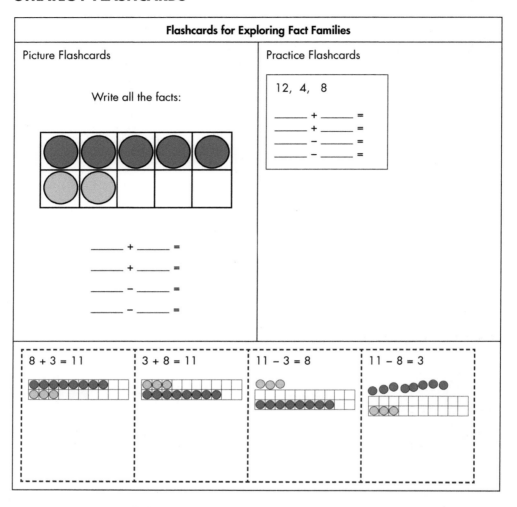

FIGURE 6.43 Strategy Flashcards

WORD PROBLEMS

In every fluency module there should be a focus on word problems. Here are a few examples of the types of word problems for fact families.			
Fact Family Story Problems Booklet	There were 8 boys and 9 girls on the playground. Ask a question about that scenario. Question: Write the set-up equation: Show your thinking with a model. Write the solution equation.	There were 4 girls and 6 boys. Ask a question about that scenario. Write the set-up equation: Show your thinking with a model. Write the solution equation.	There were 15 students. 7 were boys. Finish the story. Ask a question about the story. Write the set-up equation: Show your thinking with a model. Write the solution equation.

FIGURE 6.44 Word Problems

RESOURCES

Anchor Chart

We can use fact families to help us add and subtract. Numbers work together!
Let's take a look. 5 + 4 = 9 4 + 5 = 9 9 − 4 = 5 9 − 5 = 4

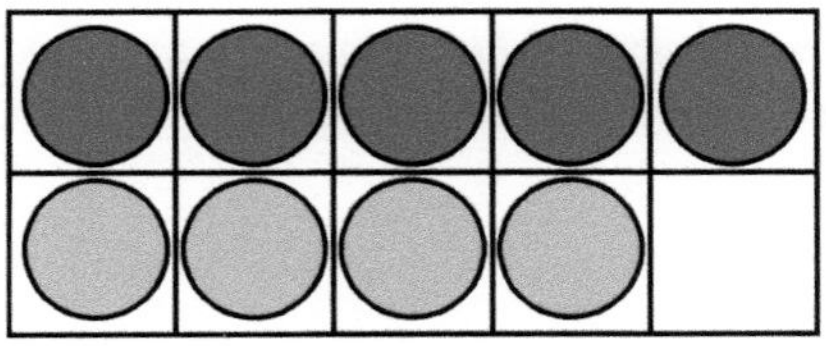

FIGURE 6.45 Anchor Chart

EXPLORING AND LEARNING TO SUBTRACT FROM 20

Students should explore a variety of ways to subtract from 20. In this section we are going to discuss fact families and counting up or down to subtract from 20 (really focusing on Bridging 10 again). Strategies developed to subtract from 20 are especially important because they will be used further down the math journey when students are subtracting from decade numbers. At this point in the progression, students should have their pairs of numbers that make 10 automatized, which will become helpful as we subtract from 20 and then other decade numbers later. Using our understanding that 3 + 7 = 10, we can extend that to know that 20 – 7 = 13, 20 – 3 = 17, 20 – 13 = 7, and 20 – 17 = 3, as well as the additive inverses of these situations. Students need to have a lot of practice using concrete objects and visually seeing this connection (see Figures 6.46–6.57).

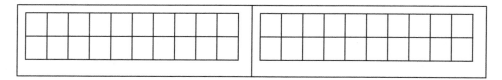

FIGURE 6.46 Twenty frames

WHOLE CLASS ACTIVITIES

Routines

Use virtual dice to roll a number and have students subtract that number from 20. Use jumbo cards and have students subtract that number from 20. Play Subtract from 20 Bingo and Tic-Tac-Toe with the whole class.

WHOLE CLASS MINI-LESSON

Introduction

Teacher:	*Today we are going to look at what happens when we subtract from 20. Everybody take out your whiteboards and markers. Let's say we have 20 marbles and 9 rolled away. How many are left?*
Marvin:	*11.*
Teacher:	*How do you know?*
Marvin:	*Well 1 more would make 10 and then 10 more makes 20.*
Teacher:	*I like your thinking! Ok, here's another one. What is 20 – 15?*
Shakhira:	*5.*
Teacher:	*How do you know?*
Shakhira:	*Because I hopped back 5.*
Teacher:	*Ok, so there are different ways to think about subtracting from 20. We could count back or count up. We are going to be thinking about the different ways and exploring them for the next few days. Any questions? Ok, let's get ready for workstations.*

SPOTLIGHT ACTIVITY

Use the double ten frame to explore patterns when subtracting from 20. Use both the twenty frame and the double ten frame. Have students make up problems and discuss what they notice about taking a number away from 10. Help them to think about what facts they can use to help them figure out the answers. For example, if they take 7 away from 20, they could think about 7 + 3 = 10 and another 10 makes 20, so it would be 3 + 10, which is 13. Give students plenty of opportunity to talk about these strategies.

MATH WORKSTATIONS

Workstations to Explore Subtracting from 20		
Concrete	**Pictorial**	**Abstract**
Show a Subtract from 20 Fact on the Double Ten Frame	Draw on Double Ten Frame Model	Subtract from 20 spin to win
Show a Subtract from 20 Fact on a Rekenrek	Draw on Rekenrek Model	Subtract from 20 War
Spin and Subtract from 20 Fact	Subtract from 20 Booklet	Subtract from 20 clip cards
Roll and Build a Subtract from 20 Fact using Cubes	Subtract from 20 on 1cm paper using Cuisenaire© rods	Subtract from 20 Tic-Tac-Toe
Pull and Build a Subtract from 20 Fact using a Number Bond	Draw Subtract from 20 on Cubes Template	Subtract from 20 Bingo
Pull and Build on a 20 Beaded Number Line	Draw on a Part-Part-Whole Mat	Subtract from 20 card sort
Roll or Pull and Build a Subtract from 20 using Cuisenaire© rods	Draw a Subtract from 20 in a Number Bond	Show Subtract from 20 on a Number Line or Open Number Line
Pull and Build on a Part-Part-Whole Mat		Show Subtract from 20 on a Numberpath
Subtract from 20 flashcards		Subtract from 20 flashcards
Split Machine		Power Towers

FIGURE 6.47 Math Workstations

CONCRETE ACTIVITIES

Subtract from 20 Concrete Activities		
Roll and Subtract that number from 20. Use Cuisenaire© rods to model.  **20 – 6**	Subtract from 20 Fact Flashcards Build on Choice of Math Tool  **20 – 8**	Pull and Build Subtract from 20 on Beaded Number Line 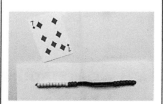 Encourage students to think of the pairs of numbers that combine to make 10 rather than counting by ones. Since 7 + 3 = 10, then 20 – 7 must be 13.

FIGURE 6.48 Concrete Activities

PICTORIAL ACTIVITIES

Subtract from 20 Pictorial Activities		
Students pull a flashcard with an expression and act it out on a rekenrek. They then record their work on the template. They draw a model and write the equation with the answer. 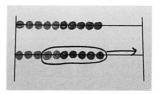 **20 – 7 = 13**	Students pull a card with an expression and act it out with a cube tower. They then record their work on the cube template. They draw a model and write the equation with the answer.  **20 – 12 = 8**	Draw on a Double 10 Frame 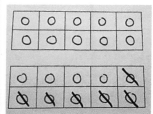 **20 – 6 = 14**

FIGURE 6.49 Pictorial Activities

ABSTRACT ACTIVITIES

Subtract from 20 Abstract Activities		
Subtract from 20 on an Open Number Line 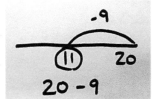 OR 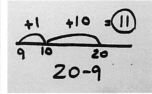	Subtract on a vertical number line. Students pull a flashcard and act out the equation on the number line. 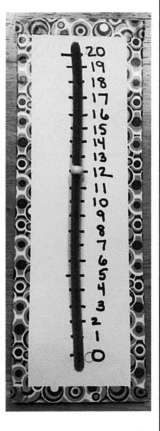 $20 - 8 = 12$	Subtract from 20 War Pull 2 flashcards and whoever has the largest difference wins that hand and gets the 2 cards. Whoever has the most cards at the end of the game is the winner. $20 - 7$ $20 - 9$

FIGURE 6.50 Abstract Activities

STRATEGY FLASHCARDS

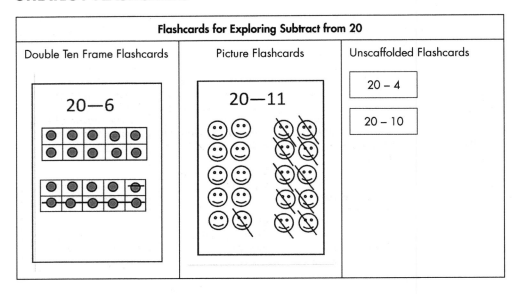

FIGURE 6.51 Strategy Flashcards

MORE STRATEGY FLASHCARDS

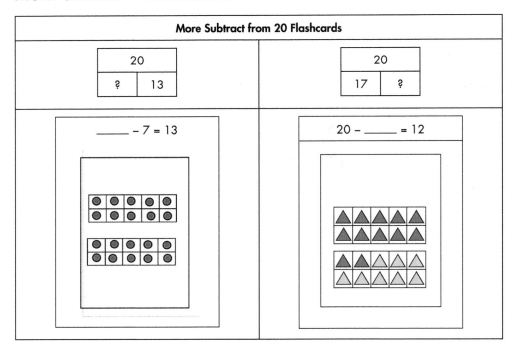

FIGURE 6.52 More Strategy Flashcards

WORD PROBLEMS

In every fluency module there should be a focus on word problems. Here are a few examples of the types of word problems for subtract from 20.

| **My Subtract from 20 Story Problems Booklet** | **There were 20 vegetables on the table. 6 were carrots and the rest were green beans. How many green beans were there?**

Write the set-up equation:

Show your thinking with a model.

Write the solution equation. | **There were 20 people waiting in line for a roller coaster that fits 12 riders. How many will not be able to ride the next time?**

Write the set-up equation:

Show your thinking with a model.

Write the solution equation. | **Walt had 20 tickets to the carnival and Lili had 8. How many more tickets did Walt have than Lili?**

Write the set-up equation:

Show your thinking with a model.

Write the solution equation. |

FIGURE 6.53 Word Problems

RESOURCES

Videos

Videos about Subtract from 20
Ann Elise's video on Subtracting Bridge 20: https://youtu.be/NsVGOaXTXPM

FIGURE 6.54 Videos

Online Games

Online Games about Subtract from 20
https://www.mathplayground.com/ASB_MinusMission.html
https://www.mathplayground.com/math_monster_subtraction.html
https://www.mathplayground.com/puzzle_pics_subtraction_facts_to_20.html
https://www.multiplication.com/games/subtraction-games
https://www.topmarks.co.uk/maths-games/5-7-years/addition-and-subtraction

FIGURE 6.55 Online Games

Anchor Chart

There are many different ways to subtract from 20.

We can count up!

We can count back!

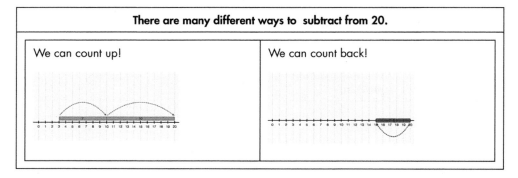

FIGURE 6.56 Anchor Chart

Quiz

Subtracting from 20 Quiz

Name: Date:

20 – 2 = Model with a drawing.	20 – 6 = Model on the double 10 frame. (blank double ten frame) 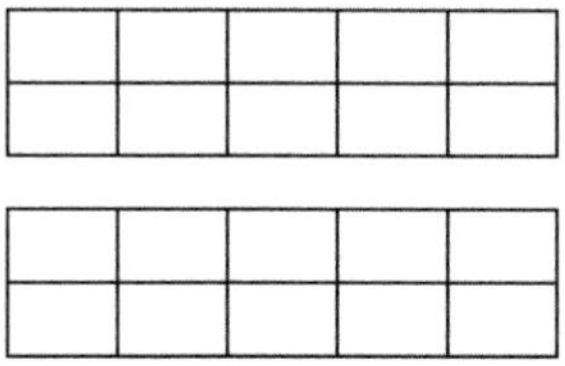	Solve. Rose had 20 beads. She gave 7 of them to her friends. How many did she have left? Write the equation: Answer: _____
Solve. There were 20 sea creatures on the beach. 11 of them were sea stars and the rest were crabs. How many of the sea creatures were crabs? Write the equation: Answer: _____	Solve. 20 – _____ = 15 _____ – 2 = 18 3 = 20 – _____ _____ = 20 – 9	Which addition problem can help you solve 20 – 3? a. 20 + 3 b. 3 + 17 c. 12 + 5 d. none of these

20 – 4 =

Model on the number line.

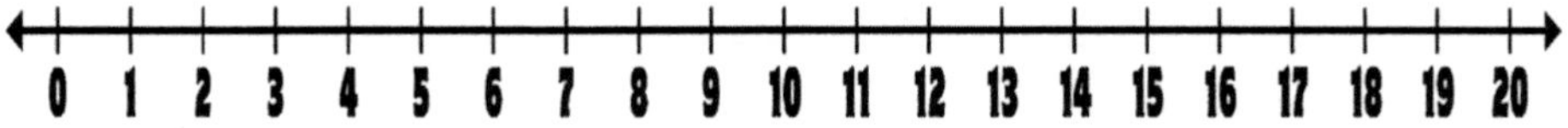

What is the Subtract from 20 strategy? Explain with numbers, words and pictures.

Circle how good you think you are at doing Subtract From 20 facts!

Great   Good   OK, still thinking

FIGURE 6.57 Quiz

KEY POINTS

Subtraction continuum:
- facts above 10 in the subtraction continuum subtracting a 1 or 10 from a teen number
- subtracting using a half facts strategy
- subtracting using a Bridging 10 strategy
- subtracting using fact families
- subtracting from 20.

SUMMARY

Subtraction within 20 is a foundational set of skills. Students need several opportunities to work with these number combinations. Scaffolding them in the research-based continuum helps students to work and practice with one set of ideas before moving on to a more advanced set of ideas. Scaffolding the activities and allowing for student independent practice allows everyone to work in their zone of proximal development so that everyone can get to where they need to be by the end of the year. Activities should be scaffolded so that students can build conceptual understanding, work on pictorial representations, and make sense of the abstract representations.

REFLECTION QUESTIONS

1. How is your personal strategic competence with subtraction? What did you learn in this chapter?
2. How will this impact your pedagogy?
3. Where will you begin?

REFERENCES

Henry, V., & Brown, R. (2008). First-grade basic facts: An investigation into teaching and learning of an accelerated, high-demand memorization standard. *Journal for Research in Mathematics Education*, 399(2), 153–183.

Van de Walle, J. A. (2007). *Elementary and middle school mathematics: Teaching developmentally*. Boston, MA: Pearson/Allyn and Bacon.

PART IV

Other Crucial Elements

CHAPTER 7

Assessing Basic Fact Fluency

Teachers who use timed tests believe that the tests help children to learn basic facts. Children who perform well under time pressure display their skills. Children who have difficulty with skills, or who work more slowly, run the risk of reinforcing wrong learning under pressure. In addition, children can become fearful and negative towards their math learning.

(Burns, 2000, p. 157)

Assessment is a pivotal piece in the instruction cycle. There are many different types of assessment (see Research Connection). In this chapter we want to look at how to develop an assessment cycle that informs what we do and how we do it every day. Students should be part of the process and involved in the conversations and plans based on the assessments. We will use the five elements of mathematical proficiency (Kilpatrick et al., 2001) to inform our discussion. Within this discussion we will look at the ways to assess the five elements of fluency: accuracy, flexibility, efficiency, appropriateness, and automaticity.

ASSESSING CONCEPTUAL UNDERSTANDING

Assessing for conceptual understanding involves looking at what students know about the concept. Do they understand the math that they are doing? Can they explain the math that they are doing? Here are some examples.

RESEARCH CONNECTION

NCTM (2000) notes that "students exhibit computational fluency when they demonstrate *flexibility* in the computational methods they choose, *understand* and can explain these methods, and produce accurate answers *efficiently*. The computational methods that a student uses should be based on mathematical ideas that the student understands well, including the structure of the base-ten number system, properties of multiplication and division, and number relationships"

(p. 152)

SHORT ESSAYS

There are different types of short essays that you can do with students (see Figure 7.1). You can give them one of these prompts and then they can write about it.

What is addition? Show your thinking with numbers, words and pictures.	What are doubles facts? Why do we use them?	Why do we use math addition strategies?
What is subtraction? Show your thinking with numbers, words and pictures.	How can thinking about 7 + 7 help you with 7 + 6?	Why do we use math subtraction strategies?

FIGURE 7.1 Short Essays

There is also a twist to this structure called the one-minute essay (see Figure 7.2).

Format for 1-Minute Essay

Step 1: Give the students a writing prompt.

Step 2: Let them write for 1 minute.

Step 3: They then stop and switch papers with someone.

Step 4: Give the students "1 minute" to write during the switch – they write in a different color and add to their partner's essay.

Step 5: Then "Switch" Back. The students have another 30 seconds to add to their essay.

FIGURE 7.2 One-Minute Essay

ASSESSING PROCEDURAL FLUENCY

Assessing for procedural fluency gives the student an opportunity to show that they know how to do the math they are doing (see Figure 7.3). These types of assessments require that students do the math, explain what they are doing, and look at the math that others are doing and give helpful observations, ask good questions, and give advice on procedures.

How do you do the "count on strategy?"	How can you show the "counting on strategy" on the number line?	Can you explain how you use "doubles" to help with "doubles plus 1 facts"?
How could you model addition using the number line?	What is the answer to 5 + 7? How do you know that you are correct?	Can you explain how to use 7 + 7 to help with 14 − 7?

FIGURE 7.3 Procedural Fluency

When students have a solid understanding of the concept and they have been working with the procedure for a while, we eventually expect them to have "automaticity." Automaticity is the instant recall of a fact. Research defines it as knowing the answer within three seconds (Kling and Bay-Williams, 2015).

We want all of our students to eventually have instant recall so that they are not bogged down in the small steps of a larger mathematical problem. If students don't have automaticity, especially when working with multi-digit numbers, they get bogged down calculating each individual fact and they are exhausted and have no energy left to think through the rest of the problem (Bjorklund et al., 1990). When students know their facts automatically, it frees up cognitive space to concentrate on the other parts of a math problem (Poncy et al., 2006). But recall isn't the first thing that you teach, nor should it be the most important aspect of learning basic math facts. The research resoundingly states that computational fluency is multidimensional (speed and accuracy, flexibility and efficiency) (Kilpatrick et al., 2001; Brownell, 1956/1987; Brownell & Chazal, 1935; Carpenter et al., 1998). As Boaler (2015) points out, "The brain researchers concluded that automaticity should be reached through understanding of numerical relations, achieved through thinking about number strategies (Delazer et al., 2005)."

> We strongly believe that students learn and own their basic facts through a combination of exposure to others, working it out for yourself, playing with concrete materials, experimenting with different forms of representation, and then rehearsing the acquired knowledge unit within your immediate memory, transferring it into long-term memory, and having it validated thousands of times.
>
> (Hattie & Yates, 2014, p. 57)

ASSESSING ADAPTIVE REASONING

Assessing for reasoning is about seeing if students can think logically. So, asking them questions that require them to think and explain their reasoning is an important part of the assessment cycle. Oftentimes, we give procedural assessments but we need to make sure that we are assessing all of the areas of mathematical proficiency. Worked examples are great ways to do reasoning conversations.

WORKED EXAMPLES

Worked examples are activities where the students are literally given a "worked example." (See Figures 7.5, 7.9, 7.10, 7.13, and 7.16.) They are told whether the worked example is correct or incorrect and then the students are asked a series of questions about the worked example. Immediately after, they are given another example to practice. The caveat here is not to give the incorrect worked example to students before they fully understand the actual concept. This being said, these are great activities to do with students to get them to reason about the math they are doing. Worked examples should be given, discussed in depth, and then a new problem given to the students to practice. It is important to center the discussion around the "why" and not to just discuss the "what" of the worked example (McGinn et al., 2015). In the worked example the teacher is trying to further deepen conceptual understanding and procedural fluency of the topic through reasoning.

On the Zones Math blog (http://zonesmath.weebly.com/) they have great examples of modifying language for English Language Learners. I added the word bank that they have on their examples because I think that it is a great idea for all learners. Remember that math is a second language for native English speakers and a third language for students who are learning English. It is important that we scaffold math language at all grades for all students (see Figure 7.4).

Original Problem	Worked Answer	Question	Corrected Answer	New Prompt
2 + _____ = 10	Joe said the answer was 12. He is incorrect.	Who can tell me why he is incorrect? Why do you think he did that? What should he have done?	So Nancy is saying that he added both sides. That is how he got 12. But 2 + 12 does not equal 10. So we have to go back to the idea that the equal sign means "the same as". We need to make this side (the left side) the same as the right side. So 2 + what number makes 10? How could we figure that out? How could we use our tools to model our thinking?	Well let's try this one: 4 + _____ = 9

FIGURE 7.4 Worked Example

What's the Mistake?

Look at this problem.
Kayla made a mistake.
Do you see her mistake?
What did she do wrong?
How can we fix it?

12 + 4 = 8

Words to use:	
Addition	**Add**
Equal sign	**Count up**
Same as	**Number line**
Addend	**Double ten frame**

Explain what she did wrong. Now do it correctly.

4 + _____ = 8

FIGURE 7.5 What's the mistake?

ASSESSING FOR REASONING THROUGH QUESTIONING

Open Questions: There are several types of problems and questions that we can ask our students (see Figure 7.6). Depth of knowledge is a framework that encourages us to ask questions that require that students think, reason, explain, defend, and justify their thinking (Webb, 2002). Here is a snapshot of what that can look like in terms of fluency work.

DOK Levels	Addition	Subtraction	Word Problems	Equality
DOK Level 1 (these are questions where students are required to simply recall/ reproduce an answer/do a procedure)	What is the sum? 4 + 5 = __	What is the difference? 10 – 5 = __	Kate had 10 rings. She gave away 5. How many does she have left?	5 + 3 = 3 + __ Fill in the blank to make the equation true.
DOK Level 2 (these are questions where students have to use information, think about concepts and reason)	What is the missing addend? 4 + __ = 9	What is the missing number? 10 – __ = 5	Tell me a subtraction story where the answer is 5.	5 + __ = 5 10 – __ = 10 What number makes both equations true? 1) 1 2) 2 3) 0
DOK Level 3 (these are questions where students have to reason, plan, explain, justify and defend their thinking)	What addends could we use to make 9? __ + __ = 9	What 2 numbers could we use to make the equation true? __ – __ = 5	Tell a story about this model. Write an equation. Explain your thinking. Justify your answer. 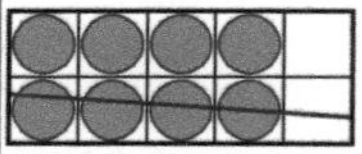 	2 + 3 = __ – __ Fill in the blanks to make the equation true.

FIGURE 7.6 Depth of Knowledge

A great resource for asking open questions is Marion Small's *Good Questions: Great Ways to Differentiate Mathematics Instruction in the Standards-Based Classroom* (2017).Also see (Kaplinsky: https://robertkaplinsky.com/tag/depth-of-knowledge-dok/; Kentucky: www.centralriversaea.org/wp-content/uploads/2017/03/G_math_samples-Revised-5.26.17.pdf)

STRATEGIC COMPETENCE

Assessing for strategic competence involves looking at student thinking about how to work with numbers. We are looking to see if they are flexible and efficient. Being flexible requires that students can think about numbers in a variety of ways. It means that they can look at structure and pattern and think about different ways to take apart, put together, and combine numbers. Efficiency means that students can see quick and easy ways to take apart, put together, and combine numbers. These two things actually go hand in hand; meaning that in order to be efficient, you have to be flexible. It is the flexibility that allows students to be efficient. Here are some prompts to assess for both these things (see Figure 7.7).

Flexibility	Flexibility	Efficiency	Efficiency
How can we add 8 + 6 in two different ways?	If your friend was stuck on 9 + 5, what would you tell them to do?	What is an efficient way to solve 7 + 6?	What is an efficient way to think about 14 – 7?

FIGURE 7.7 Fluency (see Kling &; Bay-Williams, 2014 &; 2019; Also see https://howwe teach.com/17-prompts-for-writing-in-mathematics-and-why-it-even-matters/)

PRODUCTIVE DISPOSITION

A productive disposition is just as important as the other four elements. We need students to be confident, competent, risk-taking mathematicians. Students must learn in environments where they are required to be public mathematicians – meaning that they must think out loud, discuss their ideas, and think about and respond to others' thinking. There are four major factors that impact a productive disposition: (1) the teacher, (2) past mathematical experiences, (3) the family, (4) peers and culture (Mtetwa & Garofalo, 1989).

What happens between the teacher and the students and what happens in terms of the mathematical environment greatly impacts what students can and will do. We have to help students by not "helping them immediately" but by getting them to help themselves. We have to teach them to use their tools to think. We have to let them engage in the productive struggle rather than stealing the struggle (see Research Connection). Remember there are three types of struggle: (1) productive struggle, (2) no struggle, (3) unproductive struggle. We know that when students engage in productive struggle they learn and soar to new heights of knowledge. We must scaffold the struggle. We need students to continually think about what they are learning, how they are doing in learning it, and what they might need to help them. Throughout the learning of facts, students are asked to reflect on what they know, what they are learning, and how they are doing (see Figure 7.8).

Don't Steal the Struggle!
When students are stuck – don't save them! Let them struggle productively.

In a productive struggle, on the other hand, students grapple with the issues and are able to come up with a solution themselves, developing persistence and resilience in pursuing and attaining the learning goal or understanding, says Jackson. In productive struggles, kids have developed the necessary strategies for working through something difficult. They can also take a teacher's suggestions for help and run with them (Jackson & Lambert, 2010) (http://inservice.ascd.org/how-to-tell-when-learning-struggles-are-productive-or-destructive/).

RESEARCH CONNECTION: PRODUCTIVE STRUGGLE

What is easy about addition?

What is tricky about subtraction?

Circle the way that you feel when you think about subtraction?

FIGURE 7.8 Productive Disposition

The research shows that students begin to develop a mathematical disposition at an early age. It is therefore essential that we start thinking about and teaching in ways that develop and foster a productive disposition (Ramirez et al., 2013). It is essential that throughout the process of becoming fluent, students are self-monitoring and assessing their behavior. Students should keep track of where they are and where they need to go next. For example:

		Goal	Practicing	Fluent	
_____ 's Math Addition Fluency Goal Checklist Part A					
 SPLATT!		Adding Zero			
 ZAP!		Adding 1			
 WHAM!		Adding within 10			
		Adding to make 10			

FIGURE 7.9 Self-Monitoring A

Source: Newton, 2016.

+	0	1	2	3	4	5	6	7	8	9	10
0	0 + 0	0 + 1	0 + 2	0 + 3	0 + 4	0 + 5	0 + 6	0 + 7	0 + 8	0 + 9	0 + 10
1	1 + 0	1 + 1	1 + 2	1 + 3	1 + 4	1 + 5	1 + 6	1 + 7	1 + 8	1 + 9	1 + 10
2	2 + 0	2 + 1	2 + 2	2 + 3	2 + 4	2 + 5	2 + 6	2 + 7	2 + 8	2 + 9	2 + 10
3	3 + 0	3 + 1	3 + 2	3 + 3	3 + 4	3 + 5	3 + 6	3 + 7	3 + 8	3 + 9	3 + 10
4	4 + 0	4 + 1	4 + 2	4 + 3	4 + 4	4 + 5	4 + 6	4 + 7	4 + 8	4 + 9	4 + 10
5	5 + 0	5 + 1	5 + 2	5 + 3	5 + 4	5 + 5	5 + 6	5 + 7	5 + 8	5 + 9	5 + 10
6	6 + 0	6 + 1	6 + 2	6 + 3	6 + 4	6 + 5	6 + 6	6 + 7	6 + 8	6 + 9	6 + 10
7	7 + 0	7 + 1	7 + 2	7 + 3	7 + 4	7 + 5	7 + 6	7 + 7	7 + 8	7 + 9	7 + 10
8	8 + 0	8 + 1	8 + 2	8 + 3	8 + 4	8 + 5	8 + 6	8 + 7	8 + 8	8 + 9	8 + 10
9	9 + 0	9 + 1	9 + 2	9 + 3	9 + 4	9 + 5	9 + 6	9 + 7	9 + 8	9 + 9	9 + 10
10	10 + 0	10 + 1	10 + 2	10 + 3	10 + 4	10 + 5	10 + 6	10 + 7	10 + 8	10 + 9	10 + 10

FIGURE 7.10 Self-Monitoring B

Many people have used the addition grid to help students keep track of how they are progressing. There are different ways to do this.

Give the students an addition grid and as they learn the facts, they color them in. You want students to make connections between facts. Students should realize that if they know 1 + 4 then they also know 4 + 1. Figure 7.11 shows one way it could look as students are coloring in the facts.

+	0	1	2	3	4	5	6	7	8	9	10
0	0 + 0	0 + 1	0 + 2	0 + 3	0 + 4	0 + 5	0 + 6	0 + 7	0 + 8	0 + 9	0 + 10
1	1 + 0	1 + 1	1 + 2	1 + 3	1 + 4	1 + 5	1 + 6	1 + 7	1 + 8	1 + 9	1 + 10
2	2 + 0	2 + 1	2 + 2	2 + 3	2 + 4	2 + 5	2 + 6	2 + 7	2 + 8	2 + 9	2 + 10
3	3 + 0	3 + 1	3 + 2	3 + 3	3 + 4	3 + 5	3 + 6	3 + 7	3 + 8	3 + 9	3 + 10
4	4 + 0	4 + 1	4 + 2	4 + 3	4 + 4	4 + 5	4 + 6	4 + 2	4 + 8	4 + 9	4 + 10
5	5 + 0	5 + 1	5 + 2	5 + 3	5 + 4	5 + 5	5 + 6	5 + 7	5 + 8	5 + 9	5 + 10
6	6 + 0	6 + 1	6 + 2	6 + 3	6 + 4	6 + 5	6 + 6	6 + 7	6 + 8	6 + 9	6 + 10
7	7 + 0	7 + 1	7 + 2	7 + 3	7 + 4	7 + 5	7 + 6	7 + 7	7 + 8	7 + 9	7 + 10
8	8 + 0	8 + 1	8 + 2	8 + 3	8 + 4	8 + 5	8 + 6	8 + 7	8 + 8	8 + 9	8 + 10
9	9 + 0	9 + 1	9 + 2	9 + 3	9 + 4	9 + 5	9 + 6	9 + 7	9 + 8	9 + 9	9 + 10
10	10 + 0	10 + 1	10 + 2	10 + 3	10 + 4	10 + 5	10 + 6	10 + 7	10 + 8	10 + 9	10 + 10

Color Coded Strategies					
Plus 0	Counting on Facts: Adding 1,2,3	Makes 10	Adding 10	Doubles, Doubles + 1 Doubles + 2	Bridging 7, 8 & 9

FIGURE 7.11 Self-Monitoring C

Another way to do it is to give the students a blank chart. As they learn the facts, then they fill in the facts (see Figure 7.12).

+	0	2	3	4	5	6	7	8	9	10
0										
1										
2										
3										
4										
5										
6										
7										
8										
9										
10										

FIGURE 7.12 Self-Monitoring Blank Chart

SELF-MONITORING FLUENCY SELF-CHECK

Fluency Self-Check

Name: _____

Date: _____

After you take the quiz, think about the statements in the table below. Check the boxes to show what you think.

	Doing Great! 	Doing Good! 	Working on it! 
Accuracy I get the right answer often.			
Flexibility I can think about a problem in more than one way.			
Efficiency I can decide on quick ways to solve a problem.			
Instant Recall I know the answer right away.			

I feel _____ about learning my math facts.

The easy part is …

The tricky part is …

FIGURE 7.13 Self-Monitoring Fluency Self-Check

Source: Newton, 2015 (personal communication).

When students finish a level they get a small certificate; something to celebrate their success (see Figure 7.14)!

FIGURE 7.14 Certificates

MATH RUNNING RECORDS: INDIVIDUAL PROFILES

Math Running Records are the GPS of Math Fact Fluency (Newton, 2016). They help us to know where students are, where they should be going next, and how to help them get there. There is a Math Running Record for every operation. The Running Record has three parts. The first part assesses for automaticity and accuracy. The second part assesses for flexibility and efficiency. The third part taps into the student's mathematical disposition.

Math Running Records are given from the end of kindergarten through middle school (see Figure 7.15). You give them to students until they have learned all of their basic facts. It is an interview assessment that tells us about student thinking, student strategy, and student disposition. It is the beginning of the fluency journey. After the data is collected, it should drive the instruction. Teachers now know what ideas to work on when they do routines, in small guided math groups, in math workstations, and homework. Math Running Records allow us to get very specific about student fact power and they allow us to scaffold steps to success. NCTM (2000) states that "Effective math teaching requires understanding what students know and need to learn and then challenging and supporting them to learn it well."

Math Running Record

Part 1 Student Page

0 + 1	7 + 7
2 + 1	5 + 6
3 + 2	7 + 5
2 + 6	9 + 6
4 + 6	8 + 4

Research-based problems

Part 1 Teacher Page

Addition Running Record Recording sheet

Student: ______________ Teacher: ______________ Date: ______________

Part 1: Initial Observations

Teacher: We are now going to administer Part I of the Running Record. I am going to give you a sheet of paper with some problems. I want you to go from the top to the bottom and tell me just the answer. If you get stuck, you can stop and ask for what you need to help you. If you want to pass, you can. We might not do all of the problems. Let's start.

Part 1	Codes: What do you notice?	Initial Observations of Strategies	Data Code Names
0 + 1 a 5s pth	ca fco cah coh dk wo sc asc	0 1 2 3 4M 4	A0 — add 0
2 + 1 a 5s pth	ca fco cah coh dk wo sc asc	0 1 2 3 4M 4	A1 — add 1
3 + 2 a 5s pth	ca fco cah coh dk wo sc asc	0 1 2 3 4M 4	Aw5 — add within 5
2 + 6 a 5s pth	ca fco cah coh dk wo sc asc	0 1 2 3 4M 4	Aw10 — add within 10
4 + 6 a 5s pth	ca fco cah coh dk wo sc asc	0 1 2 3 4M 4	AM10 — add making 10
10 + 4 a 5s pth	ca fco cah coh dk wo sc asc	0 1 2 3 4M 4	A10 — add 10 to a #
7 + 7 a 5s pth	ca fco cah coh dk wo sc asc	0 1 2 3 4M 4	AD — add doubles
5 + 6 a 5s pth	ca fco cah coh dk wo sc asc	0 1 2 3 4M 4	AD1 — add dbls ±/-1
7 + 5 a 5s pth	ca fco cah coh dk wo sc asc	0 1 2 3 4M 4	AD2 — add dbls ±/-2
9 + 6 a 5s pth	ca fco cah coh dk wo sc asc	0 1 2 3 4M 4	AHF/C9 — add higher facts use compensation w/9
8 + 4 a 5s pth	ca fco cah coh dk wo sc asc	0 1 2 3 4M 4	AHF/C7/8 — add higher facts/use compensation with 7/8
7 + 8 a 5s pth	ca fco cah coh dk wo sc asc	0 1 2 3 4M 4	AHF/C7/8 — add higher facts/use compensation with 7/8
Codes a - automatic 5s – 5 seconds Pth – prolonged thinking time	**Types of Strategies** ca – counted all fco – finger counted on cah – counted all in head dk – didn't know wo – wrong operation sc – self-corrected asc – attempted to self-correct	**Strategy Levels** 0 – doesn't know 1 – counting strategies by ones or skip counting using fingers, drawings or manipulatives 2 – mental math/solving in head 3 – using known facts and strategies 4M – automatic recall from memory 4 – automatic recall and students have number sense	

Part 2 Teacher Recording Sheet

Part 2: Flexibility/Efficiency

Teacher: We are now going to administer Part II of the Running Record. In this part of the Running Record we are going to talk about what strategies you use when you are solving basic addition facts. I am going to tell you a problem and then ask you to tell me how you think about it. I am also going to ask you about some different types of facts. Take your time as you answer and tell me what you are thinking as you see and do the math. I am going to take notes so I can remember everything that happened during this Running Record.

Add 0 0 + 1	Add 1 2 + 1	Add within 5 or 10 3 + 2 2 + 6	Add to Make 10 4 + 6
What happens when you add zero to a number? ________ same # ________ other ________ can't articulate What would be the answer to... 3 + 0 5 + 0 8 + 0 Do they know this strategy? No/Emerging/Yes A0 Level 0 1 2 3 4M 4	What strategy do you use when you add 1 to a number? ________ next counting # ________ other ________ can't articulate What would be the answer to... 4 + 1 7 + 1 10 + 1 Do they know this strategy? No/Emerging/Yes A1 Level 0 1 2 3 4M 4	How do you solve 2 + 3? And 6 + 3? ________ count on from big # ________ other ________ can't articulate within 5 ________ within 10 1 + 3 5 + 4 2 + 2 2 + 7 Do they know this strategy? No/Emerging/Yes A10 Level 0 1 2 3 4M 4	How do you solve 5 + 5? ________ count on from big # ________ other ________ can't articulate I'm going to give you a number and I want you to give me the number that makes 10 with it. If I give you 7, how many more to make 10? If I give you ________ how many more to 10? 9? 2? 6? Do they know this strategy? No/Emerging/Yes AM10 Level 0 1 2 3 4M 4
Add 10 10 + 4 What strategy do you use when you add 10 to a number? ________ teen #s decompose to 10 and 1s ________ other ________ can't articulate How would you solve ________? 10 + 2 10 + 6 10 + 8 Do they know this strategy? No/Emerging/Yes	**Doubles 7 + 7** How would you solve 6 + 6? ________ doubles ________ other ________ can't articulate How would you solve ________? 4 + 4 8 + 8 9 + 9 What kind of facts are these? ________ Do they know this strategy? No/Emerging/Yes	**Doubles +/-1 5 + 6** How would you solve 6 + 7? ________ doubles +/-1 ________ other ________ can't articulate How would you solve ________? 3 + 4 6 + 7 8 + 9 Do they know this strategy? No/Emerging/Yes	**Doubles +/2 7 + 5** If a friend did not know how to solve 7 + 9, what would you tell her to do? ________ doubles +/-2 ________ other ________ can't articulate How would you solve ________? 2 + 4 8 + 6 9 + 11 Do they know this strategy? No/Emerging/Yes

Part 3 Mathematical Disposition

Part 3: Mathematical Disposition

Do you like math?

What do you find easy?

What do you find tricky?

What do you do when you get stuck?

FIGURE 7.15 Math Running Records

Source: Newton, 2016.

COMMON ERRORS

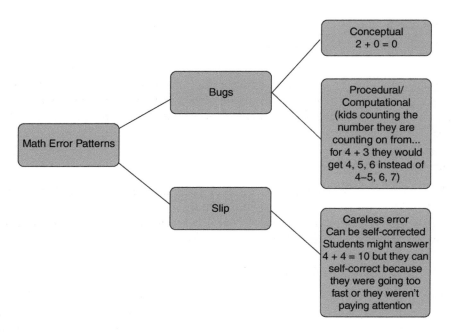

FIGURE 7.16 Common Errors

Source: Illustration of Ginsburg, 1987.

Students have various error patterns when they are adding or subtracting within 20. Here are some common errors and how to address them (Ginsburg, 1987).

Error #1: Miscounting When Adding

When adding, students will count the number they are starting from rather than jumping forward as the first count. For example 4 + 5: students might count 5, 6, 7, 8 rather than 5 … 6, 7, 8, 9.

Correct It: Have students work with life-size number paths so that they can actually see and feel the need to count on from the number. Also, every student should have a number path in their tool kit.

Error #2: Miscounting When Subtracting

When subtracting, students will count the number they are subtracting from rather than counting back from that number. For example 5 - 3: students will say 5, 4, 3 instead of 5 … 4, 3, 2.

Correct It: Have students work with life-size number paths so that they can actually see and feel the need to count on from the number. Also, every student should have a number path in their tool kit.

Error #3: Doing the Wrong Operation

Often when subtracting, students will use the wrong symbol. They will add instead of subtract. Sometimes, this occurs for addition but it is much more common for subtraction.

Correct It: Have students focus in on the symbol. With primary students we will use magic pointers (popsicle sticks or craft sticks) to indicate the symbol and discuss what it means out loud.

Error #4: 0

Students do not understand 0. So often they will say that anything plus 0 is 0 and anything minus 0 is 0.

Correct It: Use story mats and have the students act out problems with 0 so they can see that when you add or subtract 0 the number stays the same.

Error #5: Following Key Words

Students will see words like "altogether" or "total" and immediately add rather than read the problem and think about what it is asking them to do. For example: Sue had 5 marbles. Her sister had 2 more than she did. How many did they have altogether? Students who are using a key word strategy will answer 7. Students who are reading and thinking about the problem will realize that it is 5 + 5 + 2 more and that that will make 12 altogether.

Correct It: Always have students tell what the story is about and what they are looking for. Starting in 1st grade, students are supposed to be able to write an equation with a symbol for the unknown. The simple truth is that if students know what they are looking for, they are much more likely to find it.

CLASS LISTS

It is important to know where the students are as a class, so that you can form small guided math groups and workstations that meet the needs of your students. (See Figure 7.17.) There are several ways to do this. Dodge (n.d.) discusses using a "system of check-minus, check and check plus or the numbers 4, 3, 2, 1 to indicate student proficiency with the skill."

	A	B	C	D	E	F
1	Student	Teacher	Current Strat	Current Leve	Notes	Inst Focus
2	Bailey, David	Jones	03 - Aw5	1	fca	acc, flex, auto
3	Moore, Karen	Jones	03 - Aw5	1	fca	acc, flex, auto
4	Nichols, Michael	Jones	03 - Aw5	1	fca	acc, flex, auto
5	Styles, Susanne	Jones	03 - Aw5	2	cah	acc, flex, auto
6	Furlong, Donna	Jones	04 - Aw10	1	fco 1st add	acc, flex, auto
7	Duquette, Angela	Jones	04 - Aw10	1	fco larger add	acc, flex, auto
8	Frizzell, Emily	Jones	05 - AM10	1	fco larger add	flex, auto
9	Griffin, Sue	Jones	05 - AM10	1	fco larger add	flex, auto
10	Holt, Heidi	Jones	05 - AM10	1	fco larger add	acc, flex, auto
11	Manning, Benjamin	Jones	05 - AM10	1	fco 1st add	acc, flex, auto
12	Rancourt, Rosemary	Jones	05 - AM10	1	fco larger add	acc, flex, auto
13	Record, Daniel	Jones	05 - AM10	2	coh larger add	flex, auto
14	Rodrigues, Justina	Jones	05 - AM10	2	coh larger add	flex, auto
15	Schersten, Tom	Jones	05 - AM10	2	coh larger add	acc, flex, auto
16	Vig, Elizabeth	Jones	05 - AM10	2	coh larger add	acc, flex, auto
17	Williams, Kylynn	Jones	05 - AM10	2	coh larger add	acc, flex, auto
18	King, Julie	Jones	06 - A10	1	fco 1st add	flex, auto
19	Chappell, Cordelia	Jones	07 - AD	1	fco larger add	flex, auto
20	Kotkowski, Jillian	Jones	07 - AD	1	fco 1st add	flex, auto
21	Kane, Darcy	Jones	07 - AD	2	hco larger add	acc, flex, auto
22	Valliere, Meg	Jones	07 - AD	2	hco larger add	flex, auto
23	Nolin, Ann	Jones	08 - AD1	1	fco larger add	flex, auto
24	Losier, Joele	Jones	09 - AD2	1	fco larger add	flex, auto
25	Magrath, Lindsey	Jones	12 - DONE	4		auto

FIGURE 7.17 Class Notes

Source: Record's adaptation of Newton, 2016.

From this data spreadsheet of a 1st grade classroom, we can see what students know and what they need to learn. We can also decide on the groups that need to be pulled and what they need to work on. We can see that David, Karen, Michael, and Susanne should all be working on Adding within 5. We can also see that there is a large number of students who are working on their Add Make 10 pairs. If we look further, there is a subgroup of these students who are currently using their fingers and another group that is using mental math. We can then subdivide this group and respond instructionally to move them all to the next level in the progression. There are several students who are working with sums within 20. Before students work on these fluency strategies, we will want to be sure that their Subtract within and from 10 fluency is solid so that we can be sure to be exploring the inverse relationship between addition and subtraction all along the fluency journey.

KEY POINTS

- conceptual assessments
- procedural assessments
- reasoning assessments
- strategic assessments
- productive disposition assessments.

SUMMARY

Assessment should be an ongoing part of the instructional cycle. We need to consciously *assess for learning* so that we know what to do next (Stiggins & Guskey, 2007). Guskey (2007) notes that we must "use assessments as sources of information for both students and teachers" and that our assessments must be followed up "with high-quality corrective instruction" and that we must allow our students the opportunity to practice it until they can "demonstrate success."

We need to make sure that we frame our assessments around the elements of mathematical proficiency. We need to check for conceptual understanding, procedural fluency, adaptive reasoning, strategic competence, and a productive disposition. Our assessment should take many forms and provide us a "photo album" of learning rather than just a "snapshot" (Tomlinson & McTighe, 2006). Assessment doesn't just happen, we have to plan for it (see Figure 7.18).

REFLECTION QUESTIONS

1. What does your school currently use for assessment of your students' math thinking?
2. Has the information shared in this chapter changed your thinking surrounding assessments?
3. What is one assessment you would like to introduce to your classroom or school?

Assessments for Building Mathematical Proficiency				
Conceptual Understanding	Procedural Fluency	Strategic Competence	Adaptive Reasoning	Productive Disposition
Quick Quiz 1 Minute Essay Mini-Interview Entrance and Exit Slip	Quick Quiz 1 Minute Essay Mini-Interview Entrance and Exit Slip	Quick Quiz 1 Minute Essay Mini-Interview Entrance and Exit Slip	Quick Quiz 1 Minute Essay Mini-Interview Entrance and Exit Slip	Marzano self (checks) Mini-Interview Entrance and Exit Slip

FIGURE 7.18 Assessments

REFERENCES

Bay-Williams, J. & Kling, G. (2019). Math Fact Fluency: 60+ Games and Assessment Tools to Support Learning and Retention. Reston, VA: ASCD.

Bay-Williams, J. & Kling, G. (2014). Assessing Basic Fact Fluency. Reston, VA: NCTM.

Bjorklund, D. F., Muir-Broaddus, J. E., & Schneider, W. (1990). The role of knowledge in the development of strategies. In D. F. Bjorklund (Ed.), *Children's strategies: Contemporary views of cognitive development* (pp. 93–128). Hillsdale, NJ: Erlbaum.

Boaler, J. (2015). Fluency without fear. Retrieved May 15, 2019 from www.youcubed.org/evidence/fluency-without-fear/.

Brownell, W. A. (1956/1987). Meaning and skill: Maintaining the balance. *Arithmetic Teacher*, 34(8), 18–25.

Brownell, W. A., & Chazal, C. B. (1935). The effects of premature drill in third-grade arithmetic. *The Journal of Educational Research*, 29(1), 17–28.

Burns, M. (1941/2000). *About teaching mathematics: A K-8 resource*. Sausalito, CA: Math Solutions Publications.

Carpenter, T. P., Franke, M. L., Jacobs, V. R., Fennema, E., & Empson, S. B. (1998). A longitudinal study of invention and understanding in children's multidigit addition and subtraction. *Journal for Research in Mathematics Education*, 29(1), 3–20. https://doi.org/10.2307/749715.

Dodge, J. (nd). *25 quick assessments for a differentiated classroom*. New York: Scholastic.

Ginsburg, H. P. (1987). How to assess number facts, calculation, and understanding. In D. D. Hammill (Ed.), *Assessing the abilities and instructional needs of students* (pp. 483–503). Austin, TX: Pro-Ed.

Guskey, T. (2007). Using assessments to improve teaching and learning. In D. Reeves (Ed.), *Ahead of the curve: The power of assessment to transform teaching and learning* (pp. 14–29). Bloomington, IN: Solution Tree.

Hattie, J., & Yates, G. C. R. (2014). *Visible learning and the science of how we learn*. Abingdon, Oxon & New York: Routledge.

Kilpatrick, J., Swafford, J., & Findell, B. (2001). *Adding it up: Helping children learn mathematics*. Washington, DC: National Academy Press.

Kling, G., & Bay-Williams, J. M. (2015). Three steps to mastering multiplication facts. *Teaching Children Mathematics*, 21(9), 548.

McGinn, K., Lange, K., & Booth, J. (2015). A worked example for creating worked examples. *Mathematics Teaching in the Middle School*, 21(1), 26–33.

Mtetwa, D., & Garofalo, J. (1989). Beliefs about mathematics: An overlooked aspect of student difficulties. *Academic Therapy*, 24(5), 611–618.

National Council of Teachers of Mathematics. (2000). *Principles and standards for school mathematics*. Reston, VA: National Council of Teachers of Mathematics.

Newton, R. (2016). *Math running records*. Abingdon, Oxon & New York: Routledge.

Poncy, B. C., Skinner, C. H., & O'Mara, T. (2006). Detect, practice, and repair: The effects of a classwide intervention on elementary students' math fact fluency. *Journal of Evidence Based-Practices for Schools*, 7(1), 47–68.

Ramirez, G., Gunderson, E. A., Levine, S. C., & Beilock, S. L. (2013). Math anxiety, working memory, and math achievement in early elementary school. *Journal of Cognition and Development*, 14(2), 187–202.

Small, M. (2012). *Good questions: Great ways to differentiate mathematics instruction*. New York: Columbia University, Teachers College, Bureau of Publications.

Stiggins, R., & Guskey, T. (2007). Assessment for learning: An essential foundation of productive instruction. In D. Reeves (Ed.), *Ahead of the curve: The power of assessment to transform teaching and learning* (pp. 59–78). Bloomington, IN: Solution Tree.

Tomlinson, C. A., & McTighe, J. (2006). *Integrating differentiated instruction & understanding by design: Connecting content and kids.* Alexandria, VA: Association for Supervision and Curriculum Development.

Webb, N. (2002). An analysis of the alignment between mathematics standards and assessments for three states. Paper presented at the annual meeting of the American Educational Research Association, New Orleans, LA.

CHAPTER 8

Doing Daily Fluency Routines

Number flexes are daily routines that focus on building fluency. They are called number flexes because they build flexibility. These routines emphasize accuracy, flexibility, and efficiency. In this chapter we will discuss ten number flexes (see Figures 8.1–8.10). Research says that teachers should do fluency practice every day for at least ten minutes (IES, 2009).

NUMBER FLEX 1: SUBITIZING

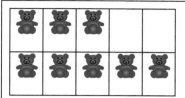

Subitizing – Quick Images

Activity: *Subitizing is a routine that is done throughout the grades. In k-2, the focus of subitizing is for students to recognize quick images at first at a perceptual level (seeing and recognizing small amounts) and then at a conceptual level where they can talk about the ways in which they see the given number such as 3 and 2 make 5.* Clements points out that for students who can do this, "this more advanced ability to group and quantify sets quickly in turn supports their development of number sense and arithmetic (1999, p.401)." For example: Teacher flashes the dice:

Students might say: I see 3 and 3 and 1. That makes 7.

I can statement:
I can reason about numbers and explain and justify my thinking. I can listen to, understand and respond to the thinking of others and decide whether or not their reasoning makes sense.

Purpose
➤ Reason
➤ Generalize math concepts
➤ Defend their thinking

Materials and Tools
Teachers should use both the concrete cards as well as the virtual sets for subitizing.

Concrete Cards	Virtual Sets

Protocol
Overview: The teacher flashes a number card and the students have to state what they saw. The teacher flashes a number on the cards or digitally. The teacher tells the students to take "private think time" to think about what they saw. The teacher asks the students "What did you see?" Notice that this is different than "How many were there?" The first question gets at breaking apart the numbers and analyzing them. Students respond with things like "I see 2 and 2 and that makes 4".

Questions:
• **What do you see?**
• **How did you see it?**
• **Is there another way to see it?**

FIGURE 8.1 Subitizing

NUMBER FLEX 2: WHAT DOESN'T BELONG?

2 + 2	3 + 1
4 + 4	5 + 5

10 – 5	11 – 6
2 + 3	3 + 2 + 0

What Doesn't Belong?	
Activity: *The What Doesn't Belong Routine* is a routine that focuses on reasoning across different mathematics topics. Students are presented with a variety of options and they have to figure out *which one is not like the others.* They can work by themselves, in pairs, small groups and as a whole group to determine what doesn't belong. Resources: http://wodb.ca/	**I can statement:** **I can** reason about numbers and explain and justify my thinking. I can listen to, understand and respond to the thinking of others and decide whether or not their reasoning makes sense. **Purpose:** ➢ **Reason** ➢ **Generalize math concepts** ➢ **Defend their thinking** **Materials and Tools** Students should have a variety of tools to think and reason about the ideas being discussed. They should use their toolkits. Students can use manipulatives, drawings and mental math.
Protocol Overview: The teacher puts the square template on the board and asks the students which one doesn't belong. The students have to reason about which one doesn't belong and justify their answer. Sometimes there is more than one answer.	**Questions:** • **How do you know that?** • **Are you sure about that?** • **Can you prove it?** • **Can you show me another way?** • **Does that make sense?** • **Does this always work?**

FIGURE 8.2 What Doesn't Belong?

NUMBER FLEX 3: I WAS WALKING DOWN THE STREET

 *I was walking down the street!*

Activity: This routine is about getting students to be flexible with their numbers. It requires them to compose and decompose numbers in a variety of ways quickly. The teacher basically tells a story in which an answer is given. The students have to think about and then discuss what was the question.	**I can statement:** **I can** think flexibly about numbers. **Purpose** • **Compose and decompose whole numbers** **Materials and Tools** Students should have a variety of tools to think and reason about the numbers being discussed. They should use their toolkits. Students can use manipulatives, drawings and mental math.
Protocol Overview: The teacher gives the students a number and asks them how they could compose it. For example: Teacher: I was walking down the street and I heard Tom say 12. I was wondering what was the question? Student A: 6 + 6 Student B: 14 − 2 Student C: 4 + 4 + 4 The teacher can set different criteria like: there were only 3 numbers or they didn't use addition.	**Questions:** ✓ **What could be the question?** ✓ **What are some ways to make this number?** ✓ **What are some ways to break this number up?** ✓ **Are you sure?**

FIGURE 8.3 I Was Walking Down the Street

NUMBER FLEX 4: NUMBER TALKS

Number Talks	
Activity: Number talks are teacher led discussions that occur for about 5 -10 minutes where students discuss different ways to solve problems. The teacher gives the students an expression to think about and solve mentally. Then students share and discuss their strategies. Resources: http://mathperspectives.com/number-talks/ Making Number Talks Matter – Humphries and Parker Number Talks – Sherry Parrish	**I can statement:** *I can add and subtract numbers using strategies.* **Purpose:** • Think and reason about numbers. • Develop flexibility, efficiency, accuracy and automaticity with whole numbers, fractions and decimals **Materials and Tools** Students should have a variety of tools to think and reason about the numbers being discussed. They should use their toolkits. Students can use manipulatives, drawings and mental math.
Protocol: The teacher gives the student an expression and the students talk about different ways to solve the problem. For example: Teacher: Let's talk about 8 + 9 today. If you have a strategy show me 1 finger, if you have 2 strategies show me 2 fingers. (wait time) Ok. Who has an answer? Teacher records answers: 17 18 19 (without any reaction to responses) Ok, who wants to defend one of the answers. Student A: I did 8 + 8 and that is 16 and 1 more makes 17. Student B: I did 9 + 9 and that is 18 and then I took away 1, that is 17. Student C: I counted up from 9 and I got 17. Teacher: Ok let's think and talk about these strategies. Mica, what do you call the strategy you used? Mica: Doubles Plus 1 *(conversation continues).*	**Questions:** ✓ **Who wants to defend their thinking?** ✓ **What did you do exactly?** ✓ **Can you lead us through the steps?** ✓ **Tell us why you did that?** ✓ **What are some different ways that you might solve this problem?**

FIGURE 8.4 Number Talks

NUMBER FLEX 5: TRUE OR FALSE?

 True or False?

Activity: True or False is a routine that focuses on reasoning. Students are presented with mathematical statements that are either true or false. They must reason about those statements, with themselves, in pairs, small groups and as a whole group to determine whether or not the statements make mathematical sense.

True	False
$3 + 5 = 8$	$11 = 5 + 7$
$4 + 2 = 7 - 1$	

$4 + 5 = 9$
$5 + 7 = 14 - 3$

I can statement:
I can reason about numbers and explain and justify my thinking. I can listen to, understand and respond to the thinking of others and decide whether or not their reasoning makes sense.

Purpose
- Reason alone
- Reason with others and follow their thinking
- To determine whether something is true or false
- To defend one's thinking
- To defend the thinking of another

Materials and Tools
Students should have a variety of tools to think and reason about the numbers being discussed. They should use their toolkits. Students can use manipulatives, drawings and mental math.

Protocol
Overview: The teacher puts some mathematical concept on the board and the students have to vote whether or not it is true or false.
- The teacher puts a mathematical concept on the board.
- The teacher tells the students to take "private think time" to think about the concept.
- After about 30 seconds the teacher tells the students to "turn and talk to a neighbor."
- Everyone comes back together and students raise their hand:
    - thumbs up if they think it is true
    - thumbs down if they think it is false
    - thumbs sideways if they are not sure.
The teacher calls on various students to explain their thinking.

Questions:
- **How do you know that?**
- **Are you sure about that?**
- **Can you prove it?**
- **Can you show me another way?**
- **Does that make sense?**
- **Does this always work?**

FIGURE 8.5 True or False?

NUMBER FLEX 6: I LOVE MATH

The *I Love Math* Routine

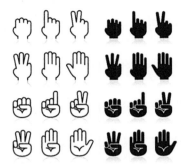

5 + 3

Game:	I can statement:
This is a quick game for students to work on their basic fact fluency. It is played like Rock Paper Scissors. Instead of throwing rock, paper or scissors the students throw a number in the form of fingers. Depending on the grade the winner is decided in different ways. For example, students each throw out a number on 1 hand; whoever says the sum of the two numbers first wins. They just keep playing over and over again. It is important for students to start with throwing out just 1 hand (and practicing fluency within 10) and then eventually throwing out 2 hands (and practicing fluency within 20).	I can state my math facts. **Purpose:** To work on addition and subtraction facts with fluency. **Materials and Tools:** Students just use their hands.
Protocol Overview: The students get in pairs (often with teacher direction) and they play. 1. Get in pairs. 2. Say "I Love Math". 3. Then throw out 1 hand. (Start with 1 hand and then work up to two hands.) 4. Whoever calls out the sum or product first wins.	**Questions:** What strategies did you use today? What facts were easy? What facts were challenging?

FIGURE 8.6 I Love Math

NUMBER FLEX 7: VIRTUAL DICE

 Virtual Dice

Activity: *Virtual dice rolls are just meant to build flexibility. There are several virtual dice sites on the internet as well as some that are built into different interactive boards. The teacher or the students roll the dice and then the teacher asks a variety of questions based on the grade level.*
http://www.curriculumbits.com/ mathematics/virtual-dice/(a personal favorite with sound effects)
http://dice.virtuworld.net/
https://www.random.org/dice/?num=2
https://www.freeonlinedice.com/#dice

I can statement:
I can reason about numbers and explain and justify my thinking. I can listen to, understand and respond to the thinking of others and decide whether or not their reasoning makes sense.

Purpose:
➤ Reason about numbers
➤ Explain their thinking
➤ Justify their answers

Materials and Tools
Students should have a variety of tools to think and reason about the numbers being discussed. They should use their toolkits. Students can use manipulatives, drawings and mental math.

Protocol
Overview: There are at least 3 different dice rolls to choose from: single dice, double dice or triple dice. These dice allow for the teacher to ask different questions. The questions could be about flexibility, efficiency, appropriate strategy or accuracy.

Questions:
1. dice: How many more to 10?

2. dice: What strategy would you use to solve this problem?

3. dice: What is the most efficient way to solve this problem?

FIGURE 8.7 Virtual Dice

NUMBER FLEX 8: SPLAT!

This is work by Steve Wyborney (a math genius). He graciously allowed us to discuss two of his number sense routines. He has so many others. Check them all out at http://www.stevewyborney.com/ http://www.stevewyborney.com/?p=893 (splat)

Activity: Splat is a game where students are working with various number combinations. Teacher pulls up a powerpoint and shows it to the students. Each slide has the questions already on it. The students have to figure out what is the missing number and how to decompose it in various ways.	**I can statement:** **I can** reason about numbers and explain and justify my thinking. I can listen to, understand and respond to the thinking of others and decide whether or not their reasoning makes sense. **Purpose:** ➢ Reason ➢ Explain and Justify thinking ➢ Composing and decomposing numbers **Materials:** Splat powerpoints. There are several different versions. There are 5 different powerpoints for each one.
Protocol: Teacher shows the powerpoint. Students discuss it. If there are 7 blue circles in all and we are seeing 3 of them, how many must be under the splat?  In 2-Color splat, if there are 10 circles and we are seeing 5 of them, what are the possibilities of circles that could be under each splat if they have to be different numbers? 	**Questions:** 1. How many do you see? 2. What is a way to figure this out? 3. What are the different ways to make this missing number? 4. What is a strategy that we could use?

FIGURE 8.8 Splat!

Source: Steve Wyborney (used with permission from https://stevewyborney.com/2017/02/splat/).

NUMBER FLEX 9: THE POWER OF COLOR

This is work by Steve Wyborney as well. He graciously allowed us to discuss two of his number sense routines. He has so many others. Check them all out at http://www.stevewyborney.com/

Activity: Teacher gives the students paper with the circles and crayons. The students shade the circles in different colors and write down equations to represent those shadings.	**I can statement:** I can model equations. **Purpose:** ➤ Reason ➤ Explain and justify thinking ➤ Composing and decomposing numbers **Materials:** Power of color powerpoints. There are several different versions.
Protocol: The teacher would give the students this grouping of circles. The students would shade the circles. After they shade the circles, they discuss the equations that match their representations.	**Questions:** 1. Tell us what you saw. 2. Did anybody see it a different way? 3. What are some other possibilities? 4. What would be a really long equation that you could make with this? 5. What could be an equation that had a 0 as an addend? 6. What could be an equation that had a 1 as an addend?

FIGURE 8.9 The Power of Color

Source: Steve Wyborney (used with permission from https://stevewyborney.com/2016/03/the-power-of-color/).

NUMBER FLEX 10: CIRCLE MAP FACTS

Circle Map Facts	
Activity: *Circle maps are a way for students to show the many different ways that they can think about numbers. Students get to think of their own work as well as the work of others because they get the opportunity to look at each others' work.*	**I can statement:** **I can** reason about numbers and explain and justify my thinking. I can listen to, understand and respond to the thinking of others and decide whether or not their reasoning makes sense. **Purpose:** ➢ Reason ➢ Explain and justify thinking ➢ Composing and decomposing numbers **Materials and Tools** Students should have a variety of tools to think and reason about the numbers being discussed. They should use their toolkits. Students can use manipulatives, drawings and mental math.
Protocol Overview: Students get a circle map. They get a minute to think and write about ways to make that number. Then they pass the map to a friend who adds to it. Then they get it back and must add 1 more way. 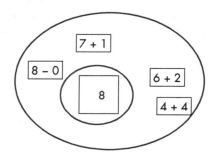	**Questions:** 1. What are some ways to make your target number? 2. What are some ways to make your number by adding? 3. What are some ways to make your number by subtracting? 4. How could you make your number with 3 numbers?

Figure 8.10 Circle Map Facts

KEY POINTS

Number flexes specifically address computational fluency (strategies, models, procedures, flexibility; and efficiency):
- Subitizing
- What Doesn't Belong?
- I Was Walking Down the Street
- Number Talks
- True or False?
- I Love Math
- Virtual Dice Roll
- Splat!
- The Power of Color
- Circle Map Facts.

SUMMARY

Every day, for ten minutes, students should work on fluency. It is the distributed practice across time that allows students to develop a strong sense of number. Engaging students in a variety of energizers and routines where they have to think, reason, listen to others, and justify their answers, builds communication skills. Implementing a variety of activities where there is more than one answer also builds flexibility and efficiency. The many examples included here may be used in any grade and should change and evolve throughout the year to best match current areas of study. Teachers should think about where their students are in the learning trajectory and plan to do these standards-based, academically rigorous, engaging activities throughout the year.

REFLECTION QUESTIONS

1. What routines do you currently use specifically to build fluency?
2. What are three different routines that you might try immediately from this chapter?
3. How well do you emphasize representation of the facts with different models?

REFERENCES

Clements, D. (1999). Subitizing: What is it? Why teach it? *Teaching Children Mathematics*, 5(7), 400–405.

Humphreys, C., & Parker, R. (2015). *Making number talks matter: Developing mathematical practices and deepening understanding*. Maine: Stenhouse.

IES/What Works Clearinghouse. (2009). Retrieved March 23, 2019 from https://ies.ed.gov/ncee/wwc/practiceguide/2.

Parrish, S. (2010). *Number talks: Helping children build mental math and computation strategies, grades K-5*. Sausalito, CA: Math Solutions.

CHAPTER 9

Parental Involvement

MAKING THE MOST OF THE HOME–SCHOOL CONNECTION

Generally speaking, most parents really want to support their kids at home. Research shows, however, that parental involvement in math may be less common than with other subjects such as reading (Sheldon et al., 2010). This is especially true now with all of the changes to the standards. Parents no longer recognize the math that their students are learning. This can make them feel powerless and helpless, which leads to great frustration when trying to help with homework. Because so many math concepts may be foreign to parents, and we may not expect them to be able to support their children at home, it might seem like a no-brainer that we can at least have them support fluency with basic facts. Those are straightforward, right? Wrong … well, sort of.

While it may be tempting to put out the call to parents to support math facts at home, the fact is that while *we* now know that drill and kill will not get the job done, parents may not. Think about how they probably learned, and what their perception of fluency might be. These factors make it highly probable that if left to their own devices, parents will eagerly break out the trusty strategy flashcards and get their drill on. Worse, they will likely focus on speed which, again, is what they probably remember as the focus in their own experience. When they time their kids and drill them, it is all with the best intentions. Therefore, if we want parental support, we must educate them on our goals, share our strategies, and equip them with resources that will support what is happening in the classroom. Research indicates that this is an important part of making the home component more effective (Van Voorhis, 2007).

GETTING PARENTS ON BOARD

Many parents may need to know the rationale for all of these strategies. It all seems so progressive and bizarre. Why not just memorize? We are frequently asked why we are taking this approach, since, after all, the "old way" worked just fine when they were in school. Believe it or not, we welcome that question because if it goes unanswered, it's likely that the support coming from home will undermine what we are trying to accomplish in the classroom. When confronted with that question, or perhaps at Open House if you choose to put it out there, you can try this two-part response.

Part one: give an example of kids getting stuck because they try to memorize instead of reason about numbers. This makes a strong statement. We certainly never want a student to answer like that again nor do we want students to think that the "times tables" are something to learn without a purpose. That purpose is to be able to attack more complex calculations, discover the relationships between numbers, and learn how to manipulate numbers in different situations. Remember, one of the big goals is flexibility. Parents need to understand this.

Part two: ask parents how *they* feel about math. When we have a large audience and ask those who love math to raise their hands, it is always the same: a few sad little hands go up. This speaks volumes about the impact of the former standards and the traditional instruction that accompanied them. The exercise is great because it always provides the opening to share with parents that we are not here to repeat the mistakes of the past. We want better for their kids and so should they. Try this with a group of parents, or maybe at a party with your friends, and see what happens. In our experience, it always has tremendous impact and ends the debate about why we are changing things up.

SHARING THE STRATEGIES

Research consistently indicates that the beliefs and expectations of parents in math predict student achievement in elementary and middle school (Entwisle & Alexander, 1996; Gill & Reynolds, 1999; Halle et al., 1997; Holloway, 1986). Parents are strangers to these strategies, just as most of us were until recently. If we don't clue them in to what the strategies are, they can't participate in the conversation. They need to know the language. If you have the ability to begin a movement in your school, then I suggest starting right out of the gate in kindergarten. The earlier you get parents on board, the easier it is to generate and sustain the momentum needed to get kids fluent by the end of elementary school.

STEP ONE: SHARE THE FOLLOWING WITH PARENTS UP FRONT

- *The names of the strategies.* This is actually an important step as students refer to strategies by name and parents need to know what their kids are talking about. We are pretty sure that Bridging to Ten or Doubles Plus1 doesn't come up in everyday adult conversation unless you're a teacher!
- *What the strategies look like including examples of the strategies in action.* For example for some facts more than one strategy may apply. Parents need to recognize that 9 + 8 can be a double plus 1, a double minus 1, or a bridge to 10. Visuals like ten frames and number lines are helpful to make the connections for them.
- *How you will teach the strategies in your classroom?* What will your students see and hear? What will you use in your instruction? Parents need to know what a rekenrek is, what a ten frame is, how a number line is used, and whatever else you may be doing. One way of sharing this is to have the students write a weekly memo home explaining what they learned. This may include drawings, key vocabulary, and even photos if students are using the computer.

To really bring parents into the process, it is best to include visuals whenever possible and keep the dialogue going throughout the year as strategies are introduced. This could take place in the form of a newsletter, handbook, web page, or series of videos that you produce with your students. (That last suggestion may sound intimidating but can be easily done on a cell phone … no need to be fancy!!) If you really want to generate momentum, consider hosting a parent night where you personally explain the progression of facts, take parents through the strategies, and have their kids show them the models used in the classroom. Again, research has indicated that parents who participate in teacher-led training have students who make greater gains in mathematics (Shaver & Walls, 1998; Starkey & Klein, 2000). While it will take a bit of time to prepare and execute, you will get a huge return on your investment and get parents on your team.

STEP TWO: CREATE A HOMEWORK PLAN

One of the best ways to capitalize on the support of parents is to get them involved in the process every night. As noted by Epstein (2001), communicating with parents, getting them involved, and equipping them with the tools to effectively support learning at home, increases student success. There are many ways to make practice with basic facts meaningful, fun, and way more than just the exercise of flashcards or practice tests that it often has been in the past. Below is a menu of possibilities. What works for others may not work for you, so it may take a bit of trial and error, and possibly customizing an idea to make it your own before you find exactly what system you will use. Keep in mind that successful plans include two-way communication and accountability, so that both you and your parents feel valued in the process.

- *Family games of the week/month.* There are many, many games available for free on the internet that you can easily reproduce. They are fabulous for reinforcing the strategy you are working on while at the same time providing important, purposeful practice for your students. Usually all you need are some dice, perhaps a paper clip for a spinner, something to use as a game piece and you're good to go! This is a favorite suggestion for fact practice because it's engaging, fun, and really gets parents involved in the process.
- *Strategy flashcards.* A step beyond traditional flashcards, strategy flashcards reinforce the strategy along with a visual representation (such as a ten frame, dice model, or array). With strategy flashcards, you can create rings, wallets, or just use old-fashioned baggies. When creating rings of cards for your students, you can differentiate so that they are only practicing what they have yet to learn. As they master facts, they come off the ring. The wallets are similar in that the facts they know are on one side and the facts they are still working on are on the other.

   If you're about keeping it super simple, baggies labeled "all set" and "not yet" help students organize their cards. Because they are strategy flashcards, each time students practice they reinforce the visual model, the strategy used, as well as the solution. Whichever option you choose, you should include an accountability sheet to track and monitor practice each night.
- *Partner games.* With nothing more than a deck of cards, tons of opportunities abound. Whether it be playing War (for addition, subtraction, or multiplication), Salute, or Fact Family Scatter, kids will love practicing their facts. For a really easy partner activity that takes the focus off answer getting and onto strategic reasoning, parents can use traditional flashcards or strategy flashcards, but rather than seek the solution instead question which strategy the child would use and why.
- *Get creative.* Have students and parents work together to make their own activities. Some examples include making Concentration cards (math fact on one card, solution on the other), making board games, or writing questions for a "Who am I?" game (give clues about a specific fact or strategy). For those interested in movement, suggest passing a ball around like a hot potato, but attaching a math fact to it or perhaps making up their own kinesthetic game.

- *Embrace technology.* We are constantly in competition with technology for the attention of our students. If you can't beat them, join them Many parents love to pass off their devices to their kids to keep them busy and entertained. By sharing carefully selected apps (way too many are just drill and kill), and/or websites, you will equip parents with the proper tools to work on math facts.

PROVIDE ONGOING FEEDBACK

For a successful home–school partnership, it is critical to maintain a dialogue with parents (Epstein, 2001). You are continually gathering formative assessment data regarding the progress of their children in terms of fluency with basic facts. Don't wait until report card time to share what you know! Regardless of how you collect your data (hopefully not timed tests, but no judgments!) if parents know what their kids need to work on, they won't waste time working on what they already know. Keeping them in the loop need not be a laborious process. Below are some suggestions for communicating progress.

- *Weekly progress note ~ with a twist.* This note home is not written by you, but by the student! For younger students, you can create a form letter that they simply fill in. The note can share the strategy they are working on, what facts they have mastered, and which they should focus on in the coming week. This is very informative and very validating for students as they master more facts.
- *Communication log.* A communication log can be part of your homework protocol. It can be a two-way form where you quickly jot down a comment, or simply circle facts, to help direct parents to where you have noticed growth and where they should practice more.
- *Pen pal letter.* Allow students to practice their writing skills while sharing their reflections on the week. The letter to their parent(s) should include thoughts about the homework activities for the week (what they liked about the games, how they are feeling, what was tricky, etc.), what facts they want to focus on next week, and where they have felt successful. An additional element that often provides great information is a suggestion by the student about what they think would help them with their math facts.
- *Work samples.* Parents always like to see what their child is working on in school. Simply sending home evidence of what the student has done that week can really help parents to see where their efforts are paying off and where they should be spending more time.
- *Technology.* Platforms such as ClassDojo are great for maintaining communication with parents. Students can also use apps such as Explain Everything to talk through strategies and show how they use tools to support their reasoning.

ADDRESSING PARENTAL CONCERNS

With clear grade-level objectives in most states regarding fact fluency, it is normal for parents to grow concerned when it appears that their child is not progressing at the anticipated rate. Sometimes this is a slippery slope because parents may not honor the time it may take for students to engage in a strategy, and get frustrated because an answer is not produced instantaneously. Although it is the goal for students to become automatic, we know that there are stages that students progress through, and that they will not all progress at the same rate. While there may be different levels of intervention and support available in your school, there are certain ideas that you can share with parents to put their minds at ease.

First and foremost, parents need to understand that children develop at different rates and that each brain is unique. With this in mind, you may discuss different strategies for practice that cater to the learning style of the student. This may include more hands-on manipulation of objects, more written practice, or more daily review while driving in the car, over dinner, or at bedtime. The bottom line, however, is that you may need to reiterate what fluency means and stress that speed is not necessarily indicative of fluency.

Parents may need a gentle nudge to reflect upon how committed they are to the homework process. Do they really put in the suggested amount of time each night? Do they show their child that they believe that practice is important by taking the time to play games or ask questions? In addition to those questions, it is helpful for you to solicit feedback from parents. Ask them questions about where they think their child is struggling and welcome any suggestions that they may offer. You don't have to take them, but they may have some helpful tidbits that you can use. In our opinion, we don't do this enough and as a result we may miss out on valuable insight into the situation that we would otherwise not know.

Depending on the grade level, some parents with concerns may just need to be reassured that their child is fine and that you, the teacher, are not concerned. For example, many parents of 1st graders have unrealistic expectations of what their kids should know and do, and sometimes just knowing that you are comfortable with their progress is enough to ease their worries. This often requires a phone call or a face-to-face conversation to be truly effective. That said, if you follow the aforementioned advice about maintaining ongoing communication, this should not be an issue for you.

If you are the one with concerns, ask yourself what they are based on. If you are strictly going by a timed test, we would caution you about making that the only basis of your evaluation. It is critical to interview students and collect data from daily interactions in class and observations while working in small groups and with partners (Newton, 2016). Get to know how they are thinking and how they respond without the pressure of time. If you have concerns, it is ideal to administer a Math Running Record, since it will give you terrific insight into what strategies students are using, what facts they know, what facts are tricky, and how they are feeling about math. Having that collection of information allows you to have a more complete picture of where the student is and what intervention may be needed. If, even after you have a more thorough picture, you still have concerns, involve parents in the discussion and take stock of resources you may have available in your school such as teacher assistants, math specialists, or parent volunteers who can help out in the classroom. Having the extra set of hands may help to create more one-on-one opportunities for intervention. If those resources are not an option, consider employing a workshop model so that you will have more time to meet with students in small guided math groups.

PARENTS AS PARTNERS

It's really important to pause and ask yourself how you see the parents of your students. Hopefully, you see them as valuable partners in the education of the students you have been entrusted with. We all have a lot on our plates and since there never seems to be enough hours in the day, parents can really be a secret weapon in helping to achieve your goals. Of course, this requires you to educate them accordingly and show them that they are valuable to you. If you demonstrate that you appreciate their limited time by providing feedback and support that allows them to maximize homework time, they will feel that their contributions are valued. While not all parents are able or willing to be involved as much as you may like, it's in your best interest to try to get as many parents in your camp as possible.

In making this happen, do not underestimate the power of technology. A quick email here and there really can make all the difference in getting parents on your team. A website with a few photos or videos related to strategies and what fluency looks like, or a list of apps and websites, are little things that mean a lot. If this seems like a big job, enlist your peers, or even your students, and share the work. It doesn't matter *how* you do it, just *that* you do it! Remember that if you don't take a little time to teach your students' parents, you could spend *lots* of time undoing the well-intentioned "teaching" that they do to help at home. I think that many of us have learned this the hard way!

KEY POINTS

- home–school connection
- getting parents on board
- sharing strategies
- addressing concerns
- parents as partners.

SUMMARY

Parents and guardians play an important role in the acquisition of fluency with basic math facts. We need to ensure that parents can support their children in ways that foster flexibility, honor thinking, and de-emphasize speed as an indicator of success. The home–school connection must be cultivated in intentional ways so that parents are empowered to reinforce the experiences that students are having at school. We hope that you will use the ideas presented here to open the lines of communication with parents and truly engage them as partners in this process. Keep in mind that many may not have fond memories of math, and some may even be math-phobic. This may mean it will take some convincing, but if you stick with it and help them to understand why and how you approach this, you will get a great return on your investment!

REFLECTION QUESTIONS

1. What are you currently doing around fact fluency, homework, and parent support?
2. What does your current communication with parents around fluency look like?
3. What new ideas have you gained from this chapter?

REFERENCES

Entwisle, D. R., & Alexander, K. L. (1996). Family type and children's growth in reading and math over the primary grades. *Journal of Marriage and Family*, 58(2), 341–355.

Epstein, J. L. (2001). *School, family, and community partnerships: Preparing educators and improving schools.* Boulder, CO: Westview Press.

Gill, S., & Reynolds, A. J. (1999). Educational expectations and school achievement of urban African American children. *Journal of School Psychology*, 37(4), 403–424.

Halle, T. G., Kurtz-Costes, B., & Mahoney, J. L. (1997). Family influences on school achievement in low-income, African-American children. *Journal of Educational Psychology*, 89(3), 527–537.

Holloway, S. (1986). The relationship of mothers' beliefs to children's mathematics achievement: Some effects of sex differences. *Merrill-Palmer Quarterly*, 32, 231–250.

Newton, N. 2016. *Math running records in action*. New York: Routledge.

Shaver, A. V., & Walls, R. T. (1998). Effect of Title 1 parent involvement on student reading and mathematics achievement. *Journal of Research and Development in Education*, 31(2), 90–97.

Sheldon, S. B., Epstein, J. L., & Galindo, C. L. (2010). Not just numbers: Creating a partnership climate to improve math proficiency in schools. *Leadership and Policy in Schools*, 9(1), 27–48.

Starkey, P., & Klein, A. (2000). Fostering parental support for children's mathematical development: An intervention with head start families. *Early Education and Development*, 11(5), 659–680.

Van Voorhis, F. L. (2007). Can math be more meaningful? Longitudinal effects of family involvement on student homework. Paper presented at the annual meeting of the American Educational Researchers Association, Chicago, IL.

CHAPTER 10

Action Plan

Every school should have a mission statement and vision of fluency that everyone who is a stakeholder understands and can articulate. A mission statement is a short written statement about your goals and philosophies regarding math fluency in your school. The mission statement should discuss what your school does to develop mathematicians, how it does it, and why it does it. It is really an expression of your values around teaching and learning math. In order to get a clear understanding of the mission around fluency, you should have teachers submit a quick statement either on a piece of paper or through an online survey system, like SurveyMonkey or Poll Everywhere. Then, discuss the statements and come up with a shared mission statement. It should be clear, concise, specific, and useful so that everyone can understand and execute it (see Figures 10.1–10.3).

After you know what the mission is, then you can create a vision statement, which describes exactly what it looks like. Your vision statement should be short, definitely under 20 words. It should clearly communicate what you are striving towards as a school in a way that everyone (all stakeholders, secretaries, custodians, parents, students, teachers) understands, can remember, and can then tell others about.

After you have a vision statement, then you can create a fluency plan. A fluency plan articulates the exact steps that you are going to take to achieve the mission and reach the vision. Schools need a fluency plan that guides teachers both horizontally and vertically. In this chapter we are going to look at some templates to help you plan. The mission statement and vision must be communicated to and shared with all stakeholders, and each one should clearly understand their role. Below is an example of a mission statement, a vision statement, and a fluency plan.

MISSION STATEMENT

Our school's math goals are to foster the growth of mathematically-minded students. We want to provide an academically rigorous, standards-based, engaging, real-life connected curriculum that inspires and encourages students to do their very best and enjoy mathematics. We aim to provide high-quality instruction that allows all students to experience the joy of success and the love of being a lifelong learner who sees math in action in their everyday lives.

FLUENCY VISION STATEMENTS

- To make math enjoyable, engaging, and achievable for all students!
- That all students at our school will be fluent with their basic math facts!
- That all students at our school will achieve grade-level math fact fluency!
- Every student in our school is given the scaffolding they need to achieve basic fact fluency!

FLUENCY PLANS AND TEMPLATE

Box of Facts Fact Fluency Plan		
	Kindergarten (facts to 5)	**1ˢᵗ Grade (facts to 10)**	**2ⁿᵈ Grade (facts to 20)**

	Kindergarten (facts to 5)	**1ˢᵗ Grade (facts to 10)**	**2ⁿᵈ Grade (facts to 20)**
September	-subitizing dot cards -begin Count on 1+ (concrete) (0+1, 1+1, 2+1, 3+1, 4+1)	-review facts to 5 -Count on/Count back 1 +/- (concrete and number line)	-review facts to 10 (count on, doubles facts and friends of 10) -Count on/Count back 1+/- to 20 -turnaround facts
October	-subitizing five frames -continue Count on 1+ (concrete and number line)	-Count on/Count back +/-1 (5+1, 6+1, 7+1, 8+1, 9+1 and all inverse and turnaround facts)	-Count on/Count back 2+/- to 20 -Count on/Count back 0+/- to 20
November	-subitizing ten frames -Count back 1- (concrete) (5-1, 4-1, 3-1, 2-1, 1-1)	-Count on/Count back +/-2 (5+2, 6+2, 7+2, 8+2 and all inverse and turnaround facts)	-10+ Facts (10+1, 10+2, 10+3, 10+4, 10+5, 10+6, 10+7, 10+8, 10+9, 10+10 and all inverse and turnaround facts)
December	-subitizing ten frames -Count on 2+ (concrete) (0+2, 1+2, 2+2, 3+2)	-Count on/Count back +/-0 (5+0, 6+0, 7+0, 8+0, 9+0, 10+0 and all inverse and turnaround facts)	-Doubles 10-20 (6+6, 7+7, 8+8, 9+9, 10+10)
January	-Count back 2- (concrete) (5-2, 4-2, 3-2, 2-2)	-Friends of 10 (0+10, 1+9, 2+8, 3+7, 4+6, 5+5 and all turnarounds) -Friends of 10 (inverse) (10-9, 10-1, 10-8, 10-2, 10-7, 10-3, 10-6, 10-4, 10-5)	-Doubles +/-1 (5+6, 6+7, 7+8, 8+9 and all turnaround and inverse facts)
February	-Count on 0+ (concrete) (5+0, 4+0, 3+0, 2+0, 1+0, 0+0)	-Doubles (+) 0-10 (3+3, 4+4, 5+5)	-Doubles +/-2 (3+5, 4+6, 5+7, 6+8, 7+9 and all turnaround and inverse facts)
March	-Subtract 0- (concrete) (5-0, 4-0, 3-0, 2-0, 1-0, 0-0)	-Half facts(-) 0-10 (6-3, 8-4, 10-5)	-Review all doubles facts (addition and subtraction)
April	-Doubles 0-5 (0+0, 1+1, 2+2)	-Doubles +/-1 (3+4, 4+3, 4+5, 5+4, 7-3, 7-4, 9-4, 9-5)	-Bridge 10+ (4+7, 4+8, 4+9, 5+8, 5+9, 6+9, 7+4, 8+4, 9+4, 8+5, 9+5, 9+6)
May	REVIEW ALL FACTS	REVIEW ALL FACTS	-Bridge to 10- (11-4, 11-7, 12-4, 12-8, 13-4, 13-9, 13-5, 13-8, 14-5, 14-9, 15-6, 15-9)
June	REVIEW ALL FACTS	REVIEW ALL FACTS	REVIEW ALL FACTS

FIGURE 10.1 Fluency Plan A

Grade	Beginning of the Year September	1st marking period November	2nd marking period February	End of the Year May
K	Check Number Recognition to 10; Addition and Subtraction within 5	Check Number Recognition to 10; Picture Scaffolds	Kindergarten Fluency addition and subtraction within 5 (mixed scaffolds)	Kindergarten Fluency addition and subtraction within 5
1	Kindergarten Fluency addition and subtraction within 5	1st Grade Fluency within 10	1st Grade Fluency within 10	1st Grade Fluency within 10
2	1st Grade Fluency addition and subtraction within 10	2nd Grade Fluency addition and subtraction within 20	2nd Grade Fluency addition and subtraction within 20 and addition and subtraction within 100	2nd Grade Fluency addition and subtraction within 20 and addition and subtraction within 100
3	2nd Grade Fluency addition and subtraction within 20 and 100	3rd Grade Fluency addition and subtraction within 1000	3rd Grade Fluency addition and subtraction within 1000 and multiplication and division within 100	3rd Grade Fluency addition and subtraction within 1000 and multiplication and division within 100
4	3rd Grade Fluency addition and subtraction within 1000 and multiplication and division within 100	4th Grade addition and subtraction within 1 million *Also test multiplication and division within 144	4th Grade addition and subtraction within 1 million *Also test multiplication and division within 144	4th Grade addition and subtraction within 1 million *Also test multiplication and division within 144
5	4th Grade addition and subtraction within 1 million	Multi-digit Multiplication with 2-digit Numbers	Multi-digit Multiplication with 2-digit Numbers	Multi-digit Multiplication with 2-digit Numbers

FIGURE 10.2 Fluency Plan B

Fluency Assessment Analysis Sheet and Instructional Plan   Teacher:

Subject: _Designated Math Fluency_   Grade: _____ Class: _____ Date: _____

Special Note:				
Key Resource:				
Multi-Level Approach				
Standards that need to be reviewed:	Spiral in Do Now (Energizers and Routines)	Number Talks	Spiral Review in Homework	Spiral in Quizzes or Tests
Small-Group Instruction: What are quick activities for review		Workstations	Instructional Plan: How or When Will You Structure Small Group Instruction	
Students of Major Concern		What Do They Need The Most Help With?	Evidence Along the Way	

FIGURE 10.3 Fluency Plan Template

Source: Newton, 2015 (personal communication).

Here are some questions to get you started (see Figures 10.4–10.8).

QUESTION 1: WHAT IS YOUR FLUENCY PLAN?

1. Where are your students right now?	2. What evidence do you have of where they are?
3. What do you need to do to know where they are?	4. Do your assessments address all 4 elements of fluency: accuracy, flexibility, efficiency and automaticity?

FIGURE 10.4 Fluency Plan

QUESTION 2: WHAT ARE YOU DOING ABOUT ONGOING ASSESSMENT?

1. What are you doing right now to assess on a regular basis?	2. How do you keep track of your ongoing assessments?
3. What types of exit slips do you do that assess fluency?	4. What sort of system do you have so that students can track their own individual progress?

FIGURE 10.5 Ongoing Assessment

Source: Newton, 2018 (personal communication).

QUESTION 3: HOW DO YOU GET ALL THE STAKEHOLDERS ON BOARD?

1. Does your school have a fluency vision? Is there a fluency mission statement?	2. Is everyone at your school operating from the same understanding of fluency?
3. What are you doing so that parents can effectively help your students develop fluency, including accuracy, flexibility, efficiency and automaticity?	4. What are you doing to empower all your students around ideas of being and becoming fluent?

FIGURE 10.6 Stakeholders

Source: Newton, 2018 (personal communication).

QUESTION 4: WHAT DOES THE BIG PICTURE LOOK LIKE?

1. What will be easy about starting a scaffolded fluency program in your classroom?	2. What is something that you can do right away?
3. What do you see as some of the biggest challenges in starting or tweaking your fluency program?	4. How will you address these challenges?

FIGURE 10.7 Big Picture

Source: Newton, 2018 (personal communication).

Mission Statement: The mission statement should discuss what your school does to develop mathematicians. 1) How it does it: 2) Why it does it: 3) What are the underlying values:	Vision Statement: Describes exactly what it looks like:
Fluency Plan: What are the first steps: Step 1) Step 2) Step 3)	What are the easy parts of implementing these ideas? What are the challenges of implementing these ideas?

FIGURE 10.8 Template

Source: Newton, 2018 (personal communication).

KEY POINTS

- mission statement
- vision statement
- fluency plan.

SUMMARY

It is important to plan with dates, otherwise it's just talk. Remember that a goal without a plan is only a wish! So, if you are serious about raising the achievement levels of your students with basic fact fluency, then you need a detailed plan. A plan starts with a shared mission statement, continues with a shared vision statement, and culminates with a fluency plan. The fluency plan is a detailed articulation of what is going to happen and when that is based on the current data. If you do these things, you will absolutely start a movement towards greater student achievement with their basic facts! Think of how great it will be if every grade level achieves their mastery objectives and you can hit the ground running!

REFLECTION QUESTIONS

1. What have you learned about a mission statement in this chapter?
2. What have you learned about a vision statement in the chapter?
3. What have you learned about a fluency plan in this chapter?